*Rick:*

SNAP

# Reykjavík

# CONTENTS

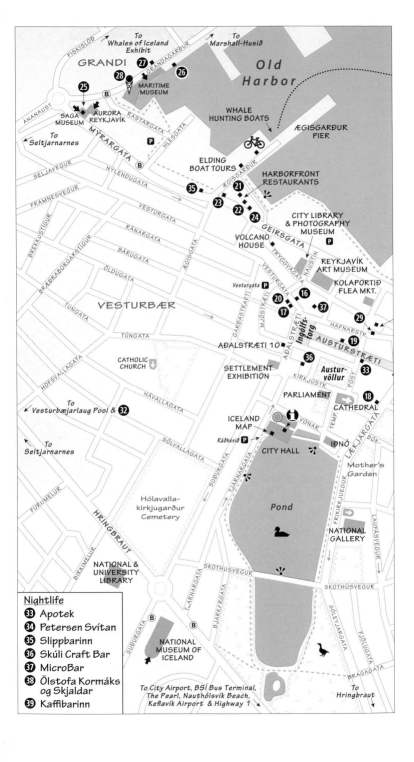

Old Harbor

GRANDI

To Whales of Iceland Exhibit
To Marshall-Husið

MARITIME MUSEUM

WHALE HUNTING BOATS

ÆGISGARÐUR PIER

SAGA MUSEUM
AURORA REYKJAVÍK

To Seltjarnarnes

ELDING BOAT TOURS

HARBORFRONT RESTAURANTS

CITY LIBRARY & PHOTOGRAPHY MUSEUM

VOLCANO HOUSE

REYKJAVÍK ART MUSEUM

KOLAPORTIÐ FLEA MKT.

VESTURBÆR

AÐALSTRÆTI 10

Ingólfstorg

SETTLEMENT EXHIBITION

Austur-völlur

CATHOLIC CHURCH

PARLIAMENT

CATHEDRAL

To Vesturbæjarlaug Pool & ③②

ICELAND MAP

Ráðhúsið

CITY HALL

IÐNÓ

Mother's Garden

To Seltjarnarnes

Hólavalla-kirkjugarðurs Cemetery

Pond

NATIONAL GALLERY

NATIONAL & UNIVERSITY LIBRARY

### Nightlife
③③ Apotek
③④ Petersen Svítan
③⑤ Slippbarinn
③⑥ Skúli Craft Bar
③⑦ MicroBar
③⑧ Ölstofa Kormáks og Skjaldar
③⑨ Kaffibarinn

NATIONAL MUSEUM OF ICELAND

To City Airport, BSÍ Bus Terminal,
The Pearl, Nauthólsvík Beach,
Keflavík Airport & Highway 1

To Hringbraut

Streets labeled: FISKISLÓÐ, GRANDAGARÐUR, ANANAUST, MÝRARGATA, RASTARGATA, HLÉSGATA, SELJAVEGUR, NYLENDUGATA, FRAMNESVEGUR, VESTURGATA, BREKKUSTÍGUR, RÁNARGATA, BÁRUGATA, ÆGISGATA, ÞRÁÐBORGARSTÍGUR, ÖLDUGATA, TÚNGATA, HOFSVALLAGATA, HÁVALLAGATA, SÓLVALLAGATA, FURUMELUR, HRINGBRAUT, BIRKIMELUR, SUÐURGATA, TJARNARGATA, BJARKARGATA, SKOTHÚSVEGUR, FRÍKIRKJUVEGUR, LAUFÁSVEGUR, SÓLEYJARGATA, FJÓLUGATA, BRAGAGATA, GEIRSGATA, TRYGGVAGATA, VESTURGÖTU, NAUSTIN, GARÐASTRÆTI, MJÓSTRÆTI, AÐALSTRÆTI, HAFNARSTR., AUSTURSTRÆTI, KIRKJUSTR., LÆKJARGATA, VONAR.

# Reykjavík Center Restaurants

1. Sjávargrillið
2. Snaps Bistro
3. Pizza Place with No Name; Mikkeller & Friends
4. Dill
5. Ostabúðin
6. Kaffi Vínyl
7. Brauð & Co
8. Reykjavík Roasters
9. Sandholt
10. Íslenski Barinn
11. Gló
12. Kryddlegin Hjörtu
13. Kex Hostel Café
14. To Hlemmur Food Market
15. Grillmarkaðurinn
16. Fiskfélagið
17. Matarkjallarinn
18. Messinn
19. The Laundromat Café
20. Stofan Café
21. Kopar
22. Sægreifinn
23. Hamborgarabúllan
24. Café Haiti
25. Matur og Drykkur
26. Kaffivagninn
27. The Coocoo's Nest
28. Valdís Ice Cream
29. Hornið Pizza
30. Krua Thai
31. Bónus Supermarket (2)
32. To Kaffihús Vesturbæjar

# INTRODUCTION

This Snapshot guide, excerpted from my guidebook *Rick Steves Iceland*, introduces you to Iceland's capital city, Reykjavík. Its colorful, pedestrian-friendly downtown has fine museums, a stroll-worthy harbor, and a dozen thermal swimming pools, perfect for a rejuvenating soak among Icelanders. The capital's restaurants are surprisingly good, and its nightlife scene is legendary.

Reykjavík is also the natural jumping-off point for exploring Iceland's dramatic countryside. It's an easy hop from Reykjavík inland to the Golden Circle route, studded with natural and historical attractions (from geysers to thundering waterfalls), or south to the legendary Blue Lagoon thermal baths (on the Reykjanes Peninsula, near the international airport at Keflavík).

Iceland's countryside is famously spectacular. While it's hard to have a bad time here, it's easy to underestimate the famously changeable weather, blow through too much money, or waste time by not making a good plan. But if you equip yourself with good information (this book) and expect to travel smart, you will.

To help you have the best trip possible, I've included the following topics in this book:

• **Planning Your Time,** with advice on how to make the most of your limited time

• **Orientation,** including tourist information (abbreviated as TI), tips on public transportation, local tour options, and helpful hints

• **Sights** with ratings:

      ▲▲▲—Don't miss

      ▲▲—Try hard to see

      ▲—Worthwhile if you can make it

**No rating**—Worth knowing about
   • **Sleeping** and **Eating,** with good-value recommendations in every price range
   • **Connections,** with tips on buses and driving
   **Practicalities**, near the end of this book, has information on money, staying connected, hotel reservations, transportation, and other helpful hints.

It's my hope that this guide will make your trip more meaningful and rewarding. Traveling like a temporary local, you'll get the absolute most out of every mile, minute, and dollar.

*Góða ferð!* Happy travels!

*Rick Steves*

# REYKJAVÍK

# REYKJAVÍK

Reykjavík, the tiny capital of a remote island-nation, is unexpectedly cosmopolitan, with an artistic, bohemian flair. It lacks world-class sights, yet manages to surprise and delight even those who use the city mostly as a home base for exploring Iceland's natural wonders.

The city's downtown streets are lined with creative restaurants, quirky art galleries, rollicking bars serving everything from craft beer to designer cocktails, and shops selling stuffed puffins, local knitwear, and Gore-Tex parkas. Reykjavík is a colorful enclave in a stark landscape: It seems every wall serves as a canvas for a vibrant street-art mural, and each corner is occupied by a cozy, art-strewn, stay-awhile café. In the old town center, colorful timber-frame houses clad in corrugated metal sheets huddle together amid a sprinkling of land-marks—such as the striking Hallgrímskirk-ja church, which crowns the town's highest point.

Reykjavík, like the rest of the country, has old roots. Viking Age farmers settled here in the ninth century. Until the 1750s, this area remained nothing more than a sprawling farm. As towns started to form in Iceland, Reykjavík emerged as the country's capital. Today, the capital region is a small city, home to two out of every three Icelanders—a population similar to that of Berkeley, California, or Fargo, North Dakota. The northernmost capital city in the world—which straddles the European and American hemispheres—feels more New World than Old.

With the recent tourism boom, these days Icelanders tend to work, live, and shop elsewhere, and make fun of Reykjavík's downtown core with all its "puffin shops" selling souvenirs. But that doesn't mean you should avoid downtown: Visitors find just about everything they need in this small, walkable zone. You can take in the vibe of the pithy city in a leisurely two-hour

stroll, and it's an enjoyable place to simply hang out. While museums aren't a priority here, those seeking sights can easily fill a day or two.

Step into Hallgrímskirkja's serene church interior, and ride the elevator up its tower for a view over Reykjavík's rooftops. Learn about this little nation's proud history at the National Museum, and about the city's humble Viking Age roots at the Settlement Exhibition—built around the surviving walls of a 10th-century longhouse. Art lovers can visit a half-dozen galleries highlighting Icelandic artists (early-20th-century sculptor Einar Jónsson is tops). Naturalists can go on a whale-watching cruise, or ride a ferry to an island getaway. Modern architecture fans can ogle the award-winning Harpa concert hall, then walk along the shoreline to the iconic *Sun Voyager* sculpture.

Explore the city's pricey but well-done private museums: At Whales of Iceland, ogle life-size models of gigantic marine mammals; at the Saga Museum, meet the Viking protagonists of the Icelandic sagas face-to-waxy-face; and at the Aurora Reykjavík exhibit, watch mesmerizing time-lapse footage of the northern lights. More sights await in the suburbs, including another city view at a domed building called the Pearl, and family-friendly activities (open-air museum, zoo, botanic gardens). To recharge, the capital area has plenty of relaxing—and very local—thermal swimming pools.

But don't focus too much on the capital. On a short summertime getaway to Iceland, I might not even devote a full day to Reykjavík. Instead, use the city as a springboard for Iceland's glorious countryside sights, taking advantage of its accommodations, great restaurants, and lively nightlife. Even on a longer visit, drivers may prefer sleeping at a distance, dropping into town only for occasional sightseeing, strolling, and dining. To save money and have a more

REYKJAVÍK

local experience, consider sleeping in suburban Reykjavík—which has fewer hotels, but ample Airbnb options.

## PLANNING YOUR TIME

On a short visit, savor Reykjavík's strolling ambience in the morning and evening, maybe drop into one or two sights early or late, and use your precious daytime hours to tour sights in the countryside (see the Near Reykjavík chapter for an overview of your options). My self-guided Reykjavík Walk offers a helpful town orientation (and crash-course in Iceland) that can be done at any time of day or night.

On a longer trip—or in winter (when countryside options are limited)—Reykjavík warrants more time. The following schedule is designed to fill two full days in Reykjavík itself. With less time, mix and match from among these options. My plan ignores weather—in practice, let the weather dictate your itinerary. If it's blowing hard and drizzling, prioritize indoor sights. Use the good weather well.

**Day 1:** Start with my self-guided walk around downtown, and (if the line's not too long) ride up the tower of Hallgrímskirkja church. Then find a nice lunch in the Laugavegur/Skólavörðustígur area. Walk down to the *Sun Voyager* sculpture for a photo op, then follow the shoreline to the Harpa concert hall (peek in the lobby, and stop by the box office to survey entertainment options). Follow the moored boats around to the Old Harbor, where you can comparison-shop whale watching and other boat tours for tomorrow. Then continue along the harbor to the Grandi area, where you can drop into your choice of exhibits: Whales of Iceland, Saga Museum, Maritime Museum, or Aurora Reykjavík. Return to the downtown area for dinner and after-hours strolling.

**Day 2:** Begin your day at the Settlement Exhibition. If that compact exhibit whets your appetite for Icelandic history, take a walk along the Pond (the city's little lake) to the National Museum. After lunch, take your pick of activities: boat trip (either whale or puffin watching, or simply a ride out to Viðey Island); suburban sights in Laugardalur (botanic garden, zoo) and/or Árbær Open-Air Museum, with a stop at the observation deck/museum called the Pearl; or explore the city's many art museums. In the late afternoon, unwind with the Icelanders in one of Reykjavík's thermal swimming pools, before another dinner in the center.

If you're in town on a weekend, squeeze in a visit to the Kolaportið flea market, downtown.

## Orientation to Reykjavík

Reykjavík's population is about 125,000, but the entire capital region has nearly double that (220,000). The compact core of Reykjavík radiates out from the main walking street, which changes names from Austurstræti to Bankastræti to Laugavegur as it cuts through the city. You can walk from one end of downtown Reykjavík (Ingólfstorg square) to the other (the bus junction Hlemmur) in about 20 minutes. Just northwest of downtown is  the mostly postindustrial Old Harbor zone, with excursion boats, salty restaurants, and a few sights.

Greater Reykjavík is made up of six towns. Hafnarfjörður ("harbor fjord"), to the south, has its own history, harbor, and downtown core. Kópavogur and Garðabær, between Reykjavík and

Hafnarfjörður, are 20th-century suburbs. Mosfellsbær, once a rural farming district along the road running north from Reykjavík, has turned into a sizable town of its own. And Seltjarnarnes is a posh enclave at the end of the Reykjavík Peninsula. While I haven't recommended specific hotels or restaurants in these neighborhoods (except in Hafnarfjörður)—finding an affordable Airbnb in one of these areas can provide a very local home base.

## TOURIST INFORMATION

The city-run **TI** is in City Hall, by the Pond (daily 8:00-20:00, Tjarnargata 11, tel. 411-6040, www.visitreykjavik.is). It has three desks: one for impartial information; the "Guide to Iceland" desk, which sells tours and excursions; and a "Safe Travel Iceland" desk, which offers advice and answers questions about driving, weather, and other risks and concerns. Around downtown you'll see several booking services billed as tourist information offices. These are primarily tour-sales offices, but can be helpful.

The *Reykjavík Grapevine,* a free informative English-language paper and website, provides a roundup of sightseeing hours, music listings, helpful restaurant reviews, and fun insights into local life. They also publish a quarterly *Best of Reykjavík* booklet with lots of reviews (www.grapevine.is). The local blog IHeartReykjavik.net also has helpful insights about both the capital region and all of Iceland.

**Sightseeing Pass:** The **Reykjavík City Card** may make sense for busy museum sightseers on a longer stay, but is not worth it for a short visit. It covers bus transport, city-run museums, Reykjavík swimming pools, and some other attractions (24 hours-3,700 ISK, 48 hours-4,900 ISK, 72 hours-5,900 ISK; sold at hotels and City Hall TI).

## HELPFUL HINTS

**Money:** You'll use credit cards more than cash in Iceland. If you do need cash, several big banks downtown have ATMs, and can exchange money (banks closed Sat-Sun). The downtown branch of Landsbankinn at Austurstræti 11 is convenient and along my self-guided walk.

**Useful Bus App:** If you'll be using public buses, use the **Strætó app** to avoid having to carry exact bus fare. Download the app, then change the default language to English under "Settings." At the prompt to enter your mobile number, include "001" for the US country code. You'll receive a PIN number on your mobile phone—once you enter the PIN, you can enter your credit card details to buy bus tickets.

**Pharmacy:** A downtown pharmacy is at Laugavegur 16 (Mon-Fri 9:00-18:00, Sat 11:00-16:00, closed Sun, tel. 552-4045, www.

REYKJAVÍK

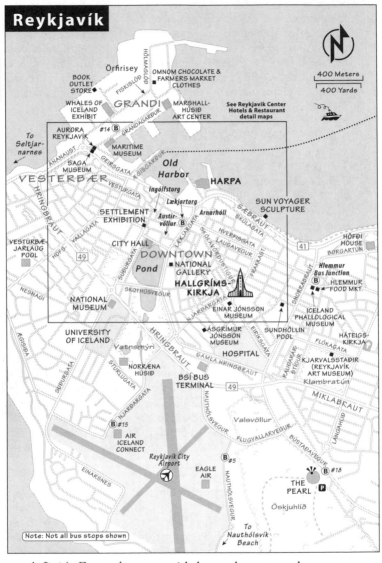

# Reykjavík

Örfirisey

HOLMASLÓÐ

BOOK OUTLET STORE◆

FISKISLÓÐ

OMNOM CHOCOLATE & FARMERS MARKET CLOTHES

WHALES OF ICELAND EXHIBIT

**GRANDI**

GRANDAGARÐUR

MARSHALL-HÚSIÐ ART CENTER

See Reykjavík Center Hotels & Restaurant detail maps

400 Meters

400 Yards

AURORA REYKJAVÍK  #14 Ⓑ

To Seltjar-narnes

ANANAUST

MARITIME MUSEUM

GEIRSGATA

EGISGARÐUR

SAGA MUSEUM

*Old Harbor*

**VESTURBÆR**

VESTURGATA

**HARPA**

HRINGBRAUT

*Ingólfstorg*

Lækjartorg

SÆBRAUT

SUN VOYAGER SCULPTURE

SETTLEMENT EXHIBITION

Austur-völlur Ⓑ

*Arnarhóll*

SKÚLAGATA

VESTURBÆ-JARLAUG POOL

HOFS-

VALLAGATA

SUÐURGATA

**CITY HALL**

LÆKJARGATA

SKÓLAVÖRÐUSTÍGUR

HVERFISGATA

LAUGAVEGUR

FRAKKASTÍGUR

HÖFÐI HOUSE

BORGARTÚN

41

49

**DOWNTOWN**

Pond

■ NATIONAL GALLERY

**HALLGRÍMS-KIRKJA**

SNORRABRAUT

*Hlemmur Bus Junction*

Ⓑ HLEMMUR FOOD MKT.

NESHAGI

ÆGISÍÐA

SKOTHÚSVEGUR

**NATIONAL MUSEUM**

NJARÐARGATA

EINAR JÓNSSON MUSEUM ■

ICELAND PHALLOLOGICAL MUSEUM

**UNIVERSITY OF ICELAND**

*Vatnsmýri*

HRINGBRAUT

◆ÁSGRÍMUR JÓNSSON MUSEUM

EIRÍKSGATA

SUNDHÖLLIN POOL

HÁTEIGS-KIRKJA

FLÓKAGATA

NORRÆNA HÚSIÐ

STURLUGATA

GAMLA HRINGBRAUT

**HOSPITAL**

RAUÐARÁR

STÍGUR

KJARVALSSTAÐIR (REYKJAVÍK ART MUSEUM)

SUÐURGATA

NJARÐARGATA

BSÍ BUS TERMINAL   49

*Klambratún*

BÚSTAÐAVEGUR

LANGAHLÍÐ

**MIKLABRAUT**

Ⓑ #15

*Valsvöllur*

AIR ICELAND CONNECT

NAUTHÓLSVEGUR

FLUGVALLARVEGUR

EINARSNES

*Reykjavík City Airport* ✈

EAGLE AIR

Ⓑ #5

Ⓑ #18

**THE PEARL**

🅿

*Öskjuhlíð*

Note: Not all bus stops shown

*To Nauthólsvík Beach*

---

lyfja.is). For a pharmacy with longer hours, try the ones at Lágmúli 5 in outer Reykjavík (tel. 533-2300) and Smáratorg 1, under the Læknavakt after-hours medical service near the Smáralind shopping mall (tel. 564-5600).

**Local Guidebook:** Look for historian Guðjón Friðriksson's great little book *Reykjavík Walks,* which describes six building-by-building routes around the downtown center.

**Laundry:** The downtown **Laundromat Café,** has four washers and four dryers in its basement (long hours daily, Austurstræti 9,

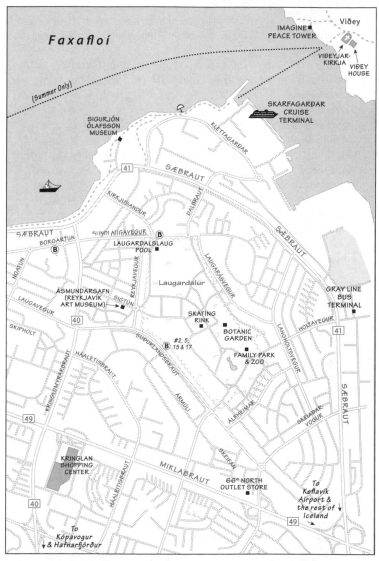

www.thelaundromatcafe.com). It's also a popular comfort-food restaurant (described later in this chapter)—turning your chore into a fun night out.

**Bike Rental: WOW Citybike** provides basic rent-and-return bikes at several self-service stations around the city center (400 ISK/one-way trip up to 30 minutes; www.wowcitybike.com). For a better-quality and longer-term rental, **Reykjavík Bike Tours** rents from its location on the pier in the Old Harbor (3,500 ISK/4 hours, 4,900 ISK/24 hours; in summer daily at least

9:00-17:00, in winter by appointment; Ægisgarður 7, mobile 694-8956, www.icelandbike.com). They also run tours (see "Tours in Reykjavík," later).

**Taxis:** The two long-established companies are **Hreyfill** (tel. 588-5522, www.hreyfill.is) and **BSR** (tel. 561-0000, www.taxireykjavik.is). Both offer flat rates to Keflavík Airport. For early-morning rides, call the evening before to reserve. Icelanders generally order taxis by phone, but there are a few taxi stands downtown and at major transportation hubs. In general, though, taxis are expensive—even a short ride in Reykjavík will cost 2,000 ISK—so use them only when there's no better option (cabbies expect payment by credit card but not a tip). Services such as Uber and Lyft don't operate in Reykjavík.

**Online Translation Tip:** A few of the websites I list in this chapter are in Icelandic only. To view them in English, use Google's Chrome browser (for automatic translation) or paste the URL into the translation window at Translate.google.com.

## GETTING AROUND
### By Car

North Americans will feel at home in Reykjavík, as it's largely a car city. If you'll be renting a car to explore the countryside, you may want to keep it for part of your time in Reykjavík. Outside of downtown, parking is generally free and easy.

That said, you don't need a car to enjoy your visit. And if you are staying in the center (inside the street called Hringbraut) and visiting only downtown sights, a car can be a headache. But many interesting and authentic things to do in town are outside the center, accessible only by car or bus. If you plan to have your own wheels in town, consider looking for accommodations with free parking a little outside the center.

**Parking:** Downtown, on-street parking is metered (Mon-Fri 9:00-18:00, Sat 10:00-16:00; free outside these times). Pay with credit cards or coins at machines (look for the white and blue "P" sign), and display your ticket on the windshield. Parking in the P1 zone is the most expensive (275 ISK/hour); parking in P2 through P4 costs about 150 ISK/hour. You can prepay for an entire day, so even if overnighting in the center, you don't have to worry about returning to feed the meter. A few coin-op-only parking meters still survive.

There are several small public parking garages downtown (check up-to-the-minute availability at www.bilastaedasjodur.is/#bilahusin). The Traðarkot garage at Hverfisgata 20 is the best option and close to the end point of my Reykjavík Walk (80-150 ISK/hour, daily 7:00-24:00). Progressively closer in, but typically full on weekdays, are the Kolaport garage, near the Harpa concert hall at Kalkofnsvegur 1; the Ráðhúsið garage, underneath City Hall at Tjarnargata 11; and—closest to my Reykjavík Walk's starting point—the Vesturgata garage at Vesturgata 7 (on the corner with Mjóstræti).

You can also park just outside downtown in a neighborhood with free on-street parking, such as behind Hallgrímskirkja church or near the BSÍ bus terminal. A free parking lot is along Eiríksgata at the top of the hill by Hallgrímskirkja church, but it's often full. Or look for metered on-street parking closer in (along Garðastræti and its side-streets, just a couple of blocks above Ingólfstorg). There's also plenty of free parking in the Grandi box-store zone to the far side of the Old Harbor.

### By Public Transportation

Greater Reykjavík has a decent bus *(strætó)* system. In this high-rising city, buses run from about 6.30 on weekdays, 8:00 on Saturdays, and 10:00 on Sundays, with last departures between 23:00 and 24:00. Service is sparse on evenings and weekends, when most buses only run every half-hour.

Bus routes intersect at several key points, notably Hlemmur, at the eastern end of Laugavegur, Reykjavík's downtown shopping street; Lækjartorg, at the western end of Laugavegur; Mjódd, in the eastern Reykjavík suburbs; and Fjörður, in the town of Hafnarfjörður. The English journey planner at Straeto.is makes using the system easy, and recognizes addresses without Icelandic characters (you can omit all the accent marks and use *th*, *d*, and *ae* instead of *þ*, *ð*, and *æ*). To get help from a real person, call 540-2700.

You can pay for the bus in cash (440 ISK), but few do this, and drivers don't give change. Instead, buy a pass, a shareable perforated strip of paper tickets, or use the Strætó app (app described in "Helpful Hints," earlier; one-day pass-1,560 ISK; three-day pass-3,650 ISK; 20 tickets-8,300 ISK and more than most visitors will need). Buses are also covered by the Reykjavík City Card (described earlier).

Tickets and passes are sold at 10-11 convenience stores, most swimming pools, information desks at the Kringlan and Smáralind shopping malls, and at the Mjódd bus junction (but not from bus drivers). Without a pass, ask the driver for a free transfer slip if you need to change buses.

# Tours in Reykjavík

While you'll see bus tours advertised in Reykjavík, I wouldn't take one. The city is easy and enjoyable by foot.

# Reykjavík at a Glance

**▲▲▲Thermal Swimming Pools** Bathe with the locals at more than a dozen naturally heated municipal pools. See page 160.

**▲▲Hallgrímskirkja** Iconic Guðjón Samúelsson-designed Lutheran church, with crushed-volcanic-rock exterior, serene and austere interior, and bell tower with sweeping views. **Hours:** Daily 9:00-21:00, Oct-April until 17:00. See page 33.

**▲▲National Museum of Iceland** Well-curated Icelandic artifacts that illustrate the nation's history. **Hours:** Daily 10:00-17:00, mid-Sept-April closed Mon. See page 44.

**▲▲Harpa** Boldly modern harborfront concert hall, with a fun-to-explore lobby and regular schedule of cultural events. **Hours:** Lobby open daily 8:00-24:00. See page 48.

**▲▲Whales of Iceland** Pricey but captivating exhibit with life-size models of the gentle giants in Icelandic waters. **Hours:** Daily 10:00-18:00, off-season until 17:00. See page 53.

**▲The Settlement Exhibition** Modern museum showcasing the actual ruins of a millennium-old, Viking Age longhouse. **Hours:** Daily 9:00-18:00. See page 37.

**▲Kolaportið Flea Market** Lively, market hall just off the Old Harbor, with fun food section. **Hours:** Sat-Sun 11:00-17:00. See page 40.

**▲Einar Jónsson Museum and Garden** Talented sculptor's house and studio, with free back garden decorated with his works. **Hours:** Tue-Sun 10:00-17:00, closed Mon. See page 43.

## On Foot

**I Heart Reykjavík,** run by local blogger Auður and her associates, offers excellent two-hour small-group walking tours that start at Hallgrímskirkja church and end in front of the parliament building. While you'll get a good historical overview of the city, this tour's strength is its personal approach and insights on daily life in Reykjavík (5,500 ISK/person, at least one morning tour per day, more in summer, book on website, tel. 511-5522, www.iheartreykjavik.net, hello@iheartreykjavik.net).

**CityWalk,** more conventional and typically with bigger groups, has two-hour tours starting in front of the parliament building several times a day year-round. While advertised as "free," you pay whatever you feel the tour is worth; book in advance on their website. They also run a pub crawl (2,500 ISK/person, Fri-Sat

▲*Sun Voyager (Sólfar)* Modern, harborfront sculpture by Jón Gunnar Árnason evoking Iceland's earliest settlers. See page 48.

▲**Old Harbor** Modern harbor with waterfront eateries and sight-seeing cruises. See page 49.

▲**Saga Museum** Viking Age mannequins reenact the legendary early-history sagas. **Hours:** Daily 10:00-18:00. See page 52.

▲**Aurora Reykjavík** Modest but enjoyable exhibit on the northern lights, starring a mesmerizing film of the aurora borealis. **Hours:** Daily 9:00-21:00. See page 53.

▲**The Pearl (Perlan)** Domed building in the suburbs with fine views over Reykjavík's skyline and the new Museum of Icelandic Natural Wonders. **Hours:** Observation deck open daily 8:00-20:00, museum until 19:00. See page 57.

▲**Viðey Island** An easy ferry ride to a smattering of attractions, including the John Lennon Imagine Peace Tower (lit in fall). Ferries depart daily in season from the Old Harbor (none off-season) and Skarfagarðar (off-season Sat-Sun only). See page 58.

▲**Árbær Open-Air Museum** Collection of old buildings in the suburbs, offering a glimpse of traditional lifestyles. **Hours:** Daily 10:00-17:00, Sept-May by guided tour only. See page 60.

at 22:00) and a running tour (mobile tel. 787-7779, www.citywalk. is, citywalk@citywalk.is).

For something a little different, take the 2.5-hour **"Walk the Crash"** tour with Magnús Sveinn Helgason, a journalist and historian. Starting at the parliament building, he'll walk you around downtown and relay a lively inside story of Iceland's 2008 financial crash—one of the largest in world history—and how the country has recovered since. Magnús worked for the government commission that investigated the crash, so he knows his stuff (3,500 ISK/person, 1-2 tours a week, usually Mon and/or Fri—email or check website for times, www.citywalk.is, magnus@citywalk.is).

**Food Tours:** To learn more about Icelandic cuisine and cooking—from traditional dishes to modern interpretations—you can take a three- to four-hour guided walk with stops at a half-dozen local eateries. Two companies offer the tours (each one around 15,000 ISK): **Wake Up Reykjavík Food Tour** (www.wakeupreykjavik.com) and **Your Friend in Reykjavík** (www.yourfriendinreykjavik.com).

## By Bike

**Reykjavík Bike Tours** takes you on a 2.5-hour, fairly flat guided bike tour that starts on the Old Harbor pier and does a circuit through downtown and all the way over to the university and residential areas on the other side of the peninsula. This is a nice way to get to know more of the city than the downtown core (7,500 ISK, mid-May-Sept daily at 10:00, off-season Fri-Sat only at 10:00 or 11:00, confirm times by phone or on website; Ægisgarður 7, mobile 694-8956, www.icelandbike.com).

# Reykjavík Walk

This self-guided walk, rated ▲▲▲, introduces the highlights of downtown Reykjavík, as well as some slices of local life, in about two hours. While a few indoor sights may be closed early or late, the walk can be done at any time—allowing you to fit it in before or after your day-trips. The walk starts at Reykjavík's central square, Ingólfstorg, and finishes at Hallgrímskirkja, the big, landmark church on the hill. As Reykjavík is likely your first stop in Iceland, I've designed this walk as a crash course not only for the city, but for the whole country—introducing you to names, customs, stories, and themes that will come in handy from here to the Eastfjords.

**Getting There:** By **bus,** the Ráðhúsið, MR, and Lækjartorg stops are each a five-minute jaunt from the beginning of this walk (it's easy to find Ingólfstorg; the main street, Austurstræti, runs right into it). If coming by **car,** see "Getting Around," earlier, for parking options.

• *Begin on the modern, sunken square called...*

## ❶ Ingólfstorg (Ingólfur's Square)

While this somewhat dreary square isn't much to look at, it packs a lot of history and myth. Ingólfstorg is named for Ingólfur Árnason, the early Scandinavian explorer who—according to the Icelandic sagas—settled at Reykjavík in A.D. 874.

In the middle of the square, look for the two nondescript **stone pillars** (one of them marked *874*). These recall the much-told legend about Ingólfur: As he sighted the southeast coast of Iceland, he followed an old Scandinavian custom and threw the two carved wooden pillars from his best chair overboard—vowing to establish his farm wherever they washed ashore. In the meantime, he set up a temporary settlement on the South Coast and sent two of his slaves on a scavenger hunt all over the island. Three years later (in 874), they discovered the pillars here. Ingólfur called this place Reykjavík, meaning "Smoky Bay"—likely for the thermal vapor he saw venting nearby.

While the details of this story are a mix of fact and legend (see the "Sagas of the Icelanders 101" sidebar in this chapter), archaeologists confirm that the original Reykjavík farm was just a few steps from where you're standing. And for most of its history, Reykjavík remained nothing more than a farm—set between the sea and a pond a few hundred yards inland (we'll go there in a few minutes). But in the 18th century, Reykjavík gradually emerged as the logical seat of Iceland's government.

Ingólfstorg was not an open space until 1944, when a big hotel that used to stand here burned down. The lot was left vacant and became a seedy hangout where Reykjavík teens would drink, smoke, and do other things they didn't want their parents to know about. Locals called it Hallærisplan (which means, roughly, "Messed-Up Square"). Only in 1993 was it cleaned up, redesigned, and respectably renamed. Today, this square is designed for skateboarders, and hosts outdoor concerts and performances in summer. Lining the square are cafés and fast-food joints where you can pick up a hot dog, a slice of pizza, a toasted sub sandwich, or an ice-cream cone (or even a decadent *bragðarefur*—a giant cup of soft serve with mix-ins, like a supersized McFlurry).

The big, glass-fronted, **eight-story building** that dominates the square represents the latest chapter in Reykjavík's story: its re-

cent tourism boom. Long the headquarters of Iceland's biggest newspaper, those offices recently moved out to the suburbs, and the building is now a hotel. A generation ago, downtown Reykjavík was mostly offices, government institutions, cheap housing, and lots of students. But with the flood of tourism over the last decade, most of these have been replaced by hotels, bars, restaurants, shops, and tour operators; the number of Icelanders who actually live downtown has dropped sharply.

• *Let's take a little back-streets detour. Facing that big building, turn right, then walk to the end of the square. The street leaving the square is...*

REYKJAVÍK

# Reykjavík Walk

1. Ingólfstorg (Ingólf's Square)
2. Vesturgata
3. Mjóstræti
4. Aðalstræti (Main Street)
5. City Hall
6. The Pond (Tjörnin)
7. Austurvöllur (Parliament Sq.)
8. Austurstræti
9. Lækjartorg (Creek Square)
10. Bankastræti & Laugavegur
11. Skólavörðustígur
12. Hallgrímskirkja Church
13. Leifur Eiríksson Statue
14. Einar Jónsson Sculpture Garden

HARPA CONCERT HALL

To Sun Voyager Sculpture, Skarfagarðar, Keflavík Airport & Highway 1

KALKOFNSVEGUR

B

Kolaport

Arnarhóll

INGÓLFUR ARNARSSON STATUE

PRIME MINISTER'S OFFICE

BANKASTRÆTI

10

CULTURE HOUSE

NATIONAL THEATER

GAMLA BÍÓ THEATER

Traðarkot

LAUGAVEGUR

11

Garden

FORMER JAIL

MAL & MENNING BOOKSTORE

BÍÓ PARADÍS CINEMA

LAUGAVEGUR

BOOKS

12 TÓNAR

ICELANDIC HANDKNITTING ASSOCIATION

GRETTISGATA

PINGHOLT

NJÁLSGATA

To Hlemmur Bus Junction

BRAUÐ & CO. BAKERY

SKÓLAVÖRÐUSTIGUR

COFFEE

AUSTURBÆR

LEIFUR EIRÍKSSON STATUE

WALK ENDS

13

GARDEN ENTRANCE

12

14

EINAR JÓNSSON MUSEUM & SCULPTURE GARDEN

HALLGRÍMS-KIRKJA

EIRIKSGATA

## ❷ Vesturgata, Reykjavík's Original Shoreline

This lovely lane (literally "West Street") is lined by colorful buildings from the early 20th century. The **yellow building** (today the Restaurant Reykjavík) was once the base of the town pier, back when the waterfront came all the way up to this point. The entry to the pier ran under the building's tower (beneath the round window). In 1874, when the king of Denmark visited Iceland, his fleet anchored in the harbor, and he came ashore on little boats right here. Around 1910, land reclamation created the modern harborfront zone, just beyond the taller modern buildings. Today, this so-called Old Harbor area has some appealing sights (see page 49).

In the sidewalk immediately in front of the yellow building, notice the brass plaque marking the **"hub of Reykjavík"**—both the symbolic gateway to the city, and the spot from where the city's address numbers radiate.

Around the left side of the yellow building, you can spot faint remains of the **original wharf,** and a little tidal pool that's still connected, underground, to the harbor. Several recommended restaurants are on or near this square (see "Eating in Reykjavík," later).

• *Now continue along Vesturgata. Just past the bright red building on the left corner, turn left onto...*

## ❸ Mjóstræti, Back-Streets Reykjavík

Even in the bustling downtown of Iceland's capital, you're never more than a block or two away from a sleepy residential area. Stroll a couple of blocks along Mjóstræti ("Little Street"), appreciating some slices of Reykjavík life.

A block up Mjóstræti, look right up the hill to see a humble cottage called **Hákot.** Built in the 1890s, and beautifully renovated in the 1980s, this is one of a few old houses that survive in the neighborhood. In the 1970s, many houses were knocked down after an expressway was slated to cut through here. Locals protested, and the plans were abandoned.

Continue straight along Mjóstræti, and notice one of Reykjavík's distinctive **fire hydrants**—painted in garish, McDonald's-esque red and yellow. Residents embrace these cheery hydrants, some embellished with faces, as a sort of local symbol.

You'll see many houses sided with vertical **corrugated iron** (despite the name, it's usually steel, galvanized with zinc). Since the late 19th century, corrugated metal sheets have been widely used for siding and roofing in Iceland. It stands up well to the punishing wind and sideways rain, it doesn't burn, it's easy to maintain, it's cheap and easy to transport to Iceland, and can dress up renovated old houses as well as new ones. Many locals prefer to use brightly saturated hues, perhaps to help cheer them through the gloomy winters. Around town, you may also notice a few houses with boring gray metal: Newer siding needs to weather for a few years to get rough enough for primer and paint to adhere.

As you stroll, notice lots of **propped-open windows** (often one smaller pane built into a bigger window). Icelanders mostly heat their homes with geothermal hot water—harnessing the substantial natural power of their volcanic island. There are radiators in every room, but typically no central thermostat. Heating costs are low, so when things get too warm or stuffy indoors, Icelanders just open the window to create a cross-breeze. For tourists, opening a window also helps vent the sulfur smell that accompanies the city's scalding-hot tap water, which is piped directly into the city from boreholes in the countryside. (Residents are used to the smell and don't even notice it.)

Another way Icelanders use all that hot water is to heat **swimming pools.** Every Iceland town has a municipal thermal pool complex where locals swim laps, relax, and socialize—particularly appealing in the cold and dreary winter months. These basically feel like your hometown swimming pool...except that the water is delightfully warm-to-hot, year-round. Tourists are welcome to join in the fun, and many find it the most local-feeling experience they have in Iceland. (For more about visiting pools, see "Experiences in and near Reykjavík," later.)

Any **cats** roaming? Reykjavík has a relaxed, small-town vibe, and people tend to let their cats wander free by day. Watch for clever little cat doors built into windows and doors. You won't see many dogs, though; until 1984 they were banned in the city for health reasons, and condo owners still need permission from their neighbors to keep a dog.

• *After another block, Mjóstræti dead-ends into someone's driveway. Turn left on Brattagata and head downhill. You'll pop out back at the bottom of Ingólfstorg square, on...*

## ❹ Aðalstræti, Reykjavík's First Street

While today it feels more like an alley, this "Main Street" (as its name means) was Reykjavík's first thoroughfare.

The **one-story, black house** on your right (at Aðal-stræti 10) was originally built around 1760 for the textile industry. The current version is a complete rebuild (only the location of the walls is original), but faithful to the original style. The hand pump across the street (under the arcade) is a reminder

that, until 1910, locals used pumps like this one as their sole source of drinking water.

Turn right down Aðalstræti. A few doors down on the right is the Hótel Reykjavík Centrum. When this hotel was built in 2001, workers unearthed the ruins of a 10th-century Scandinavian longhouse—part of the original Reykjavík farm. Today it's the excellent **Settlement Exhibition,** where you can step down into the cellar and walk around the ancient structure (enter at the corner; museum described later, under "Sights in Reykjavík"). The museum's other name—Reykjavík 871±2—refers to a volcanic eruption in A.D. 871, plus or minus a few years, evidence of which was found in the house.

Opposite the hotel, a statue of **Skúli Magnússon** stands in a small square with a few trees. Skúli was an Enlightenment-era entrepreneur whose enterprises seeded settlement at Reykjavík in the mid-1700s—finally transforming it from a farm into a real town, and setting the stage for its eventual capital status. While Ingólfur may have settled in Reykjavík, Skúli put it on the map. The little square was the village cemetery until 1838.

• *Ahead of you, the big yellow building is the local branch of the Salvation Army. Loop around it to the left, following Tjarnargata for a block to Vonarstræti, where you'll see, on your left, a large, modern concrete building with a curved roof and a mossy pond in front. This is the...*

## ❺ Reykjavík City Hall (Ráðhús Reykjavíkur)

Enter the blocky, curved-roofed, concrete-and-glass building (daily 8:00-20:00, free WCs; use the door at the inner corner of the fountain). The city council meets upstairs, but most city offices are outside the center, and this "City Hall" is more of a ceremonial hall for the city's residents. Its ground-floor space, normally open to the public, is rented out for concerts, exhibitions, and other cultural events.

A huge wooden **relief map of Iceland** is sometimes displayed in front of the large windows overlooking the little lake known as the Pond. The towns on the map are not labeled, but it's easy to find Reykjavík and the Reykjanes Peninsula: Look for the airport. Pick out the island's major landforms: Fjords ruffle the coastline in the northwest (the Westfjords), the east coast (the Eastfjords), and the far-north (Skagafjörður and Eyjafjörður, flanking the mountainous Tröllaskagi— "Troll Peninsula"). Glacier-covered volcanic peaks loom ominously above the South Coast, while the desolate Highlands cover the middle of the country. Trace your

own route through Iceland; spotting the roads and towns around the country is absorbing. Notebooks with topographic maps help you identify fjords, mountains, and rivers. Nearby you may see a second model, with a street map of Reykjavík and elevated models of major architectural landmarks.

Stop by the official **Reykjavík TI** here for help with your sightseeing plans, or to purchase a sightseeing or bus pass.

• *Exit the City Hall next to the TI, and walk across the pedestrian bridge that runs along...*

### ❻ The Pond (Tjörnin)

This miniature lake feels just right for this small capital of a small country. On sunny days, parents bring small children to feed the ducks and swans that live in the Pond. In the winter, if the temperatures drop to a safe range, snow on the Pond is cleared away to make a skating rink. It's a pleasant one-mile walk all the way around.

At the far end of the pedestrian bridge, you're greeted by a statue of a **faceless bureaucrat** (see photo next page).

REYKJAVÍK

The period building next to him is Iðnó, Reykjavík's old theater.

Gaze out to the far end of the Pond, where you'll see some of the **University of Iceland** buildings (that's the science center with the curved glass roof). The country's oldest and largest university, with a total enrollment of around 13,000, was founded in 1911. Before that, students had to go abroad for college (mostly to Denmark)...a reminder of just how recently this country came into its own.

Farther right, rising a couple of stories above the rooftops, is the brown tower of the recommended **National Museum,** where a thoughtfully explained collection of artifacts tells the story of Iceland (described under "Sights in Reykjavík"). Along the right side of the Pond are fine homes built by wealthy families a century ago.

• *Standing next to the bureaucrat, turn your back to the Pond, cross the street, and walk straight up Templarasund. You'll arrive at a lovely little park with a big statue in the middle. Stand by the statue and get oriented to...*

## ❼ Austurvöllur, Iceland's Parliament Square

Translated roughly as "Eastern Field," Austurvöllur is the political center of this small country. With your back to the statue, the big,

stone building facing the square is Iceland's parliament, the **Alþingi** (pronounced, roughly, "all-thingy"). While Icelanders like to call the Alþingi the "world's oldest parliament," this is an exaggeration. The Alþingi that met at Þingvellir in the centuries after settlement was very different from a modern democratic parliament. From about 1400 to 1800, it was an appeals court, not a legislature. Then there were 45 years when the Alþingi didn't meet at all. It was reestablished in Reykjavík, in a totally new and different form, in 1845. Finally, in 1874, Iceland received a constitution that gave the Alþingi its first real decision-making power—even though Iceland remained fully part of Denmark.

On the building's gable, notice the crowned 9, which represents King Christian IX (the Danish ruler in 1881, when the building was erected). Engraved over four of the upstairs windows of the

Alþingi, notice the mythical "four protectors of Iceland"—dragon, eagle, giant, and bull—which also appear on Iceland's coat of arms and many Icelandic coins. (As if to drive home Iceland's closeness to the sea, the flipsides of the coins feature cod, dolphins, crab, and lumpfish.)

The Alþingi's 63 members are a lot for a country of less than 350,000 people. Icelanders vote for a party, not for a person; each party submits an ordered list of candidates, and the top names on the list get seats. There are no public tours of the Alþingi, but if parliament is in session visitors are welcome to sit in the gallery (parliament is on vacation June-mid-Sept; otherwise confirm session times at www.althingi.is—typically Mon 15:00, Tue 13:30, Wed 15:00, Thu and sometimes Fri 10:30). The gallery entrance is around the back of the building, by a fine little walled garden that's open to the public.

Now turn your attention to the statue on the pillar: **Jón Sigurðsson** (1811-1879) was the 19th-century scholar and politician who successfully advocated for Iceland's increased autonomy under the Danish crown. Jón spent most of his life in Denmark, where he politely but forcefully pressed the case for freer trade and a constitution that would reduce the king's power. At the time, many other Europeans were agitating for the same kinds of things, and often took up arms. But Icelanders achieved their goals without firing a shot—thanks largely to the articulate persistence of this one man. The parliament building was finished just a couple of years after Jón's death. In Jón's honor, his birthday—June 17—became Iceland's National Day.

Look around the **square.** Early each summer new turf is laid and flower beds are filled in preparation for National Day ceremonies and speeches. But it was quite a different scene in the winter of 2008-2009: Thousands of Icelanders gathered here to demand the government's resignation in the wake of the country's financial collapse. Protesters banged pots and pans, and pelted politicians with eggs and tomatoes (hence the protest's nickname, the "Kitchenware Revolution"). New elections were called, and the prime minister was censured for failing in his responsibilities. Ólafur Þór Hauksson—a small-town cop who became the unyielding special prosecutor for financial crimes—emerged as something of an international folk hero. A good number of bankers were tried, convicted, and in many cases jailed for their role in the crisis.

Then, in spring 2016, thousands came to this square again after it was revealed that Iceland's then-prime minister had kept some of his considerable family wealth in an offshore account in Panama. Again, new elections were called.

To the left of the Alþingi is Reykjavík's **Lutheran Cathedral** (Dómkirkjan; generally open Mon-Fri 10:00-16:00, closed

Sat-Sun except for services, occasional concerts—look for posters, www.domkirkjan.is). Surprisingly small, it was built in the 1790s and expanded in the 1840s. The city now has larger churches, but the cathedral is still regularly used for weddings, funerals, and the opening of parliament. If you

go inside, you'll find a beautifully tranquil interior, with an upstairs gallery and finely painted ceiling. The centerpiece—directly in front of the main altar—is a marble baptismal font by renowned 19th-century Danish sculptor Bertel Thorvaldsen, whose father was Icelandic.

At the right end of the Alþingi, notice the **statue of a strong woman** on a pillar: Ingibjörg H. Bjarnason (1867-1941), who was

elected Iceland's first female member of parliament in 1922. Iceland has an impressive tradition of honoring women's rights. On October 24, 1975, 90 percent of Icelandic women went on strike to drive home their importance to society. The country ground to a halt. (Icelandic men—who very quickly learned their lesson—gave the protest the tongue-in-cheek nickname "The Long Friday," which is also what Icelanders call Good Friday.) In 1980, Iceland became the first modern, democratic nation to elect a female head of state, when single mother Vigdís Finn-

bogadóttir became president. She served for four terms (16 years) and remains a beloved figure today.

Facing the Bjarnason statue, at the corner of the park, notice the chunk of rock split in half by **"The Black Cone."** This monument to civil disobedience was placed here (somewhat controversially) in 2012—when memories of those 2009 protests were still fresh and, for some, painful.

• *Exit the square behind Jón Sigurðsson's left shoulder, and go one short block up the street called Pósthússtræti ("Post Office Street"). Pause at the intersection with Austurstræti ("Eastern Street"), in front of Apotek Hótel.*

## ❽ Austurstræti, Reykjavík's Main Street

Reykjavík's main drag begins about a block to your left (at Ingólfstorg, where we started our walk) and continues about a mile to your right, changing names as it runs through town.

Looking straight ahead, on your right is the red **post office** building. Across the street on the left, the old-meets-new building is **Landsbankinn,** founded as Iceland's national bank in 1886. It was privatized around 2000, failed spectacularly in 2008, and then continued operations under a slightly altered name. Past that, at the end of the block, you'll see a white, boxy building that houses the **Kolaportið flea market** on weekends—a fun browse, even for nonshoppers (see page 40).

Tucked away kitty-corner from the flea market (just down this street and on the right, but not quite visible from here) is Reykjavík's

most-famous **hot dog stand.** In 2004, Bill Clinton was in Reykjavík to speak at a UNICEF event. When the proprietor of this stand offered him a free frankfurter, Clinton—a notorious connoisseur of junk food— just couldn't say no. Camera shutters clicked...and suddenly, eating at Bæjarins Beztu Pylsur ("The City's Best Sausages") became *the* thing to do when visiting Reykjavík. Now people stand in long lines to shell out 600 ISK for what is, by any honest assessment, a fairly average weenie.

Now look up, behind you, at the Art Deco-style facade of the **Apotek Hótel.** This was designed by Guðjón Samúelsson, Iceland's best-known 20th-century architect, who's responsible for many of the major landmarks around town—including his masterpiece church, Hallgrímskirkja.

Facing the hotel, across the street, is **Café Paris,** an old standby. Look up at the relief on the pediment-like gable, from the 1920s, which shows an imagined scene from the settlement of the country: An established settler—standing in front of his pack animals—shakes hands with a new arrival, whose crew is taking down the mast of his longship. While you may sometimes hear the word "Viking" used to describe those early Icelandic settlers, that's not quite right. They were contemporaries (and actually relatives) of the Vikings, but had a different modus operandi: Rather than

## Icelandic Names:
## From Magnússon to Gunnarsdóttir

Traditionally, Icelanders' last names were patronymics, formed from the father's name plus "son" or "dóttir." So if you meet a man named Gunnar Magnússon, you know his father's name was Magnús. If Gunnar has a son Jón, he'll be named Jón Gunnarsson. A daughter María will be María Gunnarsdóttir. Get it? (This system was the norm all over Scandinavia until just a few hundred years ago.) Women keep their name at marriage.

Around 1900, fashions changed, and Icelanders started to assume family names and pass them down from generation to generation, like we do in the US. Then the pendulum swung back: In 1925, family names were banned as un-Icelandic, but people who had already taken one were allowed to keep it. (You may run into a few of these today.) Things went so far that for a few decades, immigrants who wanted to take up Icelandic citizenship had to abandon their foreign surname and choose an Icelandic patronymic (this requirement was abolished only in the 1980s). Today, with immigration rising, and many marriages between Icelandic women and immigrant men, family names are on the increase in Iceland again.

These days, Icelanders can choose to form their children's last name from either parent's first name. So, if Gunnar and Katrín have a son, they could give him the last name Katrínarson. But

pillage, plunder, and rape, the first Icelanders were mostly farmers in search of good grazing land.

Now look up the street past Café Paris (back toward Ingólfstorg). On the left side of the street, notice **Vínbúðin**—one of the unobtrusive state-run liquor stores. Only weak beer can be bought at regular stores; every other kind of alcohol can be purchased only here. While nationalized liquor stores are fairly standard in Nordic countries, Iceland has at times taken a particularly hard line against alcohol. From 1915 all the way until 1989—in an attempt to curtail everyone's favorite, cheap "gateway drug"—beer with an alcohol content over 2.25 percent was illegal. Icelanders compensated by mixing spirits—which were, oddly, perfectly legal—with light beer, creating a super-alcoholic faux-brew. Today, as if making up for lost time, Iceland has a burgeoning microbrew culture (see recommendations, including many within a few steps of this walk, on the country's Personal Names Committee still controls what first names parents can give their children (from a list of 3,500 authorized names). While this seems oppressive, it's largely a grammatical concern—to ensure that names will work within the structure of the Icelandic language. Recently, politicians have moved to abolish the committee. Stay tuned.

All Icelanders address each other by first names, which may seem strangely informal. But in Icelandic, using a person's full first name actually has a ceremonial ring to it. Most Icelanders go by a nickname among family and friends, so Magnús's old schoolmates probably call him "Maggi." But strangers wouldn't dare call him anything less than Magnús. There's no real equivalent of "Mr." or "Ms." in Icelandic.

It's traditional for Icelandic parents to reveal their children's names only when the child is christened (usually a few weeks after birth, but the law lets them wait for up to six months). Many parents choose the name before the birth, but still follow custom and keep it a secret. Others appreciate the chance to get to know their child before deciding. In the meantime, parents use nicknames for their baby, like "The Short One."

What children do get within minutes of birth is a 10-digit identification number, based on their birth date, which follows them through life. This number, called the *kennitala,* is almost like an alternative name, and Icelanders use it very openly and casually to identify themselves to schools, banks, or the power company. Anyone can look up anyone else's ID number and address. This shocks Americans, who are used to keeping their social security number secret. Despite—or perhaps because of—this openness, identity theft in Iceland is practically unknown.

page 73). Also look for the Icelandic firewater called *brennivín.* In another anti-alcohol crusade, originally the *brennivín* bottle came with a health warning in the form of a black skull. While that's long gone, today the drink still carries the tongue-in-cheek nickname "Black Death" *(svartidauði).*

Turn right and walk up Austurstræti. After a few steps, on your right, look for one of the city center's three main **bookstores** (this one is run by Eymundsson—Iceland's answer to Barnes & Noble). Books are clearly valued here: A high percentage of Icelanders are published authors, and every Icelandic living room has shelves of books on display. Books also play a key role in Christmas gift exchanges: The Iceland publishers' association mails a catalog of the year's new releases each fall, just in time for holiday shopping lists.

Just past the bookstore, notice "The Hot Dog Stand"...taking

REYKJAVÍK

full advantage of its prime location to hijack hungry tourists looking for the famous place around the corner.

• *Across the street from the bookstore is a 10-11 convenience store, useful
for bus tickets or a bus pass. At the end of the street, you'll emerge into a
square called...*

## ❾ Lækjartorg (Creek Square)

This square and the adjacent, busy street (Lækjargata) are named
for a creek *(lækur)* that ran from the Pond (to your right) down to
the sea (to your left) in Reykjavík's early days. It still flows, but was
buried in an underground culvert more than a century ago.

As Reykjavík grew in the mid-1700s, the first building constructed of materials more permanent than turf or timber was
not a church or palace but a
prison, built across the creek
from the village center. (Look
across Lækjargata to find the
white stone building with five
windows on the second story.)
Today it's the **office of Iceland's
prime minister.** The "no parking" sign out front indicates
the spot reserved for the prime
minister.

But no matter how high you rise in Icelandic society, you're
called by your first name—so President Guðni Th. Jóhannesson is
known to Icelanders simply as "Guðni." That's why, in this book,
I'm on a first-name basis even with big-name historic Icelanders.
This isn't necessarily because Icelanders are more casual than the
norm—it's because of the unique way they form their last names.
(For more on this tradition, see the "Icelandic Names" sidebar, earlier.)

Flanking the prime minister's office are two streets: **Bankastræti** (on the right) runs uphill for a couple blocks, and then
changes its name to Laugavegur. This has long been the main
downtown shopping street; we'll head up this way soon. **Hverfisgata** (on the left), a more heavily trafficked commercial street, is
where city buses run on their way between the two main bus stops
downtown: Lækjartorg (where you're standing) and Hlemmur (just
under a mile to the east).

On the hill to the left of Hverfisgata are many government
offices, including Iceland's supreme court, ministry of finance, and
central bank. The large white building with multiple chimneys is
the former city library; today it's the **Culture House,** with a modest
exhibit (including a precious 14th-century illuminated manuscript;
see page 41). Behind it rises the flyspace of the dark-gray **National**

**REYKJAVÍK**

**Theater,** whose color comes from crushed obsidian mixed into its roughcast coating—a popular look in Icelandic architecture.

Out by the water, you may just be able to see the corner of the dark, glassy, boxy building called **Harpa**—Reykjavík's concert hall and conference center. Don't trek out to Harpa now; at the end of this walk, you can head to Harpa to enter the hall's futuristic lobby for a good look at its multicolored windows.

• *Cross the busy street and walk uphill on Bankastræti (with the prime minister's office on your left).*

## ❿ Bankastræti/Laugavegur, More of Reykjavík's Main Drag

By the end of the 19th century, Reykjavík had expanded, and most people lived on this side of the town's little creek. This stretch became the city's main shopping and business street. Today, most locals shop at malls and in the suburbs, and services along Laugavegur are geared toward tourists.

A half-block up on your left (just past the PM's backyard), notice another old stone building (marked with the *Stella* sign).

This was Iceland's first bank building, built in 1882, which gave Bankastræti its name.

Huff uphill along Bankastræti, noticing the moveable, blue **traffic barriers** (including some shaped like bicycles). In the summer, some stretches of this street are closed to cars to promote strolling—but be careful at intersections, as cross-streets still carry traffic.

As you walk along here, keep a very close eye on street signs; you'll spot tiny plastic **action figures** glued to some of them. This is the work of a mysterious street artist (dubbed Dótadreifarinn— "The Toy Spreader") who sneaks around the city center and glues figurines to signs and ledges, always just out of arm's reach. Spotting these as you stroll can be a fun scavenger hunt.

Also keep your eye out— both along this main strip, and in the residential side streets— for big **street-art murals.** This isn't eyesore graffiti, but quite the opposite: Locals have found that if you supply a blank canvas, it'll be tagged. But if you decorate it yourself, taggers leave it alone. So government and private property owners commission murals like these. Many of the most renowned Icelandic street artists are women. The back lanes are even more highly decorated than the main streets we're seeing on this walk—be sure to explore later.

After two short blocks, pause at the lively intersection where Skólavörðustígur splits off to the right. This is also where the street changes names to **Laugavegur** (roughly LOY-ga-VEH-grr, "Hot Springs Road")—once the walking route for those going to do their laundry in the Laugardalur hot springs east of downtown. We won't walk the entire length of Laugavegur right now, but you'll certainly find plenty of excuses to explore it while you're in town—many of the city's best restaurants, shops, and bars are on or within a few steps of this street. About 10 minutes' walk away, at Laugavegur's far end, is Hlemmur, the main city bus junction. While the entire drag is commercialized, the farther you go up Laugavegur, the less it feels like a tourist circus.

• *From here, head toward the distant church steeple on the angled, uphill street called...*

## ⓫ Skólavörðustígur Street

This street (SKO-la-vur-thu-STEE-grr, "School Cairn Lane") leads up to Hallgrímskirkja church. The street got its name from a pile of rocks that Reykjavík schoolchildren set up long ago atop the hill, near where the church is now. A bit broader and brighter than Laugavegur, it's lined with cafés, restaurants, and bookstores. As it's also a bit less congested, and capped with a lovely church steeple, this street is many visitors' (and shoppers') favorite place to stroll in Reykjavík.

Just a few steps up Skólavörðustígur at #4 (on the right), notice the tiny gap between the buildings. If the gate is open, step discreetly into an adorable, private little **garden** facing a bright red house—a tranquil parallel world to the bustle just a few steps away. Many downtown blocks have an interior garden, shared among the surrounding houses. Sometimes, like here, little houses are tucked behind other houses. This was a good way to increase the capacity of your lot in this city of chronic housing shortages (and loosely enforced building regulations).

Back on Skólavörðustígur, continue a block uphill. On the left, you'll see another **old stone building.** It looks a bit like the historic jail we saw earlier—and yes, it's another former jail, built in 1874 (after the city had expanded, and this area was just outside town). This remained in use until summer 2016. Run your fingers over the chunky, volcanic rock in the building's facade.

Just past the jail, also on the left, the boxy three-story building at #11 was a bank, until the financial crisis, and now houses a branch of the Eymundsson bookstore chain.

While the lower end of the street is dominated by big, glitzy shops (like Geysir, with modern Icelandic fashion, or the venerable Rammagerðin handicraft shop), as you continue uphill the shops become smaller, more characteristic boutiques. Ceramic and jewelry shops—often with a small workshop in the back—are popular along here. At #15 (on the left), 12 Tónar is Reykjavík's most beloved music store, specializing in Icelandic tunes. A few doors up at #19 (with the metal balcony) is the Handknitting Association of Iceland's shop, where you can browse expensive but top quality handmade Icelandic sweaters and other woolens. For more recommendations, see "Shopping in Reykjavík," later.

• *The last couple of blocks of the street are increasingly residential. It's fun to explore the side-streets in this neighborhood, where you'll find more corrugated metal siding, propped-open windows, street art, hidden gardens, and cats. But for now, continue straight uphill until you run right into...*

## ⓬ Hallgrímskirkja Lutheran Church

After Reykjavík's Catholic minority built their church atop the hill west of downtown in 1929, Lutheran state church leaders felt they needed to keep up. They hired the same well-known architect, Guðjón Samúelsson, and commissioned him to build a taller, bigger response on the higher hill to the east of downtown. His distinctive Hallgrímskirkja (HAHTL-greems-KEER-kyah) was designed in the 1930s, with construction beginning in 1945, but was not completed until the 1980s. On New Year's Eve, this square is one of the best spots in town to watch fireworks.

**Exterior:** The basalt-column motif soaring skyward on the facade recalls Iceland's volcanic origins. In the winter, as you look up from Skólavörðustígur, light shining out through the windows makes the top of the 250-foot tower glow like a giant jack-o'-lantern.

Guðjón Samúelsson (1887-1950)—an Icelander who trained in Denmark—was Iceland's most influential architect. Arriving back home after finishing his studies in 1919, he was hired as the government's in-house building designer—a plum post that he kept until his death. These were good years for architects, as Iceland urbanized and the availability of concrete opened up new design possibilities. Guðjón's favored aesthetic was the functionalist style typical of the 1920s and 1930s. He attempted to forge a distinctly Icelandic architectural style...and, because he designed so many buildings here, you might say he succeeded. In Reykjavík alone, he designed this church, the main university building, the original National Hospital building, the National Theater, the Sundhöllin swimming pool, the Apotek Hótel we saw earlier, and the Hótel Borg across the square from the parliament building.

Hallgrímskirkja is named for the 17th-century Icelandic poet Hallgrímur Pétursson, who wrote a well-known series of 50 hymns retelling the story of the Passion of Christ.

**Interior:** Step inside (free, daily 9:00-21:00, Oct-April until 17:00). Temporary art installations fill the entry foyer. The church's

dramatically austere nave is a sleek space culminating in classically Gothic pointed arches—but with virtually no adornments. The glass is clear, not stained, and the main altar is a simple table. Notice how the ends of the pews echo the stairstep steeple outside.

Turn around and face the massive organ, which was "crowdfunded" in 1991; people paid to sponsor individual pipes. (To the right of the door you came in, notice the collection box shaped like an organ pipe—donations for the instrument's upkeep.) The church is a popular venue for organ and choral concerts (look for posters, and see page 70).

Notice that the pews are reversible—the seat backs can be flipped over to face the organ. Not only is this in keeping with Lutheranism—where the most important aspects of worship are the sermon (pulpit) and the music (organ)—but it's very practical. In smaller towns, you can't have both a church and a concert hall—so one building has to do double-duty.

Before leaving, consider riding the elevator (plus 33 steps) to the top of the **tower,** with a fine view over the rooftops. If there's a long line for the small elevator, consider coming back in the evening.

• *Head back outside. Prominently displayed in front of the church is a...*

### ⓭ Leifur Eiríksson Statue

Known as Leif Erikson (c. 970-1020) to Americans, this Viking Age explorer was—if we can trust the sagas—the first European

to set foot on the American continent. The sagas weave a colorful tale of Leifur's outlaw-family lineage and his clan's explorations. His grandfather, Þorvaldur Ásvaldsson, was exiled from Norway to Iceland, and his father, Eiríkur Þorvaldsson (Erik the Red), was in turn exiled from Iceland—establishing the first settlements on Greenland. Leifur carried on farther west, seeking a mysterious land that had been spotted by another Nordic sailor when he was blown off course.

Around five centuries before Christopher Columbus, Leifur and his crew landed in the New World, very possibly at L'Anse aux Meadows, in today's Newfoundland, where there are ruins of a Viking Age complex. Norsemen may have established more settlements in this area—which they called *Vínland* (meaning either "Land of Wine" or "Land of Meadows") for its relatively lush climate—but if so, they did not last. On his way home, according to the sagas, Leifur rescued the crew of another ship that had been stranded on a small island, and after that he was dubbed "Leifur heppni" (Leif the Lucky). The statue was donated by the US government to mark the Alþingi's 1,000th anniversary in 1930. The inscription delicately acknowledges Leifur as the "discoverer of Vínland"—but not of America.

If it's summertime, in the park flanking Leif the Lucky, look for three types of **flowers** that grow abundantly in this otherwise inhospitable land: the vivid purple Nootka lupine (from Alaska, introduced to Iceland in the mid-20th century to combat erosion); bright yellow European gorse, an alpine shrub with a pungent herbal fragrance in the early summer; and...dandelions. All three are considered weeds in much of the world, but most Icelanders don't remove them. As one local explained, "We're just happy when *anything* grows here."

• *We'll finish our walk with one more hidden sight. With the church at your back, turn left and head toward the bunker-like mansion. You'll curl around the right side of this building, passing a fun little metal cutout that lines up perfectly with the jagged roofline of the church—turn around and try it. Watch for a gate on the left and enter the...*

### ⓮ Einar Jónsson Sculpture Garden

Iceland hasn't produced many great artists—but Einar Jónsson (1874-1954) was one of the first and most significant. After studying in Copenhagen and Rome, Einar made his name working in big European capitals. But, like so many Icelanders, after half a lifetime of living abroad he felt drawn back to his homeland. Einar struck a deal with the Alþingi: If they built him a mansion and studio, he'd move back to Reykjavík and bequeath all that he produced to the city. He designed and built this house back when this was a naked, largely uninhabited hilltop (not even the church was built yet), seeding what has become a desirable neighborhood.

Linger over the 26 bronze works in the sculpture garden (free to enter). Einar's statues—with universal human themes—are taut with tension and angst. Einar was a fearful man, yet also very spiritual; his work suggests glimmers of hope in frightening times. You'll see motifs from Norse mythology and references to Iceland's "hidden people" (elves and the like). The men are mighty warriors, and the women (whose faces are modeled after Einar's wife, Anna) are protectors. Einar and Anna lived in a small, cozy, wood-paneled penthouse apartment at the top of the building's tower. To learn more about Einar, see some plaster casts of his work, and walk through his apartment, you can pay to enter the building (today the **Einar Jónsson Museum**—described on page 43, entrance facing the church).

• *Our walk is over. Both of the two downtown shopping streets—Skólavörðustígur and Laugavegur—are lined with eating options. To quickly get down to Laugavegur (and the Hlemmur bus junction), head down Frakkastígur, which runs to the left as you face the church from the top of Skólavörðustígur; on your way to the main drag, you'll pass an excellent top-end coffee shop (Reykjavík Roasters) and a fine bakery (Brauð & Co). Dining options are described later, under "Eating in Reykjavík."*

*If you follow Frakkastígur down to Laugavegur, then cross it and continue straight downhill through an uninviting condo zone (passing by the recommended Kex Hostel café), you can cross a busy street to reach the city's iconic* **Sun Voyager** *sculpture. From here, it's an easy five-minute walk (with the water on your right) to the* **Harpa** *concert hall. The* **Old Harbor** *zone is just beyond.*

# Sights in Reykjavík

In addition to its fine state- and city-run museums, Reykjavík has an assortment of pricey private museums (including Whales of Iceland, Saga Museum, Aurora Reykjavík, and the Phallological Museum). You might expect these to be tourist traps, but they're thoughtfully presented.

## DOWNTOWN REYKJAVÍK
### Near Parliament and Laugavegur
These sights are all within a short walk of the city's main artery. They're listed roughly from west to east.

### ▲The Settlement Exhibition (Landnámssýningin)
During downtown construction work in 2001, archaeologists discovered the remains of a 10th-century longhouse from the

original Reykjavík farmstead. These ruins were carefully preserved, and a small, modern, well-presented museum was built around them. This is the most accessible (and most central) place in Reykjavík to learn about Iceland's earliest history.

Some of the oldest building remains here were covered by tephra material from a volcanic eruption; carbon dating has narrowed the time of the eruption to A.D. 871...give or take a couple of years. That's why this museum is also called "Reykjavík 871±2." It's worth paying admission to see what's left of the old Viking Age house and the modern, well-presented exhibits that surround it.

**Cost and Hours:** 1,600 ISK, covered by Reykjavík City Card, free for kids 17 and younger, daily 9:00-18:00, Aðalstræti 16, tel. 411-6370, www.settlementexhibition.is.

**Tours:** Admission includes a guided tour on weekday mornings in summer (June-Aug Mon-Fri at 11:00, no tours on weekends or off-season). Skip the free audioguide, which basically repeats posted information.

**Visiting the Museum:** You'll descend to cellar level and walk around the stone-and-turf wall that survives from the 65-by-26-foot longhouse. The site is explained by a circle of high-tech exhibits on the surrounding walls. You'll learn how Scandinavians first settled the Reykjavík area a little before a volcanic eruption that took place around A.D. 871. This house dates from later (around 930) and may have belonged to the grandson of Reykjavík's semilegendary founder, Ingólfur Árnason (famous for throwing carved

REYKJAVÍK

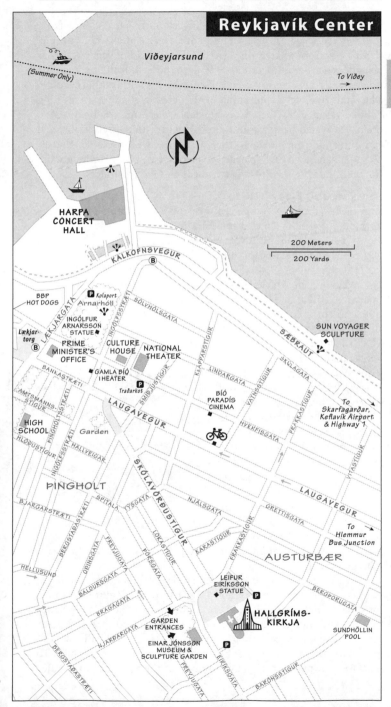

REYKJAVIK

pillars overboard to select a building site). The house of a fairly prosperous farmer, it held an extended family of about 10 people. It had a sod roof and a big hearth in the middle. The house was abandoned after only a few decades, around A.D. 1000, perhaps due to damage from a spring that still runs beneath it. Exhibits explain the landscape, flora, and fauna of this area in that era, suggesting why it was an attractive place to establish a farm. You'll see actual items excavated here: a spindle whorl with runic inscriptions, and primitive tools such as keys, fish hooks, arrowheads, and ax heads. A model and a virtual, interactive reconstruction of the longhouse further illustrate the lifestyles of these earliest Icelanders.

### ▲Kolaportið Flea Market

Reykjavík's flea market, open only on weekends, takes up the dingy ground floor of the old customs building.

**Cost and Hours:** Free entry, open Sat-Sun 11:00-17:00, closed Mon-Fri, closed or varying hours on major holiday weekends, Tryggvagata 19, tel. 562-5030, www.kolaportid.is.

**Visiting the Market:** While you'll see plenty of tourists, the market is still aimed largely at locals. It's fun to rummage through the stalls of used books and music, clothing (including knockoff Icelandic sweaters), and collectibles.

The food section serves as a crash course in Icelandic eats. Several stalls offer free samples. Look for the different kinds of smoked fish: *silungur* is trout, *bleikja* is arctic char, *lax* is salmon, and *makríll* is mackerel. If you're a bit bolder, there's *harðfiskur* (air-dried, skinless white fish that's been pounded flat—eaten as a snack with butter), crunchy fish chips, or dried seaweed (which might be labeled *hollustusnakk*—"health snack"). And  if you're even more daring, you can buy a tiny 200-ISK tub containing cubes of the notorious fermented shark, *hákarl* (you'll never eat more than this amount, and the rare restaurant that serves it charges much more).

Also look for other unusual Icelandic eats: horsemeat and horse sausage, and in summer, seabird eggs (typically from guillemots or other *svartfuglar*—birds in the auk family, which also includes puffins and murres). Look in the freezers for cod *(þorskur)*, haddock *(ýsa)*, and plaice *(rauðspretta)*, which are all Icelandic, as well as Asian imports such as *pangasius* (catfish), mussels, and squid. To cleanse your palate, grab some samples at the bakery counter (they might have a layer cake with frosting or jam), or taste-test the many different varieties of chocolate-covered licorice.

### Culture House (Safnahúsið)

Filling the stately former National Library building, this downtown branch of the National Museum features a semipermanent,

highly conceptual exhibit with objects from six national institutions. The audioguide (which you can rent, or browse on your phone using the free Wi-Fi) works hard to weave the exhibits together, but ultimately there are few highlights. Come here only if you have a National Museum ticket or Reykjavík City Card, and are curious to explore a fine old building.

**Cost and Hours:** 2,000 ISK, covered by Reykjavík City Card, includes admission to National Museum; Tue-Sun 10:00-17:00, closed Mon; Hverfisgata 15, tel. 530-2210, www.culturehouse.is.

**Visiting the Museum:** The exhibit begins with a display of 14 manuscripts of the *Jónsbók*—the law code imposed on Iceland by Norway in the late 1200s, and named "Jón's Book" after the man who compiled it. The earliest one is the priceless *Skarðsbók* from 1363, an illuminated manuscript painstakingly written on vellum (calfskin). As the original Icelandic saga manuscripts are not on public view, this is as close as you'll get to seeing pages from that era...and a very big deal to Icelanders. Other highlights include the elegant old reading room on the second floor; some eye-catching illustrations of Icelandic mountains and rivers by Samúel Eggertsson; and, on the top floor, an exhibit on the great auk—a large, flightless, penguin-like bird that was once abundant in Iceland, but hunted to extinction in the mid-19th century.

### ▲▲Laugavegur, Reykjavík's Main Drag

The city's main walking street is a delight to stroll—particularly its eastern stretch, Laugavegur. While far from "local" (you'll

rarely spot an Icelander here who doesn't work in the tourist trade), it's enjoyable to wander and browse, with characteristic old houses, vivid street art, tempting cafés and bars, and—yes—plenty of touristy puffin shops. Many visitors wind up doing several laps up and down Laugavegur, picking out new details with each pass. I've described a short stretch of Laugavegur on my self-guided "Reykjavík Walk," and listed several businesses along here in the Eating, Shopping, and Nightlife sections.

## Icelandic Phallological Museum (Hið Íslenzka Reðasafn)

This gimmicky museum near the Hlemmur bus junction (at the far end of Laugavegur) is a one-room collection of preserved animal penises that can be seen in 15 minutes, plus various depictions of phalluses in folk art. It's impossible to describe (or visit) this place without juvenile jokes, so here goes: You'll see more wieners than you can shake a stick at—preserved, pickled peckers floating in jars of yellow liquid. You'll see a seal's schlong, a wolf's wang, a zebra's zipper trout, a fox's frankfurter, a giraffe's gherkin, a dog's dong, a badger's baloney pony, a squirrel's schwanz, a coyote's crankshaft, a horse's hardware, a reindeer's rod, an elephant's equipment, and lots of whale willies. If you can't get through this description without giggling, maybe you should visit. If you're about to set down this book and write me an angry letter...don't.

**Cost and Hours:** 1,500 ISK, daily 9:00-18:00, Oct-April from 10:00, Laugavegur 116, tel. 561-6663, www.phallus.is.

## Hallgrímskirkja Area

This hilltop zone is marked by the prominent tower of Reykjavík's landmark church.

### ▲▲Hallgrímskirkja Lutheran Church

Reykjavík's most recognizable icon is the stairstep gable of this fine, modern church, designed in the 1930s by state architect Guðjón Samúelsson. It boasts a sleek interior and a tower with grand views. For more on the church and its interior, see my "Reykjavík Walk," earlier. In the summer, there are regular

performances on its booming organ (see "Entertainment in Reykjavík," later).

**Cost and Hours:** Church—free; tower—900 ISK, 100 ISK for kids under 15. Church and tower open 9:00-21:00, Oct-April until 17:00. The church sometimes closes for special events. Tel. 510-1000, www.hallgrimskirkja.is.

**Tower:** The 250-foot-tall tower offers a commanding view of the city. A six-person elevator takes you up to the belfry, where you can look down on the city's colorful roofs amidst the clang of the church bells (cover your ears at :00 and :30 past the hour). Straight ahead, look down over the colorful roofs lining Skólavörðustígur street, which stretches toward the harbor. In the distance, if it's clear, you may see the snow-capped volcanic peak at the end of the Snæfellsnes Peninsula, 50 miles away. The closer mountain, looming to the right, is the 3,000-foot Mount Esja, a popular destination for local hikers. And to the right, the island you see is Viðey, reachable on an easy cruise (see page 51). Ponder the fact that well over half of Iceland's population lives in view of this church. Lines for the elevator can be long—if there's a crowd, swing back later in the day.

### ▲Einar Jónsson Museum and Garden (Listasafn Einars Jónssonar)

The former home of gifted sculptor Einar Jónsson (1874-1954)—facing Hallgrímskirkja church—has a free sculpture garden out back (described in "Reykjavík Walk," earlier). For a more intimate look at the artist, tour the museum (entrance at the front, facing the church). Inside, you'll see his home, and several large- and small-scale plaster casts for Einar bronzes that decorate the city.

**Cost and Hours:** 1,000 ISK, Tue-Sun 10:00-17:00, closed Mon, Eiríksgata 3, tel. 551-3797, www.lej.is.

**Visiting the Museum:** Stepping into the grand **entry hall,** immediately on your right is *Outlaws* (*Útlagar,* 1901). This break-

through work, completed while Einar was a student in Denmark, is one of his trademark pieces. It depicts a convicted man who takes his wife's lifeless body to a cemetery before escaping with his child to live in the Highlands. (As many original Icelandic settlers were themselves outlaws—exiled from Norway—this theme is particularly poignant.) Just beyond that, *Dawn* (*Dögun,* 1906) illustrates a scene from an Icelandic folk tale, in which a girl tricks a troll by keeping him talking until the sun rises. He sweeps her up in his arm at the very moment the sun freezes him in stone, and he shakes his fist defiantly.

Then climb the tight spiral staircase to see the intimate **apartment** that Einar and his wife Anna shared—a cozy, human-scale contrast to the beefy building and Einar's dynamic works.

Yet more of Einar's sculptures are **downstairs.** In the red room, the striking *Rest* (*Hvíld,* completed in 1935) is an eerie, oversized bust of a young man whose face is half-covered by reptilian basalt columns. Beneath his chin stands a sculptor leaning against a giant hammer, taking a break. This recalls the notion (dating back to Michelangelo) that the sculpture already exists within the stone; it's the artist's job to chip away and reveal it. In *The Spell Broken* (*Úr Álögum*, completed 1927), a St. George-like knight—protectively cradling a woman—slays a dragon by driving his sword through its head. In the green room, the evocative *Remorse* (*Samviskubit*, completed 1947) shows a man tormented by tiny, conscience-like beings. One holds his eyes open, the other recites a litany of wrong-doings in his ear, and both ensure he can't escape whatever's wracking him with guilt.

## Beyond the Pond
### ▲▲National Museum of Iceland (Þjóðminjasafnið)
The National Museum presents a thoughtful and manageable look at the history of this island nation, making excellent use of artifacts and a top-notch audioguide that brings meaning to the exhibits. The collection is a bit dry, but rewards those with a serious inter-est and attention span. There's also a pleasant café and a classy gift shop.

**Cost and Hours:** 2,000 ISK, covered by Reykjavík City Card, includes admission to Culture House; daily 10:00-17:00, mid-Sept-April closed Mon; Suðurgata 41, tel. 530-2200, www. thjodminjasafn.is.

**Tours:** Rent the essential audioguide for 300 ISK—or down-load it for free via the museum's Wi-Fi.

**Getting There:** The museum is near the far end of the Pond, a pleasant 10-minute walk from City Hall along Tjarnargata; you can also take bus #1, #3, #6, or #14 to the Háskóli Íslands stop. If walking between the harbor area and the museum, you can short-cut along Garðastræti and through Hólavallakirkjugarður, the city's oldest cemetery.

**Visiting the Museum:** The permanent exhibit fills the two long floors upstairs, telling the story of Iceland. The exhibit is high-tech, loosely chronological, and well-explained in English.

From the ticket desk, head upstairs to begin. You'll see a few objects from the Settlement Age, including candle holders and gorgeous, oversized brass "dome brooches." Much of this floor is dominated by medieval church art, dating from after the island's conversion around A.D. 1000. The darkened room in the center displays vestments, statues, altar tapestries, and bells that were all imported from Europe—a reminder that early Icelanders were hardworking frontier farmers who had to order their luxury goods from "back east." Two locally made exceptions are wooden panels from a c. 1100 *Judgment Day* painting, and a carved crucifix from c. 1200. Nearby, examine the exquisite wood-carved door from the church in Valþjófsstaður (in eastern Iceland), illustrating the story of a knight who slew a dragon to save a lion. Like many precious

Icelandic objects, this door was taken to Denmark for safekeeping; the Danish government returned it in the 1930s, as part of a gift to Iceland in honor of the millennial celebration of the Alþingi.

Near the end of this floor, look for Guðbrandur's Bible—the first-ever Bible in Icelandic (1584). The Protestant Reformation, which began in Europe, also spread to Iceland, and to this day, the majority of Icelanders are Lutheran. The landing at the far end of the hall quickly covers the period of Danish rule, plus temporary exhibits.

The permanent exhibit continues upstairs, covering the 17th century through the present. Look for the drinking horn by Brynjólfur Jónsson, painstakingly carved with Bible scenes (1598). Following the Reformation, the Danish king also headed the Lutheran Church of Iceland, giving him tremendous power. While absolute rule by the king limited his subjects' freedom, it spurred efficiency and economic progress. Exhibits explain how, in 1703, Iceland conducted the world's first census that recorded every person's name (allowing us to know with precision that, in that year, Iceland was home to 50,358 people—99 percent of them farmers and farm workers).

Other exhibits explain how Danes maintained a monopoly on trade in Iceland. Starting around 1750, first the Enlighten-ment and then the wave of nationalism and democracy that swept Europe also reached these shores—with diverse effects, from the reconstitution of the Alþingi in 1845, to the creation of an Icelandic national costume by a local artist in

1860 (Sigurður Guðmundsson's *skautbúningur*). Meanwhile, the humble people of Iceland toiled along on chilly, smelly farms in the countryside—peer inside a typical farmhouse living room (called a *baðstofa*). Other Icelanders lived off the sea—fishing from basic, small, open rowing/sailing boats, like the one on display, all the way up to the advent of motorized vessels.

Soon Iceland was primed for self-rule, and you'll see the desk of the man who worked hardest to make it happen: Jón Sigurðsson, who loudly agitated in Copenhagen for a national constitution and an end to the trade monopoly. Nearby, look for "The Blue and White"— an early, unofficial Icelandic flag (missing the current red cross). In 1913, a young Icelander flew the flag from his small boat in Reykjavík harbor, until a Danish coast guard ship seized the "unauthorized" colors. Furious Icelanders demanded that the issue be resolved, and it eventually caught the attention of the Danish king—who agreed that Iceland deserved its own banner. Viewing tests from a distance showed that the blue-and-white flag was too easy to confuse with Sweden's, so the red cross was added. The flag was made official in 1915. Iceland became a sovereign state in 1918, and a fully independent republic in 1944.

The exhibit finishes with a look at modern Iceland. Look for the giant, white trawl wire cutters—a weapon used in the "Cod Wars" between Iceland and the UK (1958-1976), when the two countries squabbled over fishing rights. Finally, an airport conveyor belt displays various trappings of modern Icelandic life.

## REYKJAVÍK'S ART MUSEUMS

This small community has a busy arts scene, and the six local museums described next proudly show off Iceland's 20th-century artists. Iceland's artistic tradition goes back only a century or so; most Icelandic artists (even today) traveled abroad to get a solid education. Among the country's impressive artists are the early-20th-century sculptor **Einar Jónsson** (whose former home and gallery, described earlier, faces Hallgrímskirkja church), several good painters and illustrators, and the contemporary mixed media artist **Ólafur Elíasson** (based in Berlin, but with a studio along Reykjavík's waterfront, described later). The Reykjavík City Card covers all six branches, but I wouldn't dedicate much time here: These museums have a hard time competing with all the nearby natural beauty and interesting history.

**REYKJAVÍK**

### National Gallery of Iceland (Listasafn Íslands)

The National Gallery has three branches, each with separate costs and hours. The **main branch** is near the Pond, with five gallery spaces showing off a continually changing selection of pieces from their permanent collection of mainly modern Icelandic artists. They also have a few international pieces—including works by Picasso and Munch—but these are not always on display (1,500 ISK; daily 10:00-17:00; off-season Tue-Sun 11:00-17:00, closed Mon; Fríkirkjuvegur 7, www.listasafn.is).

The **Ásgrímur Jónsson Collection** highlights a rotating selection of works by this early-20th-century painter who specialized in Impressionistic landscapes of his homeland, dynamic illustrations of the sagas, and some later, Expressionistic, Munch-like pieces (1,000 ISK; summer Tue, Thu, Sat-Sun 14:00-17:00; off-season open only Sat-Sun; in his former home at Bergstaðastræti 74—a few blocks southeast of the main branch and Pond).

The **Sigurjón Ólafsson Museum** showcases the heavily stylized, sometimes abstract works of this mid-20th-century sculptor, who studied under both Einar Jónsson and Ásgrímur Jónsson (1,000 ISK; summer Tue-Sun 14:00-17:00, closed Mon; off-season Sat-Sun only, closed Dec-Jan; northeast of downtown near the Skarfagarðar cruise terminal, at Laugarnestangi 17).

### Reykjavík Art Museum (Listasafn Reykjavíkur)

This institution has three branches, each with changing exhibits focusing on modern art (for the latest lineup, see www.artmuseum.is). The **main branch,** right downtown and near the Kolaportið flea market at Tryggvagata 17, has an eclectic range of temporary exhibits, but almost always highlights a few works by Pop artist Erró—Iceland's answer to Roy Lichtenstein. The **Kjarvalsstaðir** branch exhibits some works by idiosyncratic modern painter Jóhannes Sveinsson Kjarval, who blended Icelandic landscapes with abstract and surreal flourishes (it's a 10-minute walk south of the Hlemmur bus junction, in the Klambratún park at Flókagata 24). And the **Ásmundarsafn** branch, in the eastern neighborhood of Laugardalur, highlights work by the mid-20th-century, mostly abstract, Miró-like sculptor Ásmundur Sveinsson, displayed in his architecturally striking former home (on Sigtún, near the corner of Reykjavegur).

**Cost and Hours:** All three museums are covered by a 1,600-ISK ticket for 24 hours, covered by the Reykjavík City Card, and open daily 10:00-17:00. The main branch stays open until 22:00 on Thu, and Ásmundarsafn has shorter hours off-season (13:00-17:00, www.artmuseum.is).

### Reykjavík Museum of Photography (Ljósmyndasafn)

This museum features Icelandic photography, both contemporary and historical. It's near the Reykjavík Art Museum's main branch, on the top floor of the downtown City Library (1,000 ISK, covered by Reykjavík City Card, open Mon-Thu 10:00-18:00, Fri from 11:00, Sat-Sun 13:00-17:00, Tryggvagata 15, www. borgarsogusafn.is).

## ALONG THE WATERFRONT

These sights are spread along a lengthy stretch of the city waterfront. I've listed them roughly from east to west.

## Just Below the Main Drag

These sights are just downhill from Bankastræti/Laugavegur streets.

### ▲Sun Voyager (Sólfar)

This popular outdoor stainless-steel sculpture is shaped like an old Viking boat, pointing northwest in the direction of the setting sun in summer. This ode to the sun
is a good place to watch the sea, take a selfie, and ponder the promise of undiscovered territory that brought Scandinavians to Iceland more than a thousand years ago—and the impulses that pushed them farther west, to Greenland and Canada. The sculpture, by Icelandic artist

Jón Gunnar Árnason, is a few blocks along the shore past Harpa, at the base of Frakkastígur street, about a five-minute walk below Laugavegur; drivers on the westbound waterfront highway will find a handy pull-out right at the sculpture.

### ▲▲Harpa Concert Hall

One of Reykjavík's newest landmarks, this cutting-edge performing arts and conference center feels too big for such a small city.
That's because the ambitious building was conceived during Iceland's banking mania. When the crash came in 2008, construction had already begun. Some cynics proposed that it be left half-built, as a monument to the greed and excess of unbridled capitalism. In the end, Harpa was finished, but plans

for a new residential and commercial quarter around it (including a striking bank headquarters) were shelved. By the time it was completed and opened in 2011, Harpa was hemorrhaging money, kept alive thanks only to huge subsidies (which some Icelanders feel would be better spent elsewhere). Despite the woes, Reykjavík wound up with a fine performance space, and the city will grow into it. In 2013, the building (designed by the Danish Henning Larsen firm), won the EU's prestigious Mies van der Rohe Award—achieving the goal of putting Iceland on the world architectural map.

Harpa's honeycombed facade, designed by Danish-born Icelandic artist Ólafur Elíasson, is the most-loved part of the building: In summer the window panes reflect the light in patterns, and in winter they're illuminated in pretty colors. The choice of location, parroting the harborside opera house cliché that started in Sydney, unfortunately separates Harpa from the rest of downtown across a busy four-lane road. But photographers drool over the building, and find lots of great angles to shoot. Don't miss the view from the far end of the pier that extends to the right of the building, where the facade is reflected in the harbor along with sailboats.

Be sure to step inside, where you're bathed in the light of those many windows. The dominant interior materials are black concrete and red wood, evoking the volcanic eruptions that have shaped Iceland. To enjoy the building's full effect, catch a performance (see options under "Entertainment in Reykjavík," later) or take a tour.

**Cost and Hours:** Lobby free to enter, daily 8:00-24:00; summer 30-minute tour—1,500 ISK, hourly 10:00-17:00; off-season 45-minute tour—2,200 ISK, 1-2/day; café and gift shop, tel. 528-5000, www.harpa.is.

## Old Harbor Area

Reykjavík's Old Harbor—about a 10-minute walk west of Harpa—isn't a creaky, shiplap time capsule, but an industrial-feeling port. Tucked around the busy berths and piers are a few seafood restaurants, kiosks selling boat trips, and (at the far end) a smattering of museums. To get here, walk out from downtown (10 minutes), or take bus #14 to the Mýrargata stop.

## ▲Exploring the Harbor

To get your bearings at the harbor, stand on the seaward side of the turquoise-colored sheds (which house some recommended restaurants) and face the bobbing boats. This "old" harbor was built only in the 1910s, on reclaimed land. (For much of its history—back when Reyk-
javík was a farm, then a small town—there was good anchor-
age, but no real harbor.) Today, heavy traffic has moved to the newer container terminal far-

ther along the peninsula. The harbor serves a mixture of excursion boats, small craft, the coast guard (notice the hulking gray ships with red-and-blue trim), and a few fishing trawlers that bring their catch to processing plants. A single small cruise ship can also moor in the harbor (larger ones use the cruise terminal in a different part of town).

On your left is the Ægisgarður pier, lined with ticket offices for several whale-watching tours (described next), as well as bike tours. On your right, across the harbor, you can see the angular, glass facade of the Harpa concert hall. And the dramatic mountain rising up straight ahead is Esja—six miles away and 3,000 feet high.

Stroll out to the end of the **Ægisgarður pier** to comparison-
shop excursion boats, and to get a good look at the hodgepodge of vessels that call this harbor home. At the beginning of the pier, an anti-whaling organization would love to talk you out of sampling whale meat. At the far end (on the left), you'll see part of Iceland's whale-hunting fleet moored (look for the black-and-white boats called *Hvalur 8* and *Hvalur 9*)—an odd juxtaposition with the whale watching industry all around you.

Back at the base of the pier, in front of Hótel Marina, is a slip where boats are hauled up to be painted (one of the remain-
ing vestiges of the maritime industry here). To extend your visit to the nearby Grandi area—with several sightseeing attractions and eateries—simply follow the footpath between the harborfront and Hótel Marina. For more on this area, see "Grandi," later.

### Whale Watching and Other Boat Trips

Whale watching is a popular Reykjavík activity. While it can be en-
joyable to get out on the water—and catching a glimpse of a whale is undoubtedly exciting—it's a substantial investment of time and money, particularly given that you may see nothing at all. Before deciding to go on a whale-watching cruise, read the description on page 164. As an alternative to a pricey whale-focused trip, consider

a faster and cheaper boat trip—such as to the island of Viðey (see later). And if you want to be assured of seeing "whales"—very up-close—you may prefer a visit to the Whales of Iceland exhibit, a short walk away (described under "Grandi," later). If you're traveling around Iceland, be aware there are also whale-watching opportunities in the north, in the Akureyri area and in Húsavík.

The many boat tour companies with ticket booths along the Old Harbor's Ægisgarður pier are fiercely competitive, offering much the same experience. For the latest prices, schedules, and

details, check each company's website, look for brochures locally, or stop by the sales kiosks. The most established outfit is **Elding** ("Lightning," described later); others include **Whale Safari** (www.whalesafari.is), **Special Tours** (www.specialtours. is), and **Ambassador** (www. ambassador.is). While Elding is typically the most all-around reliable choice, check the latest online reviews to survey the pros and cons of each one. For comparison's sake, I've outlined Elding's offerings here. Prices are typically a bit cheaper if you prebook directly online, where you'll usually find special offers.

**Whale Watching:** The **classic** whale-watching trip is three hours and runs daily all year, weather permitting (from 6/day July-Aug to 1/day Dec-Jan; adults 11,000 ISK, children 7-15 pay half-price, children under 7 free; Ægisgarður 5, tel. 519-5000, www. elding.is). You'll pay nearly double for an **"express"** option on a "RIB"—a rigid inflatable boat that also includes a high-speed zip across the waves. You'll be issued a warm coverall and goggles for this two-hour thrill ride (20,000 ISK, mid-April-Oct only).

**Other Boat Trips:** Elding and their competitors also run other seasonal boat trips. The **puffin-watching** cruise (mid-May-mid-Aug only) is shorter (1 hour) and cheaper (6,500 ISK adults) than whale watching—so if you're most interested in riding a boat, it's a reasonable alternative. Cheaper still is Elding's 20-minute ferry service to **Viðey Island,** which gets you out on the water while saving you the overland trip to the Skarfagarðar dock (1,500 ISK round-trip, 2/day, mid-May-Sept only; for more on what to do on the island, see page 58). In the early winter (early Oct-early Dec), when the **Imagine Peace Tower** on Viðey Island is illuminated, Elding offers a two-hour cruise for a closer look (8,500 ISK). Anglers enjoy the **sea-angling** trips (3 hours trying your luck catching cod, haddock, mackerel, and catfish, with an on-board grill party at the end, May-Aug only, 14,200 ISK). And in the dark months, you can take a two-hour, late-evening cruise in hopes of viewing the **northern lights** from the water (11,000 ISK, Sept-mid-April at 21:00 or 22:00).

## Volcano House

This attraction, a block off the Old Harbor, features a modest exhibit and a screening room that alternates between two documentaries explaining Iceland's most famous recent eruptions: the Westman Islands in 1973, which swallowed up part of the town of Heimaey (20 minutes); and Eyjafjallajökull in 2010, which halted European air traffic (25 minutes). The movies are interesting, particularly if you're not getting beyond Reykjavík and are curious about Iceland's famous volcanoes, but it's pricey.

**Cost and Hours:** 2,000 ISK, daily 9:00-22:00, last film begins at 21:00, Tryggvagata 11, tel. 555-1900, www.volcanohouse.is.

## Grandi

The long, broad peninsula that juts out beyond the far end of the Old Harbor is an up-and-coming district called Grandi. This former sandbar, built up with landfill, is an odd assortment: A spread-out strip of old warehouses and new big-box stores, but with a lively little waterfront zone (along Grandagarður) where you'll find some excellent eateries, and several sights (which I've listed in the order you'll approach them, if walking from the Old Harbor). At the far tip of the peninsula—a 15-minute walk or short drive away—is a trendy little cultural zone, anchored by the Marshall-húsið arts center.

### ▲Saga Museum

The Saga Museum is your best bet for an experience focused on the stories of the early Norsemen who turned Iceland's wilderness into a European community (even the National Museum covers the sagas only tangentially). This place does a valiant job of telescoping the sagas into an educational 35 minutes. Though epensive, it's far better than you'd expect for a walk-through of 17 Viking Age mannequin scenes depicting Iceland's Settlement Age. Each scene is rooted in textual evidence from the sagas and well-described by the audioguide (which is academic enough that it might bore younger or less interested visitors). At the end, you can dress up in Viking garb for a photo.

**Cost and Hours:** 2,100 ISK, 800 ISK for kids 6-12, daily 10:00-18:00, Grandagarður 2, tel. 694-3096, www.sagamuseum.is.

### ▲Aurora Reykjavík: The Northern Lights Center

If weather and daylight conditions are imperfect during your visit, this attraction may be more satisfying than trying to see the northern lights in person. You'll walk through some sparse exhibits, including one on legends and superstitions that attempted to explain these once-mysterious dancing lights. Then you'll learn a bit about the science of the phenomenon. But the main attraction is an extremely soothing 22-minute widescreen film featuring time-lapse footage of the aurora borealis at points around Iceland, photographed over eight years of cold nights. In the gift shop, you can slip on a pair of virtual reality goggles and spin around in a chair, tracking the lights as they flutter through the sky. (For more on the northern lights, and how to see them yourself, see the Icelandic Experiences chapter.)

**Cost and Hours:** 1,600 ISK, daily 9:00-21:00, Grandagarður 2, tel. 780-4500, www.aurorareykjavik.is.

### Reykjavík Maritime Museum (Sjóminjasafnið í Reykjavík)

This well-done but fairly dry exhibit considers Reykjavík's connection to the sea. Upstairs is the permanent exhibit, which traces Reykjavík's history from remote farm to bustling capital—partly thanks to its role as a fishing, shipping, and maritime center. Throughout you'll see plenty of well-described artifacts (including full-size boats), and life-size dioramas re-creating various chapters in the city's history. You'll learn why stockfish (naturally dried in the cold Reykjavík wind) was so important on early voyages, how boats gradually evolved from rowing and sailing to industrial trawlers, and how radios and navigational technology improved over time.

**Cost and Hours:** 1,600 ISK, daily 10:00-17:00, Grandagarður 8, tel. 411-6300, www.borgarsogusafn.is.

### ▲▲Whales of Iceland

Tucked unassumingly in a box-store zone just a five-minute walk beyond the museum strip, this attraction fills a cavernous ware-

house with life-size models of the whales found in the waters around Iceland. The models are impressively detailed and bathed in a shimmering blue light, and you're invited to wander under and among them, getting an up-close view of the graceful creatures. The essential audioguide (free to download via the exhibit's Wi-Fi) is informative and engaging. Begin with the smaller marine mammals: dolphin, narwhal, orca. Then step

## Sagas of the Icelanders 101

As with tales of Beowulf, King Arthur, and Robin Hood, scholars don't know how much of the Icelandic sagas is historically based and how much is fictionalized. But all agree that the sagas are an essential resource for understanding both Iceland's history and the cultural heritage it shares with mainland Scandinavia.

Icelanders have strong narrative traditions. Before they had a written language, legends and laws were passed down orally. With Christianity around A.D. 1000 came the Latin alphabet, which Icelandic scribes used to document their history, writing mostly in their own language.

These historical narratives, known collectively as "the sagas," were written on precious vellum (calfskin) mainly in the 13th and 14th centuries. It was the Icelanders who first wrote down the dynamic stories of the early Norsemen—from myths of Norse gods like Óðinn (Odin) and Þórr (Thor) to early histories of Scandinavian warriors and kings. Like the epic poems of the ancient Greeks, the sagas provide a cultural foundation for the Nordic people, stretching all the way through history to the present.

Here's a simplified overview of some of the most famous or influential sagas and other early writings:

The **Book of Settlements** (Landnámabók)—not strictly a "saga"—documents the earliest ninth- and tenth-century settlers in Iceland. This chronicle tells the story of Hrafna-Flóki (the Raven) Vilgerðarson, who followed a bird to Iceland after he'd been blown off-course on his way to the Faroe Islands; and the story of Ingólfur Árnason, who threw two carved pillars overboard and built his settlement where they washed up, founding Reykjavík. Remarkably, the Book of Settlements lists more than 400 different families, where each one settled, their family tree, and vivid stories of what they encountered here. The much shorter **Book of Icelanders** (Íslendingabók), written by Ari fróði ("the Wise") Þorgilsson in the early 12th century, gives a concise summary of the history of Iceland up to Ari's own time, including the establishment of the Icelandic Commonwealth and the conversion to Christianity.

The **Saga of Erik the Red** (Eiríks saga rauða) and the **Saga of the Greenlanders** (Grænlendinga saga), known together as "the Vínland sagas," tell of how Eiríkur rauði ("the Red") Þorvaldsson

(950–c. 1003), banished from Norway, then Iceland, founded a Norse settlement in Greenland; and how his son, Leifur heppni ("the Lucky") Eiríksson, explored what we now know as North America.

**Egill's Saga** *(Egils saga Skallagrímssonar)* tells the story of Egill Skallagrímsson (c. 904–c. 995). Egill is a fascinatingly complex figure: Swarthy and ugly, he was both a fearsome champion warrior and a tender-souled poet. When he was just seven years old, after losing a game, a furious Egill buried his ax in the head of his opponent—claiming his first of many victims. And yet, Egill composed his first poem at the tender age of three, and went on to author some of the loveliest verse in Icelandic literature (after two of his children died, Egill composed the heartbreaking "Lament for My Sons"). Egill's Saga tells of his tortured relationship with his equally short-tempered father, Skalla-Grímur ("Grímur the Bald"); his friendship and rivalry with his dashing brother, Þórólfr; his relationship with his foster sister, turned-sister-in-law, turned wife, Ásgerður; his run-ins with the powerful witch Gunnhildur; and his clashes with his nemesis, King Harald Fairhair of Norway.

**Njál's Saga** *(Brennu-Njáls saga)* tells the story of wise Njáll Þorgeirsson and his best friend, the gallant Gunnar Hámundarson. Things take a tragic turn—as they always do in the sagas—as early Iceland's penchant for escalating blood feuds spirals out of control, culminating in several tragic deaths. (Spoiler: The protagonist is also known as Brennu-Njáll—"Burning Njáll.")

The **Saga of the People of Laxárdalr** *(Laxdæla saga)* is a gripping love triangle. Childhood friends Kjartan Ólafsson and Bolli Þorleiksson fall in love with the same woman, the beautiful Guðrún Ósvífrsdóttir. Tragedy ensues.

Icelanders also recorded mythic histories much older than the settlement of Iceland. **Völsunga Saga,** which may have roots in the fifth-century conquests of Attila the Hun, is a sprawling, epic tale of the Völsung clan, including Sigurðr Fáfnisbani ("Slayer of the dragon Fáfnir"), which has inspired artists from Richard Wagner to J. R. R. Tolkien. The two Eddas—the anonymous **Poetic Edda** and Snorri Sturluson's **Prose Edda**—contain ancient poetry that records the myths of the Germanic pagan religion.

Snorri Sturluson (1179-1241)—who also wrote **Heimskringla,** the history of the Norwegian kings—was himself a dynamic figure whose life is described in **Sturlunga Saga.**

For a hefty (and I mean hefty) sample of some of the better-known sagas, pick up *The Sagas of the Icelanders,* a good, brick-like English translation edited by Robert Kellogg.

into a vast space to ogle the majestic giants: pilot whale, humpback whale, sei whale, bowhead whale, minke whale (the one you'll see on local menus—fittingly suspended above the museum café), *Moby Dick*-style sperm whale, and the largest specimen, the blue whale—which can grow up to 110 feet long. You'll also get to see (and heft) a whale's tooth and some baleen. While this is very expensive considering the brief amount of time most visitors spend here, it's legitimately educational and scratches your Icelandic-whale itch.

**Cost and Hours:** 2,900 ISK, 1,500 ISK for kids ages 7-14, free for kids under 7, daily 10:00-18:00, off-season until 17:00, Fiskislóð 23, tel. 571-0077, www.whalesoficeland.is.

**Getting There:** The exhibit is a little tricky to find. From the Maritime Museum and recommended Grandi restaurants along Grandagarður, walk to the end of the first long, white-and-turquoise warehouse building with eateries and boutiques, then turn left on Grunnslóð and walk one long block. You can also take bus #14 to the Grunnslóð stop, or drive (free parking right in front).

### Marshall-húsið Art Center

Filling a converted fish factory at the far tip of the pier (and of interest mainly to art lovers with a car), this arts center hosts several galleries. The big draw is the gallery of Ólafur Elíasson, the renowned Icelandic artist who was born in Denmark and keeps a (private) studio upstairs here. Ólafur—who helped design Reykjavík's Harpa concert hall—specializes in large-scale, multimedia pieces that combine technical precision with intangible elements like light, water, wind, temperature, and movement. The building also has two other artist-run gallery spaces (The Living Art Museum, www.nylo.is; and Kling & Bang, www.this.is/klingogbang) and Marshall, an appealing **$$$** café/restaurant facing the harbor (same hours as galleries, tel. 519-7766).

**Cost and Hours:** All galleries are free, Tue-Sun 12:00-18:00, Thu until 21:00, closed Mon, Grandagarður 20, bus #14 to Fiskislóð stop.

**Nearby:** This far tip of Grandi has started to attract some trendy businesses. Across the street in a nondescript warehouse zone, you'll find the flagship store of **Farmers Market,** with updated Icelandic fashion (closed Sun; city-center branch described under "Shopping in Reykjavík") and **Omnom,** a boutique chocolate factory (closed Sun, www.omnomchocolate.com).

## OUTSIDE THE CENTER

You'll need a car, a bus, or a boat to reach the sights in this section.

## Just South of Downtown
### ▲The Pearl (Perlan)

This striking observation deck/restaurant/museum was created in the 1990s at the site of the city's former water storage tanks. Come

here for the free view of the city and surroundings from the circular fourth-floor **viewing platform,** which rings a glass dome above the old water tanks. While the Hallgrímskirkja tower puts Reykjavík's rooftops at your feet, the Pearl's sweeping views take in the full 360-degree panorama of the city and its backdrop of sea and mountains (and it's free and less crowded).

Get your bearings by looking north to the rugged ridge of Mount Esja, then pan left, where you can't miss the spire of Hallgrímskirkja. Farther to the left (if it's clear) you'll spot the snowy white triangle of Snæfellsjökull on the northwest horizon, 75 miles away as the puffin flies. The view to the west is dominated by the bay of Faxaflói, and beyond that is the Denmark Strait. Sail 460 miles due west, and you'll be in Greenland. To the southwest you'll see a few small peninsulas jutting into the bay, and, in the distance, volcanic cones that mark the Reykjanes Peninsula, where the Blue Lagoon and Keflavík Airport lie.

The old tanks below the dome have been converted into a **Museum of Icelandic Natural Wonders,** with informative dis-

plays about Iceland's unique environment. Highlights include a short walk through an artificial 230-foot-long ice cave (chilled to 15°F, but don't worry—they provide warm jackets), and a simulation of what it's like to stand on top of Vatnajökull, Iceland's largest glacier. A planetarium and exhibits covering geology, sea life, birds, earthquakes, volcanoes, and the northern lights are also part of the line-up.

The Pearl is worth a quick stop for drivers, who will likely pass by on their way into and out of town. There's a convenient but pricey café on the fourth floor, an expensive restaurant on the fifth (in the dome), and a branch of the Rammagerðin gift shop.

**Cost and Hours:** Observation deck—free, daily 8:00-20:00;

exhibit—3,000 ISK, 1,500 ISK for kids 6-15, daily 8:00-19:00, last entry one hour before closing; www.perlanmuseum.is.

**Getting There:** It's easiest to drive; there's a big, free parking lot. By bus, take #18 from Hlemmur two stops to Perlan. You could also take bus #5 to Nauthólsvegur and walk up the hill along the paths.

**Nearby:** Around the Pearl is the forested **Öskjuhlíð** hill, with walking paths, World War II ruins (signboards explain them), many rabbits (descended from escaped pets), the temple for Iceland's revived pagan religion (the "first Norse temple built here in a thousand years," www.asatru.is), and a large cemetery, Fossvogskirkjugarður.

## Northeast of Downtown
### ▲Viðey Island

On a nice day, spend an afternoon enjoying the views of the sea and the mountains from this island a few hundred yards offshore. It's a sleepy sight, and takes a little work to reach, but it gets you into the Icelandic outdoors inexpensively and without a trip out of town. And the island comes with an interesting history.

**Getting There:** You have two options for reaching Viðey (schedules below). From the Old Harbor in the city center, Elding runs a direct but infrequent ferry (2/day, summer only, 20 minutes). Or—for a more frequent and much shorter connection—go to the Skarfagarðar ferry dock, by Reykjavík's cruise ship terminal, where small passenger ferries make the five-minute crossing to the island (take bus #16 from Hlemmur six stops to Skarfagarðar). Drivers park for free by the Skarfagarðar dock.

**Cost and Hours:** The ferry is 1,500 ISK roundtrip from the Old Harbor, 1,200 ISK round-trip from Skarfagarðar, covered by Reykjavík City Card; sights on the island are free. Ferries from the Old Harbor leave daily mid-May-Sept at 11:50 and 14:50 (none off-season); last return from island at 17:30. Hourly ferries from Skarfagarðar leave mid-May-Sept daily 10:15-17:15, last return from island at 18:30; Oct-mid-May Sat-Sun only 13:15-15:15, last return from island at 16:30. Ferry info at tel. 519-5000, www.elding.is.

**Visiting the Island:** Above the island's dock, the large, restored **house** from the 1750s is the oldest in the capital area. It was originally built for Iceland's Danish governor, but he chose to live in Reykjavík instead. Inside is a modest café, a free exhibit about the island, and a free WC. Next door, look into the small, traditional church, which is almost as old (from the 1760s).

From where you land, you can stroll to either end of the island in about 15 minutes. To the left, the west part of the island is empty grassland except for a series of columnar basalt statues by

American sculptor Richard Serra. To the right, the road through the east part of the island leads to an **abandoned village** that, in the 1920s, had a port almost as important as Reykjavík's. You can enter the old village school, which has a photography exhibit on the island's history.

Next to the café is the **Imagine Peace Tower**—a powerful vertical pillar of light, installed and paid for by Yoko Ono. Each year it shines from October 9, John Lennon's birthday, until December 8, the day he died (www.imaginepeacetower.com).

## In Laugardalur, East of Downtown

Though modest by international standards, the Laugardalur (LOY-gar-DA-lurr) valley—just east of downtown—makes a pleasant outing on a nice day and lets you hang out with Icelandic families and their kids. You pay to enter the zoo and amusement area (the adjacent botanic garden is free). A lovely café in the gardens serves meals. There's also an indoor ice rink, and the Reykjavík Art Museum's Ásmundarsafn branch is nearby (see listing, earlier).

**Getting There:** By bus, take #2, #5, #15, or #17 to the Laugardalshöll stop and walk 10 minutes downhill to the parking lot and entrance.

### Family Park and Zoo (Fjölskyldu-og Húsdýragarðurinn)

The park and zoo combines animal exhibits, amusement park rides, and a giant playground area. You'll see Icelandic farm animals—

pigs, cows, horses, sheep—plus a seal pool, birds, reindeer, rabbits, and a small aquarium. The website lists feeding times (click on "Dagskrá"). The park is open all year, but in winter it's a bit desolate, especially on weekdays, and most rides are closed. Quick Icelandic horse rides for little kids are offered year-round (Sat-Sun at 14:00). If you're hungry, you can grab a meal at the nondescript café, or stop by one of the hot-dog or ice-cream stands and enjoy a picnic at the outdoor tables with grills.

**Cost and Hours:** 860 ISK, covered by Reykjavík City Card, less for kids; rides cost about 250-750 ISK, or buy a day pass for 2,200 ISK; daily 10:00-18:00, mid-Aug-May until 17:00; Múlavegur 2, 411-5900, www.mu.is (yes, that's the Icelandic word for "moo").

### Botanic Garden (Grasagarður)

Next to the Family Park and Zoo, the city-run botanic garden showcases local trees, herbs, flowers, and other plants. Buried in the garden is the excellent **Flóran café** (described later, under "Eating in Reykjavík"), which makes a visit worthwhile even on a rainy day (free, daily 10:00-22:00, Sept-April until 15:00, tel. 411-8650, www.grasagardur.is).

**Nearby:** Follow the parkland five minutes downhill from the gardens past the ponds and bridges to an open grassy area. Here you can see the remains of the washing troughs and channels where city folk used to do their laundry in hot spring water, all the way up to the 1970s. Outdoor posters tell the story, and give you a feel for how fast the country has modernized.

### Ice Rink (Skautahöllin)

Next to the parking lot for the zoo and gardens is the city's indoor ice rink with public skating most afternoons—a useful bad-weather option (entry including skate rental-1,500 ISK, less for kids; closes for a few weeks in summer, confirm current hours on website; Múlavegur 1, tel. 588-9705, www.skautaholl.is).

## FARTHER EAST OF REYKJAVÍK

The first listing, for the open-air museum, is just on the outskirts of town. The other listings are farther east, roughly on the way to or from the Golden Circle loop. If you're efficient, you may be able to squeeze one of these into your Golden Circle day trip, or see the Hellisheiði Power Plant on the way to the South Coast. Or you can consider these as easy side-trips from the capital—each is about a 30-minute drive from downtown.

### ▲Árbær Open-Air Museum (Árbæjarsafn)

Reykjavík's open-air museum is a modest collection of old buildings and farm animals—meant to help visitors envision Icelandic life in the 1800s. Homes hold period furnishings and reward those with the patience to poke around and ask questions; while everything is described in English, exhibits seem designed for Icelandic families. At the far edge of the property, the four attached houses (one with a sod roof) are the only ones that were  originally located here; walking through them, you can see how each successive generation added their own wing. The grounds—tucked next to a subdivision, with a highway rumbling along the horizon—are underwhelming, especially if you've visited the lush open-air museums elsewhere in northern Europe. But the exhibits compensate.

Make an effort to time your visit to coincide with the 13:00

hour-long guided tour (included in admission). Note that off-season (Sept-May), this tour is the only time you can enter the museum. In December, in the weeks before Christmas, the museum opens with a holiday spirit on Sundays from 13:00 to 17:00.

**Cost and Hours:** 1,600 ISK, covered by Reykjavík City Card, free for kids under 17. Museum open daily 10:00-17:00, Sept-May by guided tour only—daily at 13:00. Café (waffles and snacks) open June-Aug daily 11:00-17:00 and on the Sundays before Christmas. Kistuhylur 4, tel. 411-6300, www.borgarsogusafn.is.

**Getting There:** The museum is at the end of the street called Kistuhylur, just off the busy highway 49. The easiest bus connection from downtown is #16 from Hlemmur to the Strengur/Laxakvísl stop.

### Halldór Laxness House (Gljúfrasteinn)

Iceland's most famous author, Nobel Prize winner Halldór Laxness (1902-1998), lived in a house called Gljúfrasteinn ("Canyonstone"). The house has been preserved as a museum; an audioguide explains each room. The backyard borders on a rushing stream.

**Cost and Hours:** 900 ISK, daily 9:00-17:00; Sept-Oct and March-May Tue-Sun 10:00-16:00, closed Mon; Nov-Feb Tue-Fri 10:00-16:00, closed Sat-Mon; tel. 586-8066, www.gljufrasteinn.is.

**Getting There:** It's one of the last houses on the right as you drive up the Mosfellsdalur valley on highway 36, about 25 minutes from downtown Reykjavík. You can easily combine Laxness's house with a visit to Þingvellir, but doing the house plus the whole Golden Circle in a day is too much.

**Background:** Born in Reykjavík, Halldór Guðjónsson was the eldest son of parents who started life poor. His father worked in road construction, and bought a farm at Laxnes in Mosfellsdalur when Halldór was three. Halldór grew up in the valley and started to write as a teenager. Like many Icelanders of his time, he took a surname (based on the farm where he grew up) instead of using his traditional patronymic. In the 1920s and 1930s he traveled in Europe and America, and converted to Catholicism. In 1945, he settled at Gljúfrasteinn, close to where he grew up, with his second wife. Here he lived comfortably, but not lavishly.

Over his lifetime, Laxness wrote more than a dozen novels, some brilliant...and others barely readable. *Independent People* (in Icelandic, *Sjálfstætt fólk*) is the best known. He also wrote short stories, plays, poetry, travel books, memoirs, and other nonfiction. In his writing, Laxness concerned himself strongly with social justice and the struggles of working people. Icelanders on the political right forbid their children to read his books, and cringed when he received the Nobel Prize; those on the political left loved him and

REYKJAVÍK

felt he told the truth. In the end, no one could deny that he was a gifted writer and a person of insight and compassion.

### Geothermal Exhibition at Hellisheiði Power Plant (Hellisheiðarvirkjun)

Less than a half-hour's drive from Reykjavík on the way to Selfoss, this is the only one of Iceland's seven geothermal energy plants where visitors can get a good look at some of the powerful turbine machinery at work. The hot water from the ground is piped to homes for heating, and it drives the turbines that generate electricity. (Most of Iceland's electricity, though, is produced by dams rather than geothermal sources.) But the plant isn't all good: It releases hydrogen sulfide—carrying the aroma of rotten eggs—that east winds blow into Reykjavík.

At the exhibit, you can see turbine rooms through big windows, read posters on how geothermal energy works, and see a couple of films. Free guided tours run several times a day if enough visitors gather (typically 5-person minimum).

**Cost and Hours:** 1,450 ISK, Mon-Fri 8:00-17:00, Sat-Sun from 9:00, confirm hours before heading out, tel. 591-2880, www. geothermalexhibition.com.

**Getting There:** The plant is on highway 1 about halfway across the Hellisheiði plateau that forms the pass between Reykjavík and the South Coast. Look for a turnoff marked *Hellisheiðarvirkjun*—you can't miss the plant, with steam rising from its towers.

# Experiences in and near Reykjavík

### ▲▲▲Thermal Swimming Pools

There are well over a dozen thermal swimming pools to choose from in the greater Reykjavík area, each one run by the local municipality. The more recently built pools in the suburbs are typically more spacious, with more elaborate waterslides and at least one weatherproof indoor pool, making them worth a short drive or bus ride. Any Icelander you ask will have a favorite pool and be able to rattle off its advantages and disadvantages. The recommended pools below are definite winners. (The famous Blue Lagoon is 45 minutes' drive from downtown—and described in the Blue Lagoon & Reykjanes Peninsula chapter—but that's quite a different experience...much more tourist-oriented, and much more expensive, than the pools described here.)

**How to Visit:** For essential tips on visiting Iceland's thermal pools, read the "Pool Rules" sidebar on page 160. For background on thermal pools and helpful resources, see page 159.

**Cost:** Pools in Reykjavík charge 950 ISK. The pools in Seltjarnarnes and Hafnarfjörður provide the same experience but charge only 600 and 550 ISK. In Reykjavík, a shareable 10-entry ticket costs 4,400 ISK, which saves money with only five entries (for example, a couple visiting three times). These are adult rates—kids get in for less.

**Hours:** On weekdays, most swimming pools in the capital area open early in the morning (before 7:00) and stay open until at least 20:00, except on Fridays, when most close around 18:00. Weekend hours are a little shorter (at least 9:00-17:00 or 18:00). Note that most pools close on national holidays. Pools are most crowded after work and school, in the late afternoon.

## Pools in and near Reykjavík

Nondrivers staying downtown can walk to either of the first two listings. The website for all Reykjavík pools is Reykjavik.is.

**Sundhöllin,** Reykjavík's oldest swimming pool, is the only one within the downtown zone and the only indoor pool within easy reach of the center. It was built in the 1930s, and parts of it have an antique feel, though it's well-kept. An outdoor wing was added in 2017, with a lap pool, kiddie pool, and new women's dressing room (Barónsstígur 45a, 5-minute walk from Hlemmur bus junction, limited free street parking in front, tel. 411-5350).

**Vesturbæjarlaug,** a 20-minute walk from downtown (or take bus #11, #13, or #15), is a compact 1960s-era pool in a residen-

tial area near the university, and a good all-around pool choice for those staying downtown. Though close enough to the center to catch tourists, it has a predominantly neighborhood feel. It's outdoor-only, with a small lap pool, a wading area, hot pots, and a sauna (corner of Hofsvallagata and Melhagi, free parking in front or on the street nearby, tel. 411-5150). If you're swimming here, grab a drink or meal at the recommended Kaffihús Vesturbæjar café across the street.

**Árbæjarlaug,** far from the center, wins the award for the nicest modern design (from the 1990s). A dome covers its small indoor section, the outdoor hot pools are especially comfortable, and there's a good water slide. It's near some pleasant-enough hiking trails, as well as the Árbær Open-Air Museum and the road from Reykjavík to Selfoss and the south. It's better on weekends, as the indoor section is mostly reserved for children's swim lessons on weekdays (Fylkisvegur 9, bus #5 or #16 to Fylkisvegur stop, tel. 411-5200).

**Laugardalslaug,** the country's largest pool, is a bit industrial-feeling, with outdoor-only facilities. A bus ride from the center, it's next to the official Reykjavík youth hostel and sports complex. It's a good option if you're staying nearby, if you want to go swimming late on a weekend evening, or on major holidays like Christmas or New Year's Day, when it's typically the only pool open (Sundlaugavegur 30, bus #14 to Laugardalslaug stop, tel. 411-5100).

**In Seltjarnarnes:** Sundlaug Seltjarnarness, a 10-minute drive or bus ride from the center on #11 (or a 40-minute walk), is a small, cozy, newly renovated residential pool frequented mostly by locals. It's outdoor-only, and has easy parking, nice views, a modest water slide, and a cozy wading and lounging area (on Suðurströnd in Seltjarnarnes; bus #11 to Íþróttamiðstöð Seltjarnarness stop, tel. 561-1551, www.seltjarnarnes.is).

**Indoor Bathing in Hafnarfjörður:** The best indoor pool in the capital area, and overall the best family pool, is **Ásvallalaug,** on the outskirts of the town of Hafnarfjörður. From downtown Reykjavík, it's a 20-minute drive by car (on the way to the airport), or a long 45 minutes by direct city bus. There's a full-size lap pool, a large wading pool, a large and shallow family pool, a good water slide, and hot pools. It's a great bad-weather destination with a big parking lot (Ásvellir 2, Hafnarfjörður, bus #1 to Ásvallalaug stop, tel. 512-4050, www.hafnarfjordur.is). You could stop in downtown Hafnarfjörður to eat afterward (see recommendations on page 96), or drive to the cheap cafeteria at IKEA, which is on the way back to Reykjavík.

### Heated Beach: Nauthólsvík

Nauthólsvík, maintained by the city of Reykjavík, is an artificial beach *(ylströnd)* in a sheltered part of the shoreline, where you can bathe in an area heated with excess geothermal water from the city's heating system. This can be fun on a nice summer day, although you'll find better facilities and services at the regular pools (free, possible charge for changing facilities; daily 10:00-19:00, limited hours and 600 ISK charge mid-Aug-mid-May, off Nauthólsvegur, bus #5 to Nauthóll/HR stop, free parking, or walk from here to the Pearl, tel. 511-6630, www.nautholsvik.is).

### Also Consider...

**Lágafellslaug,** a large, new pool in the town of Mosfellsbær (about 9 miles northeast of downtown Reykjavík), has a small indoor section. It's convenient if driving between Reykjavík and the Golden

Circle (Þingvellir) or the north (toward Akureyri; Lækjarhlíð 1a, Mosfellsbær, tel. 617-6080, www.mosfellsbaer.is).

**Álftaneslaug,** with a high waterslide and the country's only wave pool, is in the formerly separate town of Álftanes (on the peninsula due south of Reykjavík). This pool cost so much to build that the town went bankrupt and merged with neighboring Garðabær (Breiðmýri, Garðabær, tel. 550-2350, www.gardabaer.is).

**Sundlaug Kópavogs,** an older pool in the town of Kópavogur, is handy for those staying nearby (Borgarholtsbraut, Kópavogur, tel. 570-0740, www.kopavogur.is).

## More Experiences
### Horseback Riding
Several horse farms on the outskirts of Reykjavík run riding tours for tourists, see the Icelandic Experiences chapter for details.

### Volcanic Cave Tours
Two pricey excursions inside a volcano cave are close to Reykjavík: At **Þríhnjúkagígur** (a.k.a. "Inside the Volcano"), 30 minutes from the capital, you're lowered down into an extinct magma chamber (very expensive, at around $400 per person). More affordable (at $100) is **Raufarhólshellir** (a.k.a. "The Lava Tunnel"), where you can walk through a petrified lava tube (about 45 minutes from Reykjavík). A similar tour at **Víðgelmir**—a.k.a. "The Cave"—is more impressive, but much farther away from Reykjavík; consider taking it if you'll be in the West Iceland region. For more on these options, see the Icelandic Experiences chapter.

# Shopping in Reykjavík

While you'll find plenty of shopping opportunities, don't expect any bargains: Iceland has almost no manufacturing industry of its own, so many items are imported and quite expensive. My shopping advice emphasizes items that are produced or at least designed in Iceland.

**Store Hours:** Most shops are open at least Mon-Fri 10:00-18:00; on Saturdays, many close earlier. Sundays are unpredictable—larger or tourist-oriented shops remain open, while others close. In general, touristy shops on the main shopping streets downtown (Laugavegur and Skólavörðustígur) have longer hours in the evening and on Sundays.

## WHERE TO SHOP
Downtown Reykjavík seems designed for shoppers—you'll find plenty of temptations as you window-shop along the main drag, **Laugavegur.** Dozens of stores along here run the gamut from

gaudy "puffin shops" to high-end craft and design boutiques; a few highlights are mentioned in the next section.

Don't be so mesmerized by Laugavegur that you miss **Skólavörðustígur,** the charming street leading up from Lan-gavegur to Hallgrímskirkja. It's lined with more authentic-feeling small boutiques. I've listed some of my favorites in the next section, but here's a quick rundown: Near the bottom are large branches of Geysir (fashion), Rammagerðin (top-end souvenirs), and Eymundsson (books). Farther up—especially

around the intersection with Týsgata—you'll find an enticing assortment of one-off boutiques, including the 12 Tónar record shop and the Handknitting Association of Iceland.

Jewelry is a popular item along here, including at **Orrifin** (with funky style, at #17B) and **Fríða** (#18). This street also specializes in ceramicists; look for **Stígur** (a collective showcasing the work of seven artists, at #17) and **Kaolin** (at #5). It also has some eclectic fashion boutiques, such as **Yeoman** (at #22). **Nikulásarkot** features delicate, handmade dolls and ornaments infused with Icelandic folk culture (at #22). Many of these stores have their own little workshops attached, where you can watch artisans at work.

## WHAT TO BUY
### Sweaters and Other Icelandic Fashion

At the top of many shopping lists is a handmade Icelandic wool sweater *(lopapeysa).* Knitting is a major pastime in this nation where sheep outnumber people, and where hobbies get you through the dreary winter months. Traditional Icelandic designs—often with classy one- or two-tone patterns radiating from the neck—are both timeless and stylish. A good, handmade sweater starts at around $200; they tend to be bulky, so you'll need room in your luggage.

**Classic Sweaters:** The best place for a traditional sweater (as well as other knitwear and yarn) is the cozy little **Handknitting Association of Iceland** (Handprjónasambandið) shop; browse their website before you go (Mon-Sat 9:00-18:00, Sun from 10:00, Skólavörðustígur 19, tel. 552-1890, http://handknit.is). They also have a more souvenir-y location on the main drag (Laugavegur 53, closed Sun).

**Secondhand Sweaters:** For a quality sweater at a lower price (closer to $100-120), consider buying secondhand. For a big, well-stocked vintage clothing shop, stop by **Spúútnik** on the main drag (Laugavegur 28) or their second location, **Fatamarkaður** (at the Hlemmur bus junction, Laugavegur 118). Or, to support a good cause while you shop, the **Red Cross** charity shop has three very central locations (at Laugavegur 12B, Laugavegur 116, and Skólavörðustígur 12). Note that these places line up conveniently—allowing you to comparison-shop easily in about a 10-minute stroll along Laugavegur. There's also a **Salvation Army** branch at the corner of Garðastræti and Ránargata. You'll find plenty of sweaters at the **Kolaportið flea market**—but don't expect top quality there (Sat Sun only, see listing on page 40).

**Stylish Sweaters** (and Other Fashion): Icelandic designers enjoy updating traditional sweater designs. **Farmers Market** has a full range of fashionable clothes, including sweaters (www.farmersmarket.is). Their downtown outpost is called Farmers & Friends (Laugavegur 37), while their flagship store is at the far end of the Old Harbor's Grandi pier, near the Marshall-húsið arts center (Hólmaslóð 2). **Geysir**—another modern Icelandic fashion designer with several branches downtown (including at Skólavörðustígur 7 and Skólavörðustígur 16, www.geysirshops.is)—also has contemporary sweater styles, as do various one-off boutiques along Laugavegur.

**Other Clothes: 66°North,** Iceland's best-known outerwear brand, is *the* place to buy waterproof shells and puffy vests. A big, convenient location is right on the main drag (Mon-Sat 9:00-21:00, Sun from 10:00, Laugavegur 17). For a better deal, drivers can head to their suburban outlet store with deep discounts (buried in the back of the Skeifan shopping zone, Mon-Fri 8:00-21:00, Sat from 10:00, Sun from 12:00, Faxafen 12, bus #5 to Fen stop, tel. 535-6676, www.66north.is).

For high-end local fashion—a notch dressier than Farmers Market and Geysir, described earlier—check out **Kiosk,** a co-op run by local designers (just off the main drag at Ingólfsstræti 6, www.kioskreykjavik.com).

## Icelandic Souvenirs

Visitors enjoy browsing for keepsakes emblazoned with the Icelandic flag, or an outline of the country. Other popular items include stuffed puffins, whales, and polar bears (they don't live in Iceland, but every now and then, a stray bear drifts across from Greenland on an iceberg). Laugavegur and adjoining streets seem to specialize in tacky souvenir outlets; most of what you'll find is overpriced and made in China. Here are a few better options for more authentically Icelandic souvenirs.

Locally produced and inexpensive, edible souvenirs may be your best bet. **Icelandic candy** is unusual and hard to get outside of Iceland, but easily found at discount grocery stores (Bónus and Krónan), which are generally cheaper and have a better selection than the duty-free airport shops. Cooks on your shopping list might enjoy some of the wide variety of flavored **Icelandic sea salts** (including birch-smoked, seaweed, black lava, and arctic thyme).

Gift shops at the **National Museum** and the **Harpa** concert hall are a little more sophisticated than the norm (see listings in "Sights in Reykjavík").

**Rammagerðin,** a venerable, high-end boutique, offers extremely expensive but good-quality Icelandic handcrafts and design (www.rammagerdin.is). The main branch—with a row of taxidermied puffins looking out the window—is in the heart of the main shopping zone at Skólavörðustígur 12; other branches are just up the street at Skólavörðustígur 20, at Bankastræti 9, at the Pearl, and at the airport ("Iceland Gift Store").

Iceland, like other Scandinavian countries, has a knack for clean, eye-pleasing design; several shops along the main drag specialize in the works of local designers. The **Kraum** design shop shares a space with the "Around Iceland" booking center at Laugavegur 18; in the back is a small, free exhibit about Icelandic reindeer (www.kraum.is). **Hrím Eldhús** has a fun selection of upscale kitchen gadgets and housewares—a mix of Icelandic and international (Laugavegur 32); their sister shop just up the street, **Hrím Hönnunarhús,** has a more eclectic selection (Laugavegur 25, www.hrim.is).

## Bookstores

Some English-language books on Iceland are available much more cheaply back home from Amazon or other online retailers; others are hard to find outside the country.

**Mál og Menning,** along Laugavegur, is Reykjavík's most enjoyable-to-browse bookstore.

In the big atrium, tables are piled with intriguing choices, including many English books and travel guides, and there's a tiny café upstairs (Mon-Fri 9:00-22:00, Sat-Sun 10:00-22:00, Laugavegur 18, tel. 552-3740, www.bmm.is).

Two downtown branches of **Eymundsson,** Iceland's answer to Barnes & Noble, are at Austurstræti 18 and Skólavörðustígur 11 (same hours as Mál og Menning, www.eymundsson.is).

Those with a car or bike can visit the **publishers' outlet store** in the Grandi neighborhood beyond the Old Harbor, which has a large selection of books, maps, and posters offered at a 15 percent discount (Mon-Fri 10:00-18:00, Sat 11:00-15:00, closed Sun, Fiskislóð 39, tel. 575-5636, www.forlagid.is).

### Other Ideas

**12 Tónar,** downtown at Skólavörðustígur 15, is a local institution. Their shop specializes in Icelandic music, and they run their own label—making this a beloved outpost for indie music lovers (Mon-Sat 10:00-18:00, Sun from 12:00, www.12tonar.is).

Greater Reykjavík's two big **shopping malls** (Kringlan and Smáralind) are convenient for drivers and give you a nontouristy look at Icelandic commercial life.

# Entertainment in Reykjavík

## PERFORMANCES AT HARPA

Iceland's cutting-edge arts center (described earlier, under "Sights in Reykjavík") has several venues, big and small, that offer enter-

tainment options every night of the year. Three serious musical ensembles are based at Harpa: the **Iceland Symphony Orchestra** (Sinfóníuhljómsveit Íslands, http://en.sinfonia.is), the **Icelandic Opera** (Íslenska Óperan, http://opera.is), and the **Reykjavík Big Band,** a large jazz ensemble (Stórsveit Reykjavíkur, www.reykjavikbigband.com). All three regularly perform in the 1,800-seat main hall, called Eldborg. Harpa's smaller halls (200-1,100 seats) host many types of performances. Check the schedule for a chance to combine a show with a visit to the most architecturally exciting building in Iceland (box office open Mon-Fri 9:00-18:00, Sat-Sun from 10:00, often later during performances, https://en.harpa.is).

Among the shows at Harpa are likely to be the following tourist-oriented options (all designed for an English-speaking au-

# Icelandic Music

For centuries, there were few instruments in Iceland, and it was hard to organize an ensemble in a land with difficult travel and no towns or villages. What little music Icelanders had was mostly vocal, using simple melodies in minor keys, lyrics from old ballads and verses, sometimes accompanied by primitive string instruments. At Christmastime, Icelanders danced holding hands in a line while singing traditional verses. When the Pietist movement gained ground among Lutherans in the mid-1700s, music and dance were frowned upon.

But over time, that changed—especially in the 20th century, as Icelanders became wealthier and better tied into European culture. Young Icelanders started to take music lessons, sing in choirs, and play in bands, and both classical and popular music blossomed. Today, Icelanders love to sing along to local folk songs at birthdays or Christmas parties.

The best-known modern Icelandic musician is Björk Guð-mundsdóttir—known worldwide by her first name alone. Born in 1965 in Reykjavík to two politically active parents (her father was the head of the Icelandic electricians union for years), Björk sang in choirs as a child. She gained fame as the lead singer of the Sugarcubes, then struck out on her own in 1993. Björk is known for her eclectic musical style, unique voice (which strikes some ears as discordant), energetic performances, and avant-garde fashion sense (most famously, the swan-shaped dress she wore to the 2001 Oscars). Björk has also dabbled in acting, taking home the Cannes Best Actress prize for her lead performance in the 2000 Lars von Trier film *Dancer in the Dark.* While Björk's music

dience). While these may change, each one has been running for several years (though sometimes only in summer). All are entertaining and (aside from the first and last) designed to give visitors insights into Icelandic culture.

**Reykjavík Classics** is a daytime concert offering a 30-minute presentation of some "greatest hits" of classical music (Mozart, Beethoven, etc.) performed by a smaller ensemble from the symphony. As it's short and always in the main hall, it's an affordable way to experience Harpa without investing too much time and money...but there's very little Icelandic about it (3,000 ISK, usually at 12:30 or 15:30, www.reykjavikclassics.com).

**Pearls of Icelandic Song** presents a collection of traditional tunes sung by operatically trained soloists with piano accompaniment. The formal presentation of these informal songs may not be to everyone's taste, but it's authentically Icelandic (3,900 ISK, usually at 18:00 in the main hall, www.pearls.is).

**Icelandic Sagas: The Greatest Hits** is a frenetic two-person show that attempts to compress centuries of deep and complex Ice-is not for everybody, her fans are devout. To get a taste for Björk, some of her early albums in Icelandic are available for free on YouTube and well worth listening to. Try *Gling-Gló* (roughly, "Ding Dong"), with accessible but typically idiosyncratic interpretation of jazz standards. Later in her career, Björk moved to England, but still spends a lot of time in Iceland.

Over the last decade or so, other Icelandic bands have become known internationally. Sigur Rós and, more recently, Of Monsters And Men specialize in soaring, bombastic soundscapes (fitting for their dramatic homeland) that often turn up in Hollywood epics. Singer-songwriter Ásgeir is attempting to become the next Icelander to break out in a big way.

Icelandic music fans shouldn't miss the Icelandic Museum of Rock 'n' Roll, a five-minute drive from Keflavík Airport (see page 122). The 2013 book *Blue Eyed Pop* is also good (buy it at the museum, or from the website of the author, Gunnar Lárus Hjálmarsson, better known as Dr. Gunni; http://blueeyedpopdotcom1. wordpress.com).

Two annual festivals showcase the latest in Icelandic pop music. Iceland Airwaves takes place in Reykjavík in late October/ early November (www.icelandairwaves.is). Aldrei Fór Ég Suður (which loosely translates as "I never moved to Reykjavík") fills Ísafjörður, the largest town in the Westfjords, with young visitors for a few days at Easter (www.aldrei.is). There's also Eistnaflug, a heavy metal festival each July in the eastern town of Neskaupstaður (www.eistnaflug.is).

landic heritage into 75 minutes, with plenty of humor and costume changes. While designed to be more entertaining than educational, you'll come away with a somewhat better appreciation for Iceland's history (4,900 ISK, usually at 20:15 in the Northern Lights Hall, www.icelandicsagas.com).

**How to Become Icelandic in 60 Minutes** is a crowd-pleasing one-man comedy show designed to offer outsiders some humorous insights into the Icelandic psyche (4,500 ISK, usually at 19:00 in the smaller Kaldalón, www.h2become.com).

**Múlinn Jazz Club** hosts weekly jazz performances in an intimate setting (2,000 ISK, typically Wed at 21:00, www.facebook. com/mulinnjazzclub).

## OTHER PERFORMANCES

The Gamla Bíó theater—a classic old cinema in the heart of town—periodically presents **Saga Music 101**. A contemporary songwriter has written music designed to tell some of the saga stories with English lyrics (4,700 ISK, Wed at 20:00, www.sagamusic101.com).

The theater hosts other performances, too (check www.gamlabio. is), and its recommended rooftop bar—Petersen Svítan—is a fine venue for a before- or after-show drink.

Various **churches** around Reykjavík present low-key concerts. The big, landmark Hallgrímskirkja offers concerts (mainly on their huge organ) about four times weekly in summer (late June-late Aug, as part of the "International Organ Summer"), and sporadically at other times of year (www.hallgrimskirkja.is). And the cathedral—the modest building next to the parliament, downtown—hosts occasional concerts in its intimate, lovely space (www.domkirkjan.is).

**Movies: Bíó Paradís,** a beloved art-house cinema just off the main drag downtown, shows international films in their original language with Icelandic subtitles, as well as Icelandic films with English subtitles. Locals kick off weekend revelry at their throwback film series every Friday night—camp classics, '80s movies, interactive screenings (like the *Rocky Horror Picture Show*), and so on. Their bar/café is a popular hangout. The movie lets out just as things are getting rolling outside (Hverfisgata 54, tel. 412-7711, www.bioparadis.is).

## NIGHTLIFE

Reykjavík is renowned for its crazy nightlife. It's pretty simple: Just go downtown any Friday or Saturday night and hit your choice of bars and clubs. Typically, Icelanders come here only on weekends. Many young Icelanders drink at home first (less expensive) before heading downtown between 23:00 and midnight. Higher-end drinking places—hotel cocktail bars, craft-beer specialists, and the like—tend to close on the "early" side...which, in Reykjavík, means midnight on weeknights and 1:00 in the morning on weekends. Harder-partying places stay open until 3:00 or later.

I've recommended some well-established watering holes (see map on page 89)—but this scene changes quickly. For a more timely take, pick up the latest issue of the *Reykjavík Grapevine* (or read it online at www.grapevine.is) to find what's in, what's on, and which bands or DJs are playing where. The *Grapevine* also publishes a list of best happy hours—good to know about in this pricey city.

If you want company, go on a **guided pub crawl** such as the one offered by CityWalk (2,500 ISK, Fri-Sat at 22:00, mobile tel. 787-7779, www.citywalk.is).

### Upscale Cocktails

These options are for those who'd prefer a more sophisticated scene, and don't mind investing in a pricey (2,000-2,500 ISK) but well-crafted cocktail in a memorable setting.

**Sophisticated Art Deco Vibe:** Right in the heart of town, **Apotek** fills the ground floor of a landmark hotel by renowned architect Guðjón Samúelsson. This borderline-stuffy place loves to brag about their many "best cocktails" awards and generous happy-hour deals (half-price drinks 16:00-18:00). A bit more sedate than the rowdy party scene all around it, this is a nice choice for a genteel drink. They also serve a full menu of food—including a decent lunch special—but better restaurants are nearby; come for the drinks and the ambience (daily 7:00-late, Austurstræti 16).

**Rooftop Bar:** To reach **Petersen Svítan** ("The Petersen Suite"), you'll slip through a side door next to the classic Gamla Bíó theater, then ride the elevator up to a rooftop deck. You can sit in the Old World interior, but the main draw is the large outdoor area, overlooking city rooftops—a delight on warm evenings. Don't miss the spiral stairs up to an even higher deck (open daily from 16:00, happy hour until 20:00, Ingólfsstræti 2a).

**By the Harbor: Slippbarinn** ("Dry Dock Bar") is one of the best places in town for quality, creative cocktails. The menu is vividly described and fun to peruse, with a few mainstays and lots of seasonal concoctions. A mellow hangout by day, at night it's a big, boisterous, and colorful party. It sprawls through the spacious, creative, industrial-mod lobby of the Icelandair Hótel Marina, right along the harborfront, facing the namesake dry dock (daily 11:30-late, also serves food, occasional DJs or live music, Mýrargata 2).

## Craft Beer

Iceland has a burgeoning craft beer scene, including high-end bars where you can focus on sampling local brews. While some proudly feature Icelandic beer, most acknowledge the limits of local brewers and make a point to also offer a carefully curated range of imports. Most craft-beer bars have several taps and a chalkboard listing what's on today. Figure on paying 1,000-1,800 ISK for a pint.

**Skúli Craft Bar,** named for the statue of the original Reykjavík developer on the downtown square it faces, has a great section of Icelandic craft beers. The prices are high, but the glassy, modern, aboveground space feels inviting and attracts a few locals along with the tourists. At the bar—in front of an illuminated wall displaying bottles like trophies—you can choose between Icelandic brews (marked with red-and-blue stripes) and imports. They also have pleasant outdoor tables (Mon-Thu from 15:00, Fri-Sat from 14:00, Sun from 16:00, happy hour until 19:00, Aðalstræti 9, tel. 519-6455).

**MicroBar** fills a straightforward cellar with happy drinkers (mostly tourists, thanks to its main-drag location) enjoying an even wider selection of microbrews. They specialize in Icelandic beers—with 14 on tap, and more than 100 in bottles—and is the only craft beer place I saw that offers 5- or 10-beer sampler boards; this being

Iceland, you'll pay dearly for each sip (daily from 16:00, happy hour 17:00-19:00, Vesturgata 2, tel. 865-8389).

**Mikkeller & Friends,** at the top floor of an old house, focuses on Scandinavian craft brews (Mikkeller is a Danish brewery), with a big chalkboard menu of 20 choices. They take their beer (and themselves) very seriously, but it's an appealing setting—you'll feel like you're in a friend's attic lounge—and a good place to get beyond Icelandic beers (Sun-Thu from 17:00, Fri-Sat from 14:00, Hverfisgata 12—head to the top floor, passing a good pizzeria partway up, tel. 437-0203).

**Ölstofa Kormáks og Skjaldar** ("Kormákur and Skjöldur's Tavern") is a nice hybrid of the beer-geek places mentioned earlier, and the lowbrow Laugavegur scene described next. Because it's tucked away, it feels more local than most Laugavegur bars, with a *Cheers* vibe and a table often filled by regulars. While they do have taps and bottles from local brewers, their draft selection is limited (all from the same brewery, Borg Brugghús); visit for the atmosphere, not a deep dive into Icelandic brews (daily from 15:00, Laugavegur 59).

## Lively Late-Night Bars

These places really get rolling late at night on weekends (though you're welcome to stop by earlier in the evening, when they can already be quite crowded on weekends). Come for Reykjavík's famous social weekend experience, not the drinks.

**Kaffibarinn** is a classic dive bar right in the center. It's a local institution that still attracts a largely Icelandic clientele. Filling an old house, it can feel crowded and gets pretty wild on weekends; for a mellower visit, check it out on a weeknight (daily from 15:00, good happy-hour deals before 20:00, live DJ at prime times, Bergstaðastræti 1, tel. 551-1588).

Right along the busiest stretch of Laugavegur, you can't miss **Lebowski Bar,** with neon lights, a Dude-Walter-and-Donny bowling theme, 16 versions of white Russians...and, one would assume, owners very nervous that the Coen Brothers' legal team will catch on. It's rollicking, rowdy, and popular with young Americans (open long hours daily and nightly, Laugavegur 20b, tel. 552-2300).

A block from Ingólfstorg toward the river is a cluster of rowdy, hole-in-the-wall bars for late-night revelry. **Húrra** is the all-around favorite, with a big dance floor and great DJs (Tryggvagata 22, tel. 571-7101). **Paloma** is a late-late-late night option with a basement dance floor and a vaguely nautical vibe; it's bigger than most, so it feels less claustrophobic (Naustin 1). And **The Dubliner** is the city's most central Irish pub (Hafnarstræti 1).

In addition, several of the places listed under "Eating in Reykjavík," later, can be good places to grab a drink, including the hipster/vegetarian café **Kaffi Vínyl,** the lowbrow pub **Íslenski Barinn,** and **Kex Hostel.**

# Sleeping in Reykjavík

Reykjavík is an expensive place to spend the night. With its recent spike in tourism, the city is bursting at the seams, demand is soaring, and lots of new places are opening up (or old places expanding) each year—some of them great, others not.

I've focused my listings on relatively established hotels offering good value. Given how pricey Reykjavík's hotels are (especially in the center), I'd also give guesthouses and private rentals (such as on Airbnb) a serious look; youth hostels are especially good for solo travelers. Real hotels are very expensive, especially in the center, and can easily cost $400 a night in summer. Guesthouses (figure $200 a night) and Airbnb (closer to $100 a night) give you more value for the money and a more local experience.

Whatever you do, book any accommodations well in advance, as the best places sell out early for the peak summer months, or if your trip coincides with a major holiday.

In Iceland, prices drop a lot if you are willing to share a bathroom. If a place has the option of a shared bathroom, I've noted that in the listing—a shared bath often knocks down the price considerably.

Without a car, stay downtown. It's more convenient for restaurants, nightlife, much of the worthwhile sightseeing, and bus-excursion pickups. With a rental car, it can make better sense to stay outside the downtown core—where lodgings cost less and parking is easy. There are fewer hotels and guesthouses in the suburbs, but Airbnb and other rentals are abundant.

For car travelers, the outlying community of Hafnarfjörður is a nice compromise. It has its own downtown core and quaint old houses, but free parking and less noise and traffic than Reykjavík. It's strategically situated for those driving to and from the airport, the Golden Circle, the Blue Lagoon, and the South Coast.

City buses run to every corner of the metropolitan area, although some parts are a long ride (with a transfer) from downtown. When scoping out a place to stay, check bus access by plugging the address into the journey planner at www.straeto.is and seeing how long it takes to get to the main downtown stops (Lækjartorg and Hlemmur).

I rank accommodations from **$** budget to **$$$$** splurge. To get the best deal, contact small hotels and guesthouses directly by phone or email. If you go direct, the owner avoids a roughly 20 percent commission and may be able to offer you a discount. For more

REYKJAVÍK

# Reykjavík Center Hotels

1. The Reykjavík Residence Suites
2. Hótel Kvosin
3. Hótel Óðinsvé
4. Hótel Reykjavík Centrum
5. Icelandair Hótel Marina
6. Guesthouse Galtafell
7. Guesthouse Sunna
8. Hótel Hlíða
9. To Guesthouse Anna
10. To Igdlo Guesthouse
11. To Heiða's Home
12. Castle House Apartments
13. Embassy Luxury Apartments
14. Nest Apartments
15. Kex Hostel
16. Downtown Hostel
17. Loft Hostel

REYKJAVIK

(Summer Only)

To Viðey

HARPA CONCERT HALL

Note: See also Reykjavik Hotels & Restaurants Outside the Center map

200 Meters
200 Yards

KALKOFNSVEGUR

BBP HOT DOGS

Kolaport

Arnarhóll

Lækjartorg

INGÓLFUR ARNARSSON STATUE

PRIME MINISTER'S OFFICE

LÆKJARGATA

INGÓLFSSTRÆTI

SÖLVHÓLSGATA

SÆBRAUT

SUN VOYAGER SCULPTURE

CULTURE HOUSE

NATIONAL THEATER

BANKASTRÆTI

GAMLA BÍÓ THEATER

Traðarkot

LAUGAVEGUR

KLAPPARSTÍGUR

LINDARGATA

SKÚLAGATA

VATNSSTÍGUR

To Skarfagarðar, Keflavík Airport & Highway 1

AMTSMANNS-STÍGUR

SMIÐJUSTÍGUR

BÍÓ PARADÍS CINEMA

HVERFISGATA

FRAKKASTÍGUR

HIGH SCHOOL

Garden

PINGHOLTSSTRÆTI

HALLVEIGAR

HLÖÐUSTÍGUR

SKÓLAVÖRÐUSTÍGUR

LAUGAVEGUR

VITASTÍGUR

KEX HOSTEL

PINGHOLT

SPÍTALA-

TYGGATA

NJÁLSGATA

To

BJARGARSTRÆTI

LOKASTÍGUR

PÓSSTÍGUR

KÁRASTÍGUR

GRETTISGATA

To Hlemmur Bus Junction

BERGSTAÐASTRÆTI

ÓÐINSGATA

FREYJUGATA

FRAKKASTÍGUR

AUSTURBÆR

HELLUSUND

BALDURSGATA

NJARÐARGATA

LEIFUR EIRIKSSON STATUE

BERGÞÓRUGATA

BRAGAGATA

GARDEN ENTRANCES

HALLGRÍMS-KIRKJA

SUNDHÖLLIN POOL

EINAR JÓNSSON MUSEUM & SCULPTURE GARDEN

EIRIKSGATA

BAKÓNSSTÍGUR

FREYJUGATA

To

information and tips on hotel rates and deals, making reservations, and finding a short-term rental, see the Practicalities chapter.

## AIRBNB AND OTHER RENTAL SITES

I've intentionally listed fewer hotels and guesthouses than I normally would for a city of Reykjavík's size. That's because here, even more than elsewhere, I find Airbnb and other short-term rentals to be a much better value than hotels. The bottom line: Iceland is expensive, and staying in nontraditional accommodations can have the single biggest impact on your travel budget.

Airbnb lists plenty of options in the downtown core, and is handy for finding less-expensive suburban accommodations (easier for drivers), while providing a more authentic look at Icelandic life. A search for "Reykjavík" may turn up some of these, but for more options, search for the name of the separate town: Hafnarfjörður, Garðabær, Kópavogur, Mosfellsbær, or Seltjarnarnes.

## EXPENSIVE DOWNTOWN HOTELS

If you're going to spend a lot of money, you might as well do it with class. These hotels each offer something special.

$$$$ The Reykjavík Residence Suites, next to the National Theater, occupy a fine former private home that was built in 1912 by a local bigwig who later became prime minister. When the king of Denmark visited in 1926, this is where he stayed. It's been converted into 10 top-end suites, each with a kitchenette (Hverfisgata 21, tel. 546-1200, www.rrsuites.is, info@rrsuites.is). The same outfit also rents regular hotel rooms in a less historic location a couple blocks away, at Hverfisgata 45.

$$$$ Hótel Kvosin, across the street from parliament and the cathedral in a building from 1900, has 24 big suites with full kitchenettes and fine art on the walls (Kirkjutorg 4, tel. 571-4460, www.kvosinhotel.is, desk@kvosinhotel.is).

$$$$ Hótel Óðinsvé, with 50 stylish rooms and 10 apartments in a blocky shell, sits in a pleasant residential area a short walk from the lively Skólavörðustígur shopping and dining street (Þórsgötu 1, recommended Snaps Bistro on-site, tel. 511-6200, www.hotelodinsve.is, odinsve@hotelodinsve.is).

$$$ Hótel Reykjavík Centrum boasts a great location, in view of the parliament, in a modernized building with a period facade and 89 rooms. The Settlement Exhibition on Reykjavík's early history is in the basement, centered on archaeological ruins found when the hotel was built in 2001 (Aðalstræti 16, tel. 514-6000, www.hotelcentrum.is, info@hotelcentrum.is).

$$$ Icelandair Hótel Marina is at the Old Harbor in a long, skinny building that spent many years as the post office's sorting facility. This hotel's location is more interesting and convenient than

the other Icelandair hotel, the Natura, and it's also home to the rec-ommended Slippbarinn cocktail bar (Mýrargata 2, tel. 560-8000, www.icehotels.is, marina@icehotels.is).

## GUESTHOUSES AND SMALL HOTELS

These smaller, less expensive properties are generally in convert-ed residential buildings without elevators. Most of these listings give you the option of sharing a bathroom, which brings down the price substantially. When comparing prices, remember to factor in breakfast and parking costs.

### Closer In

**$$$ Guesthouse Galtafell** is on a quiet street in a handsome neighborhood a block above the Pond, a convenient five-minute walk from both downtown and the BSÍ bus terminal. One of Ice-land's richest merchants and fishing magnates built this attractive house with its crenellated roof in 1916. Breakfast is served in a cozy, art-filled dining room in the main house (free parking, Laufásvegur 46, mobile 699-2525, www.galtafell.com, info@galtafell.com).

**$$$ Guesthouse Sunna,** around the corner from the big Hallgrímskirkja church, is big and feels more like a hotel than a guesthouse. It offers a range of rooms with shared or private bath—some with kitchens—and some with lots of stairs. There's limited free parking in their courtyard (Þórsgata 26 at the corner of Njarðargata, tel. 511-5570, www.sunna.is, sunna@sunna.is).

**$$$ Hótel Hilda** has 15 rooms, many quite small and tight, and all with private bath. It's in a pleasant, fairly quiet residential neighborhood just a five-minute walk west of downtown. Parking in the immediate vicinity is scarce (Bárugata 11, tel. 552-3020, www.hotelhilda.is, info@hotelhilda.is).

### Farther Out

For locations, see the map on page 80.

**$$ Guesthouse Anna** is conveniently just a hundred yards from the BSÍ bus terminal, where many airport buses and day trips depart. Even so, it feels quiet and residential, and it's about a 10-minute walk from the parliament building and Laugavegur. Of the 12 rooms, 7 have private bathrooms. There are bright, south-facing common spaces and a nice backyard. The modern building was built to house the Czechoslovak Embassy, which closed after the fall of communism (free on-street parking, Smáragata 16, tel. 562-1618, www.guesthouseanna.is, info@guesthouseanna.is).

**$ Igdlo Guesthouse** (the name is Greenlandic for "igloo") is on the outskirts of downtown, about a 5- to 10-minute walk from the BSÍ bus terminal, in a converted small apartment building on a dead-end street near a busy road. It's a bit hostel-like—all rooms

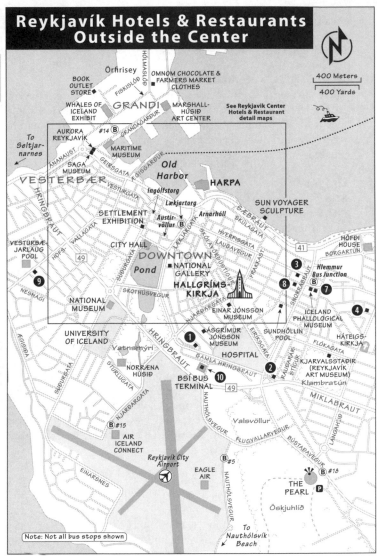

# Reykjavík Hotels & Restaurants Outside the Center

Örfirisey

BOOK OUTLET STORE

OMNOM CHOCOLATE & FARMERS MARKET CLOTHES

WHALES OF ICELAND EXHIBIT

GRANDI

MARSHALL-HÚSIÐ ART CENTER

See Reykjavik Center Hotels & Restaurant detail maps

400 Meters

400 Yards

AURORA REYKJAVÍK    #14 B

MARITIME MUSEUM

To Seltjarnarnes

SAGA MUSEUM

Old Harbor

VESTERBÆR

HARPA

Ingólfstorg

Lækjartorg

SUN VOYAGER SCULPTURE

SETTLEMENT EXHIBITION

Austur-völlur  B

Arnarhóll

HÖFÐI HOUSE

CITY HALL

VESTURBÆJARLAUG POOL

49

DOWNTOWN

Pond

NATIONAL GALLERY

HALLGRÍMS-KIRKJA

Hlemmur Bus Junction

NESHAGI

NATIONAL MUSEUM

EINAR JÓNSSON MUSEUM

ICELAND PHALLOLOGICAL MUSEUM

UNIVERSITY OF ICELAND

Vatnsmýri

ÁSGRÍMUR JÓNSSON MUSEUM

SUNDHÖLLIN POOL

HÁTEIGS-KIRKJA

HOSPITAL

KJARVALSSTAÐIR (REYKJAVÍK ART MUSEUM)

NORRÆNA HÚSIÐ

Klambratún

BSÍ BUS TERMINAL    49

MIKLABRAUT

#15

Valsvöllur

AIR ICELAND CONNECT

Reykjavík City Airport

B #5

B #18

THE PEARL    P

EAGLE AIR

Öskjuhlíð

To Nauthólsvík Beach

Note: Not all bus stops shown

share a bathroom, and most rooms have multiple beds. The exterior and location are ho-hum, but prices are low, downtown is a 15-minute walk away, and there's usually plenty of free on-street parking (kitchen, laundry facilities, rental bikes, family rooms, Gunnarsbraut 46, tel. 511-4646, www.igdlo.com, booking@igdlo.com).

**$ Heiða's Home** rents 14 tight double rooms (no sinks), with shared bathroom and kitchen facilities. It's close to the Hlemmur bus junction, occupying an older building along a busy urban-

REYKJAVÍK

**Accommodations**
1. Guesthouse Anna
2. Igdlo Guesthouse
3. Heiða's Home
4. Northern Comfort Apartments
5. Reykjavík City Hostel
6. Galaxy Pod Hostel

**Eateries**
7. Hlemmur Food Market
8. Noodle Station
9. Kaffihús Vesturbæjar
10. Mýrin Mathús
11. Flóran
12. Múlakaffi

feeling street at the east end of downtown (no breakfast, pay on-street parking, lots of stairs, Hverfisgata 102, tel. 553-6435, mobile 692-7654, www.heidashome.is, heida@heidashome.is).

## APARTMENTS

These apartments are good for a longer stay, or if you want your own kitchen.

**$$ Castle House Apartments** at Skálholtsstígur 2a and **Embassy Luxury Apartments** at Garðastræti 40 offer a dozen well-appointed, mostly one-bedroom apartments with kitchenettes in two super downtown locations well-described on their shared website. They also have cheaper studio apartments dubbed **Northern Comfort** in a lesser location at Skipholt 15, a bit outside downtown (pay on-street parking, tel. 511-2166, http://4.is, 4@4.is).

**$$ Nest Apartments** rents four units in a three-story building in a quiet spot not far from Laugavegur. The basement is generously called the "ground" floor (2-night minimum, cheaper if you stay a week, pay on-street parking, Bergþórugata 15—see map on page 77, mobile 893-0280, www.nestapartments.is, nest@ nestapartments.is).

## HOSTELS

¢ **Kex Hostel** ("Cookie")—filling an old cookie factory—is a popular choice for backpackers. While a bit pricey, it's big, close to downtown, and has a popular café that's frequented even by nonguests (lots of stairs, pay on-street parking, Skúlagata 28, a 7-minute walk from the Hlemmur bus junction—see map on page 77, tel. 561-6060, www.kexhostel.is, info@kexhostel.is).

**"Official" HI Hostels:** These three ¢ listings belong to the Hostelling International network (website for all: www.hostel. is). **Reykjavík City Hostel** is a 45-minute walk or easy bus ride from downtown, conveniently next to the Laugardalslaug swimming pool and close to the Family Park and Zoo (private rooms available, bike rental, playground, free parking, Sundlaugavegur 34—see map on page 80, bus #14 to Laugarásvegur stop, tel. 553-8110, reykjavikcity@hostel.is). **Downtown Hostel** is better suited to travelers without a car (private rooms available, Vesturgata 17—see map on page 77, bus #14 to the Mýrargata stop, tel. 553-8120, reykjavikdowntown@hostel.is). **Loft Hostel** is even more urban, occupying the top floor of a downtown building just uphill from the prime minister's office (elevator, Bankastræti 7—see map on page 77, near the Lækjartorg bus stop, tel. 553-8140, loft@hostel.is).

¢ **The Galaxy Pod Hostel** offers something different: Guests sleep in individual capsules, which give a little privacy and space to lock up valuables. The capsules are a good value for solo travelers, but two people traveling together will do better in a two-bed room at one of the HI hostels listed earlier. It's in an uninteresting neighborhood, a half-hour's walk or short drive from Parliament (elevator, breakfast optional, free parking, Laugavegur 172—see map on page 80; bus #2, #5, #14, #15, or #17 to Gamla sjónvarpshúsið; tel. 511-0505, www.galaxypodhostel.is, bookings@ galaxypodhostel.is).

## OUTSIDE REYKJAVÍK, IN HAFNARFJÖRÐUR

If you're renting a car and using Reykjavík as a base for day trips to sights in the countryside, you may find it easier to stay out-

side downtown in the southern suburb of Haf-narfjörður (HAHP-nar-FYUR-thur). While call-ing this area "charming" is a stretch, it does get you into a car-friendly zone away from the crowds, and gives you a glimpse of an authentic Icelandic

neighborhood, with restaurants and services in walking distance. And it's strategically located between downtown Reykjavík and points south: the airport, the Blue Lagoon, and the Golden Circle and South Coast.

**Hafnarfjörður Town:** Tucked just behind Hafnarfjörður's harborfront promenade is its little downtown core—a largely pedestrianized area with lots of big, modern buildings and a few historical ones. On its outskirts are rows of high-rise condos and some cozy cottage neighborhoods. Wherever you go, parking is easy.

Hafnarfjörður has good swimming pools (Ásvallalaug is one of the area's best), about a dozen restaurants and cafés downtown (including some real gems—see my recommendations in "Eating in Reykjavík," later), a big-box-store zone near the main road—handy for groceries and other shopping, and its own little TI (in the City Hall building, Mon-Fri 8:00-16:00, Sat-Sun 11:00-17:00, Vestur-gata 8, www.visithafnarfjordur.is).

Hafnarfjörður doesn't have much in the way of sights, but there are some nice places to stroll (such as Hellisgerði, a small park off Hellisgata), and a surprisingly good little town history museum (Vesturgata 6, http://museum.hafnarfjordur.is).

**Route Tips for Drivers:** Downtown Reykjavík is a 15-minute drive away, or a 25-minute ride on bus #1; airport buses stop in the center, but don't offer door-to-door pickup.

If you stay here and drive the Golden Circle or South Coast day trips, Breiðholtsbraut (highway 413) is a useful shortcut from Reykjanesbraut (highway 41) over to highway 1 in the direction of Selfoss. Your GPS or map app will guide you; otherwise, from highway 41, follow the signs for highway 413 toward highway 1.

**Sleeping in Hafnarfjörður:** While I've listed a few traditional accommodations (hotel, B&B, and hostel), you'll often get a better value via Airbnb. Before booking anything with a Hafnarfjörður address, check a map to make sure it's near downtown, rather than in the industrial zone to the east.

# Hafnarfjörður

**Accommodations**
1. Viking Village Hotel
2. To Hlíð Hótel
3. Edda's Farmhouse in Town
4. Lava Hostel

**Eateries**
5. Von & Pallett
6. Bike Cave (Burgers)
7. Súfistinn Kaffihús
8. Fjörukráin
9. Noodle Station

**$$ Viking Village Hótel,** part of the cheesy Viking-themed Fjörukráin restaurant complex, has Viking-esque common areas, but most of its 41 rooms are straightforward, on the small side, and full of heavily varnished wooden furniture; some feel a bit dated. They also have bunk-bedded cabins that sleep up to six (with private baths)—potentially cost-effective for families or small groups. There's a free sauna and hot pots, and the airport bus stops nearby (Strandgata 55, tel. 565-1213, www.fjorukrain.is, booking@

vikingvillage.is). Their "Fishermen's Village" annex, called **$$$ Hlíð Hótel,** is a little compound of woody, waterfront cabins on a rustic, sparsely populated point just north of Hafnarfjörður (a 15-minute drive from the main hotel; 20 minutes from downtown Reykjavík). It feels remote, yet is still close to the city (same contact information).

¢ **Edda's Farmhouse in Town,** in a charming and historic residential zone a short walk from downtown, has three simple, tidy rooms with a shared bathroom, and includes homemade breakfast. It's a "farmhouse" because Edda has cats, dogs, and rabbits (Vesturbraut 15, tel. 565-1480, mobile 897-1393, ekaritas@simnet.is).

¢ **Lava Hostel,** a 15-minute walk north of downtown Hafnarfjörður, is smaller and more intimate than the hostels in Reykjavík. This nonprofit hostel raises funds for the local Boy Scout troop; they also manage the adjacent campsite. As the name suggests, it's in the midst of an old lava flow (free parking, Hjallabraut 51, tel. 565-0900, www.lavahostel.is, info@lavahostel.is).

## HOTELS NEAR THE AIRPORT

It usually makes better sense to stay in Reykjavík (even when arriving or departing at odd hours). Still, given the 45-minute distance between the city and the airport, staying out here does make arrival and departure quicker: Late-night arrivals won't have to blearily pick up a rental car, or wait for an airport bus to slowly fill and rumble into town. Hotels and Airbnb lodgings in Keflavík and Njarðvík, the towns near the airport, are also a bit cheaper than in Reykjavík. But basing yourself out here makes for a much longer drive to the sights on your full days in Iceland, and drastically reduces your choice of bus tours if you're not using your own wheels. A taxi from the airport into Keflavík town can cost as much as 5,000 ISK, so figure that into your budget. For locations, see the map on page 98.

**$$ Hótel Aurora Star,** a hundred yards from the terminal, is the only hotel right at the airport, with 72 rooms. It's undistinguished but gets the job done; has family rooms, free parking, and a restaurant; and starts serving breakfast at 5:00. Prices are less expensive than downtown Reykjavík hotels, but still pricey by international standards (Blikavöllur 2, Keflavík, tel. 595-1900, www.hotelairport.is, airport@hotelairport.is).

**$ Hótel Keflavík,** near the harbor in the center of the town of Keflavík, also offers breakfast from 5:00 and free transport to (but not from) the airport. If you arrive on an early-morning transatlantic flight and get a rental car, you could have breakfast here and watch the town wake up (Vatnsnesvegi 12, Keflavík, tel. 420-7000, www.kef.is, stay@kef.is).

¢ **Alex Guesthouse,** a large one-story structure on a semirural lot between the airport and Keflavík, has two types of rooms: hotel-style rooms with shared bath and kitchen, and in summer, wooden cabins with private bath. They offer limited free transport to the airport and start serving breakfast at 4:30 (Aðalgata 60, Keflavík, tel. 421-2800, www.alex.is, alex@alex.is).

# Eating in Reykjavík

Iceland's tourist boom has equipped Reykjavík with a surprisingly good range of dining options. You'll dine well here—and it's easier than you might think to eat out without emptying your wallet. My best budget tip is to have your main meal at lunch: If you stick to drinking water, you can come away from a near-gourmet seafood lunch downtown only a little more than $25 poorer. Then, for dinner, save by picnicking, having a light meal at  a café, grabbing a cheap takeout or fast-food meal, or finding a restaurant that doesn't increase its prices in the evening—they do exist. For a few specific leads on cheap eats, see the "Budget Bites" sidebar, later.

I rank restaurants from $ budget to $$$$ splurge, based on average main-course dinner prices; many restaurants also offer a few cheaper items (like burgers or pizza). That said, you get what you pay for—in my experience, a $40 dinner is substantially better than a basic $25 dinner. For a memorable meal, consider splurging on a fixed-price, multicourse dinner (8,000-10,000 ISK). For details on restaurant pricing, see the Practicalities chapter.

## DOWNTOWN RESTAURANTS

Reykjavík's restaurants—from mom-and-pops to swanky splurges— serve weekday lunch specials for about 2,000-3,000 ISK (this may be a fixed "fish of the day," but sometimes you can choose among several options). Many places close for lunch on weekends—or, if open, have a pricier menu. Fancier restaurants become more expensive (sometimes *much* more expensive) at dinnertime.

Given the large tourist crowds, virtually any downtown restaurant (particularly in the $$$ or $$$$ price range) can book up during the busy summer months. In peak season, it's always smart to book ahead.

I've organized my listings along Reykjavík's main tourist spine, divided into three zones: to the east, along Laugavegur (the main shopping and nightlife drag) and the intersecting Skólavörðustígur (leading up to the big church); a 10-minute walk west, around Ingólfstorg and the parliament area; and a 10-minute walk farther west, near the Old Harbor area.

## Along Laugavegur and Skólavörðustígur

**$$$$ Sjávargrillið** ("The Seafood Grill") is a respected seafood house with a corner location right along Skólavörðustígur. Chef Gústav Axel Gunnlaugsson grills up delicious fish, lobster, and lamb meals. In addition to reasonable lunch specials and blow-out fixed-price dinners, they have a nice selection of lighter main courses for smaller appetites...and budgets. The cozy, tight interior is decorated with Icelandic driftwood gathered during Chef Gústav's culinary travels (Mon-Sat 11:30-14:30 & 17:00-22:30, Sun 17:00-22:30, Skólavörðustígur 14, tel. 571-1000).

**$$$ Snaps Bistro** is more Parisian-posh than Icelandic-kitsch, with a menu of mostly French-inspired dishes. The lively, sophisticated, glassed-in setting is just far enough off the main drag to attract locals alongside the tourists—particularly at lunchtime on weekdays, when their filling and artfully prepared fish-of-the-day special may be the best deal in town (around 2,000 ISK). They accept reservations only until 18:30, and it's busy at dinner—reserve to eat early, or plan to wait a bit (Sun-Thu 11:30-23:00, Fri-Sat until 24:00, Þórsgata 1, tel. 511-6677, www.snaps.is).

**Hverfisgata 12:** This classic old house, on a corner just a few steps from the main drag, hides several options for eating and drinking. From street level (along Hverfisgata), go up the stairs and let yourself inside. You'll find a cocktail bar in the basement; in the middle of the building is the **$$ Pizza Place with No Name** (good 3,000-ISK pizzas, daily 11:30-23:00, tel. 437-0203); and upstairs is the recommended **Mikkeller & Friends** bar, focusing on Scandinavian microbrews. If you're confused about which seating goes with which business...so is everyone else, so don't be afraid to ask. All have tables in comfortable wood-paneled rooms.

Just around the corner in the same building, at street level, is **$$$$ Dill**—one of Iceland's finest restaurants (and the recipient of its only Michelin star). In a clean, concrete-minimalist space, they serve up excellent, high-end, New Nordic-inspired dishes, at prices that aren't drastically higher than many other "upper-mid-range" places in this pricey town (five courses-12,000 ISK, seven courses-14,000 ISK). They often book up weeks or months ahead—reserve as early as possible (Wed-Sat 18:00-23:00, closed Sun-Tue, enter on Ingólfsstræti—look for shelves of preserve jars in the window, tel. 552-1522, www.dillrestaurant.is).

**Ostabúðin** ("The Cheese Shop") is a popular choice right near the bottom of Skólavörðustígur. In the **$$ deli,** you can assemble a

REYKJAVÍK

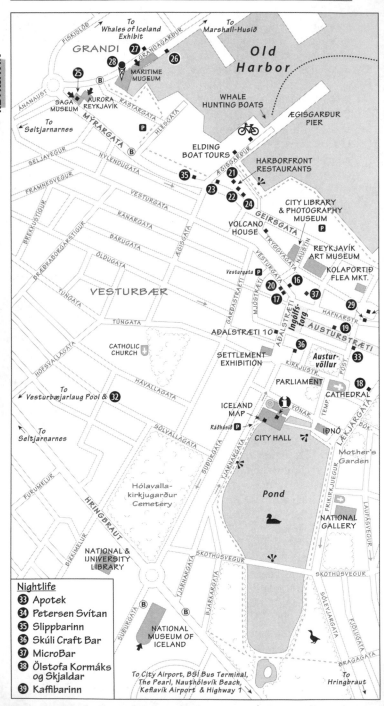

To Whales of Iceland Exhibit

To Marshall-Husið

FISKISLÓÐ

GRANDI

27

GRANDAGARÐUR

26

Old Harbor

28

25

MARITIME MUSEUM

B

ÁNANAUST

SAGA MUSEUM

AURORA REYKJAVÍK

MÝRARGATA

RASTARGATA

HLÉSGATA

To Seltjarnarnes

WHALE HUNTING BOATS

ÆGISGARÐUR PIER

SELJAVEGUR

NÝLENDUGATA

B

ELDING BOAT TOURS

ÆGISGARÐUR

HARBORFRONT RESTAURANTS

FRAMNESVEGUR

VESTURGATA

35

21

23

CITY LIBRARY & PHOTOGRAPHY MUSEUM

BREKKUSTÍGUR

RÁNARGATA

22

24

GEIRSGATA

P

BÁRUGATA

ÆGISGATA

VOLCANO HOUSE

TRYGGVAGATA

REYKJAVÍK ART MUSEUM

BRÆÐRABORGARSTÍGUR

ÖLDUGATA

VESTURGATA

NAUSTIN

KOLAPORTIÐ FLEA MKT.

TÚNGATA

VESTURBÆR

Vesturgata P

20

16

GARÐASTRÆTI

MJÓSTRÆTI

17

37

29

HAFNARSTR.

TÚNGATA

AÐALSTRÆTI

AÐALSTRÆTI 10

Ingólfs-torg

AUSTURSTRÆTI

19

CATHOLIC CHURCH

HÁVALLAGATA

SETTLEMENT EXHIBITION

36

KIRKJUSTR.

Austur-völlur

33

HOFSVALLAGATA

PARLIAMENT

POSTSTR.

To Vesturbæjarlaug Pool & 32

SÓLVALLAGATA

ICELAND MAP

TJÓNAR

18

CATHEDRAL

LÆKJARGATA

TEMP.

FÚRUMELUR

To Seltjarnarnes

SUÐURGATA

Ráðhúsið P

CITY HALL

IÐNÓ

LÆKJARGOT

Mother's Garden

FRÍKIRKJUVEGUR

TJARNARGATA

Hólavalla-kirkjugarður Cemetery

Pond

NATIONAL GALLERY

LAUFÁSVEGUR

HRINGBRAUT

BIRKIMELUR

NATIONAL & UNIVERSITY LIBRARY

SKÓTHÚSVEGUR

SKÓTHÚSVEGUR

SÓLEYJARGATA

FJÖLUGATA

B

SUÐURGATA

TJARNARGATA

BJARKARGATA

NATIONAL MUSEUM OF ICELAND

To City Airport, BSÍ Bus Terminal, The Pearl, Nauthólsvík Beach, Keflavík Airport & Highway 1

BRÁGATA

To Hringbraut

REYKJAVÍK

# Reykjavík Center Restaurants

1. Sjávargrillið
2. Snaps Bistro
3. Pizza Place with No Name; Mikkeller & Friends
4. Dill
5. Ostabúðin
6. Kaffi Vínyl
7. Brauð & Co
8. Reykjavík Roasters
9. Sandholt
10. Íslenski Barinn
11. Gló
12. Kryddlegin Hjörtu
13. Kex Hostel Café
14. To Hlemmur Food Market
15. Grillmarkaðurinn
16. Fiskfélagið
17. Matarkjallarinn
18. Messinn
19. The Laundromat Café
20. Stofan Café
21. Kopar
22. Sægreifinn
23. Hamborgarabúllan
24. Café Haiti
25. Matur og Drykkur
26. Kaffivagninn
27. The Coocoo's Nest
28. Valdís Ice Cream
29. Hornið Pizza
30. Krua Thai
31. Bónus Supermarket (2)
32. To Kaffihús Vesturbæjar

Note: See also Reykjavik Hotels & Restaurants Outside the Center map

200 Meters
200 Yards

BBP HOT DOGS

Kolaport

INGÓLFUR ARNARSSON STATUE

Lækjartorg

PRIME MINISTER'S OFFICE

CULTURE HOUSE

NATIONAL THEATER

SUN VOYAGER SCULPTURE

SÆBRAUT

SÖLVHÓLSGATA

INGÓLFSSTRÆTI

KLAPPARSTÍGUR

LINDARGATA

SKÚLAGATA

BANKASTRÆTI

Traðarkot

SMIÐJUSTÍGUR

BÍÓ PARADÍS CINEMA

VATNSSTÍGUR

FRAKKASTÍGUR

To Skarfagarðar, Keflavík Airport & Highway 1

AMTMANNSSTÍGUR

LAUGAVEGUR

HVERFISGATA

HIGH SCHOOL

Garden

ÞINGHOLTSSTRÆTI

INGÓLFSSTRÆTI

HALLVEIGAR

ÞINGHOLT

BJARGARSTÍGUR

SPÍTALA

TÝSGATA

SKÓLAVÖRÐUSTÍGUR

NJÁLSGATA

GRETTISGATA

LAUGAVEGUR

VITASTÍGUR

To Hlemmur Bus Junction

BERGSTAÐASTRÆTI

ÓÐINSGATA

FREYJUGATA

ÞÓRSGATA

LOKASTÍGUR

KÁRASTÍGUR

FRAKKASTÍGUR

AUSTURBÆR

HELLUSUND

BALDURSGATA

BRAGAGATA

NJARÐARGATA

GARDEN ENTRANCES

EINAR JÓNSSON MUSEUM & SCULPTURE GARDEN

LEIFUR EIRÍKSSON STATUE

HALLGRÍMSKIRKJA

EIRÍKSGATA

BERGÞÓRUGATA

SUNDHÖLLIN POOL

BAKÓNSSTÍGUR

(Summer Only)

To Viðey

HARPA CONCERT HALL

pricey gourmet picnic, with cheese and meat, olives, baguettes, pestos and spreads, and premade sandwiches (Mon-Fri 10:00-18:00, Sat 11:00-16:00, closed Sun). Their **$$$ restaurant** next door has a full menu of artfully presented international dishes. It's well-priced at lunch, but gets expensive at dinnertime (Mon-Fri 11:30-21:00, Sat from 12:00, Sun from 17:00; both are at Skólavörðustígur 8, tel. 562-2772).

**$ Kaffi Vínyl,** the only real vegan restaurant downtown, is worth considering even for carnivores. The hipster-chic ambience includes mismatched furniture, old record players, and an extensive record collection (live DJs spin mostly mellow tunes Wed-Sat after 20:00). The chalkboard menu lists an eclectic selection of flavorful hot sandwiches; for a heartier meal, pay extra to add some "Oumph" meat substitute. As they also have a full bar with beer and creative cocktails, this is also a cozy spot for an evening drink (Mon-Fri 9:00-23:00, Sat from 10:00, Sun from 11:00, Hverfisgata 76, tel. 537-1322).

**Hipster Corner:** For a pastry-and-coffee break downtown, head to Frakkastígur street—between Hallgrímskirkja church and Laugavegur—where two of Reykjavík's most appealing little eateries are separated by a grungy but colorful square. The exterior of artisanal bakery **$ Brauð & Co** ("Bread & Co.") is slathered with a wild graffiti mural, but inside the pastry chefs work like clockwork—churning out hot-from-the-oven cinnamon rolls *(snúðar),* danishes *(vinarbrauð),* croissants, sourdough loaves and rolls, and seasonal pastries. Get it to go and head for the little square just up the road (daily 6:00-18:00, Frakkastígur 16, tel. 776-0553). Conveniently, that's also where you'll find **Reykjavík Roasters,** the city's best, top-end gourmet coffee shop, where each grind of  beans is weighed to ensure a perfect pull. Flip through their vintage record collection while you wait, or just hang out in the bohemian-chic interior (Mon-Fri 8:00-18:00, Sat-Sun 9:00-17:00, at intersection of Frakkastígur and Kárastígur, tel. 517-5535). Reykjavík Roasters also has a larger, less crowded second location beyond the Hlemmur bus junction (same hours, Brautarholt 2).

**$$ Sandholt,** a refined, upscale-feeling bakery has great pastries (including homemade croissants and danishes), and serves breakfast and light lunches at tables in the back (daily 7:00-21:00, Laugavegur 36, tel. 551-3524).

**$$ Íslenski Barinn** ("The Icelandic Bar"), a small and casual tavern, attracts tourists looking to try very traditional, no-frills

Icelandic fare—including some exotic items, such as fermented shark. You'll pay dearly for a small vial, and eat only a nibble. More palatable pub grub (burgers) and a wide range of drinks make it a popular pub-crawl stop. This feels like a lowbrow alternative to some of the pricier, more pretentious places nearby (daily 11:30-late, Ingólfsstræti 1a, tel. 517-6767).

**$ Gló,** a local vegetarian chain, is a smart choice for a quick, inexpensive, healthy meal in the center. While it's technically a cafeteria, the inviting space—filling the upstairs of a characteristic old Reykjavík house just steps off the main street—is classy and inviting (Mon-Fri 11:00-21:00, Sat-Sun 11:30-21:00, Laugavegur 20b).

**$$ Kryddlegin Hjörtu** ("Spiced Hearts") serves Icelandic-Indian cuisine, with some vegetarian options, a cheap soup-and-salad lunch buffet, and prices that remain affordable at dinner (Mon-Sat 11:30-21:00, Sun 17:00-22:00, Hverfisgata 33, tel. 588-8818).

**$$ Kex Hostel** runs a big café open to nonguests, serving breakfast, burgers, lunch specials, and reasonably priced dinners in an ex-industrial space with lots of nooks and couches and a water view (daily 7:30-10:00 & 12:00-23:00, close to Hlemmur and the *Sun Voyager* sculpture at Skúlagata 28, tel. 561-6060).

**Hlemmur Food Market** (Hlemmur Mathöll): Located at the Hlemmur bus junction at the far end of Laugavegur, this food hall gathers lots of great Reykjavík eating under one roof, with stalls from several respected local restaurants. Check the website for vendors; for foodies, it merits the 10-minute walk from the downtown core (Laugavegur 107, www.hlemmurmatholl.is).

### Near Ingólfstorg

**$$$$ Grillmarkaðurinn** ("The Grill Market"), tucked on a courtyard along Austurstræti, is a worthwhile splurge. It has a rustic-industrial, two-story setting, with big split-log counters and a lively energy. The whole place smells like rich smoke, and their charcoal grill imbues powerful flavor. Their creative dishes allow curious travelers to sample traditional Icelandic "novelty foods" in a way that feels modern and palatable rather than  eating on a dare. Their trio of sliders feature a few bites each of puffin, minke whale, and Icelandic lobster, and their grilled minke whale steak comes on its own little hibachi. The service is helpful and without pretense. You can eat here more affordably at lunch on weekdays (reservations recommended, Mon-Fri 11:30-14:00 &

17:00-22:30, Sat-Sun 17:00-22:30, Lækjargata 2a, tel. 571-7777, www.grillmarkadurinn.is).

**$$$ Fiskfélagið** ("The Fish Company") is in the quaint Vesturgata area just off Ingólfstorg square. It fills the dark, stony cellar of a historic house; in the summer, it has outdoor seating in a sunken courtyard by a gurgling pool. Their French-trained chefs meld a variety of cuisines—including Mediterranean and Asian—with a respect for Icelandic ingredients and traditions. They offer weekday lunch specials, a few sushi options, and eclectic fish and non-fish main dishes. Reserve ahead, especially on weekends (Mon-Sat 11:30-14:30 & 17:30-22:30, Sun 17:30-22:30, closed for lunch Sat off-season, Vesturgata 2a, tel. 552-5300, www.fiskfelagid.is).

**$$$ Matarkjallarinn** ("The Food Cellar"), also at Vesturgata, manages to be one of Reykjavík's most popular restaurants despite being in a nearly windowless cellar. It's nicely decorated and feels more contemporary and sleek than its neighbor Fiskfélagið. While pricey at dinner, it's more affordable at lunch—with set-priced meals and a good-value daily fish combo (Mon-Fri 11:30-15:00 & 17:00-23:00, Sat-Sun 17:00-23:00, Aðalstræti 2, enter from Vesturgata, tel. 558-0000).

**$$ Messinn,** in a bright space on busy Lækjargata, features an appealing menu of fish and seafood, including "fish pans" served in sizzling skillets. Portions are large—even shareable. With a pleasant, woody Westfjords ambience, it's a bit more casual and less expensive than some of the fancier places I list in this area. Reserve ahead (daily 11:30-15:00 & 17:00-22:00, Lækjargata 6b, tel. 546-0095, www.messinn.com).

**$$ The Laundromat Café** is more café than launderette, and a handy place to enjoy comfort food (burgers, sandwiches, and fish) whether or not your laundry is spinning downstairs. The open-feeling space—decorated with photographs of laundromats around the world, big maps, and a bookshelf bar—is understandably popular with travelers. There's also a children's play area in the basement (Mon-Fri 8:00-23:00, Sat-Sun from 9:00, Austurstræti 9).

**$$ Stofan Café** ("Living Room") is straightforward, central, and popular. With a cozy living-room vibe overlooking a colorful (and touristy) slice of Reykjavík, it's a tempting place to escape the drizzle for a soup or sandwich. While you'll find better deals at lunch, prices are reasonable at dinnertime (daily 9:00-23:00, Vesturgata 3, tel. 546-1842).

## Old Harbor Area

**$$$ Kopar** ("Copper"), looking out over the harbor from one of the turquoise sheds, emphasizes fish and shellfish but also serves lamb and horse. They have competitively priced weekday lunches and more expensive dinners (Mon-Fri 11:30-14:00 & 17:00-22:30, Sat-Sun 17:00-22:30, Geirsgata 3, tel. 567-2700).

**$ Sægreifinn** ("The Seabaron") is a local institution, beloved for its affordable lobster soup and its late, colorful owner (who lives on in the form of a creepy wax statue in the dining room). Now the old man's daughter runs the place and keeps things simple: Line up at the register; order your soup and/or seafood skewers (including whale); then find a seat at a shared table in the sprawling interior. If you stop by on the first Saturday of the month in winter and notice a peculiar odor, they're cooking up a batch of *skötustappa*— putrefied skate wings in a sheep-innards stew (daily 11:30-23:00, children's play area, Geirsgata 8, tel. 553-1500).

**Quick Meals at the Harbor:** For a fast and affordable bite, try **$ Hamborgarabúllan** (look for "Burger Joint" signs; part of the local Tommi's chain) for a good-sized burger (daily 11:30-21:00, Geirsgata 1, tel. 511-1888). **$ Café Haiti,** Icelandic with a Caribbean twist, has inexpensive lamb and fish soups, plus sandwiches and a big coffee selection (long hours, Geirsgata 7b, tel. 588-8484).

## At the Far End of the Harbor, in Grandi

The peninsula called Grandi—which defines the far (western) end of the harbor area—has sprouted some trendy eateries, which are a notch less touristy and "ye olde" than choices closer to the whale-watching piers.

**$$$ Matur og Drykkur** ("Food and Drink"), inside the Saga Museum, prides itself on time-tested recipes that other restaurants

might dismiss as old-fashioned. Here, chefs update those traditional dishes for modern tastes. Try the trademark "halibut" soup (not made with halibut—which is illegal, for complicated reasons), cod's head (more delicious than you'd imagine), or arctic char smoked over burning sheep's dung (ditto). You'll also find lots of barley and seaweed on the menu. Despite the casual, rustic bistro ambience, the food is high-end and dinner can be spendy (when reservations are important); it's much more affordable at lunch, and pairs well with daytime sightseeing nearby (daily 11:30-15:00 & 17:00-22:00, Grandagarður 2, tel. 571-8877, www.maturogdrykkur.is).

**$$ Kaffivagninn** ("The Coffee Cart") perches on a pier overlooking bobbing boats. The understated nautical decor is charming, and the seaward glassed-in patio is tempting on a sunny day. The main dishes are Icelandic home-cooking classics like fish cakes, *plokkfiskur* (fish gratin or hash), and cod, plaice, and arctic char filets; on weekdays, soup and coffee are included (Mon-Fri 7:30-18:00, Sat-Sun from 9:30, Grandagarður 10, tel. 551-5932, http://www.kaffivagninn.is).

**$ The Coocoo's Nest** is a somewhat trendier-feeling café just across the street from Kaffivaginn, and lacks its view. But it does have a cozy, split-level, stay-awhile interior and a tempting, brief menu—ideal for escaping the elements and enjoying soup, salad, or sandwiches. It serves a rotating menu—tacos one night, pizza the next, then Italian (Tue-Sat 11:00-22:00, Sun until 16:00, closed Mon, Grandagarður 23, tel. 552-5454).

**Ice Cream: Valdís,** a couple of doors down, offers creative flavors. The name is a pun—it's a girl's first name, but can also be read as "Power Ice Cream" (daily 11:30-23:00, Grandagarður 21).

## OUTSIDE DOWNTOWN

These places are best for drivers (all have free parking) but can also be reached by bus.

### West and South of Downtown

**$ Kaffihús Vesturbæjar,** an inviting neighborhood café across the street from the Vesturbæjarlaug swimming pool, is the kind of place that makes you want to hang out and pretend you live here. They serve good lunches from a small menu chalked on the board. While I wouldn't make a special trip, it's definitely worth a visit if you happen to be nearby (Mon-Fri 8:00-23:00, Sat-Sun from 9:00, hot food served 11:30-15:00 & 17:00-21:00, at Melhaga 20 at corner of Hófsvallagata, walk or take bus #11 to Melaskóli or #15 to Vesturgarður, easy parking, tel. 551-0623, www.kaffihusvesturbaejar.is).

**$ Mýrin Mathús,** a grill restaurant set unatmospherically inside the BSÍ bus terminal, is worth a visit mostly if you want to eat *svið* (sheep's head) served with mashed potatoes and turnips. You'll get a half sheep's head grinning at you on a plate (neatly sawed down the midline, brains not included), and a fork and a knife. You eat the cheek meat; those who dare can try the eyeball and tongue. They also dish up other classic Icelandic stick-to-your-ribs fare all day long, like fish cakes, salted lamb, and stuffed cabbage. These dishes come with soup and beverages (Mon-Fri 7:30-21:00, Sat-Sun 6:00-21:00, *svið* and other hot food served daily 10:30-20:30, small kids eat free with their parents, Vatnsmýrarvegur 10, tel. 552-1288, see map on page 80).

### Near the Botanic Garden

For locations, see the map on page 80.

**$$ Flóran,** the relaxing café inside Reykjavík's botanic garden, has an eclectic, inventive menu, with main dishes and meal-

# Budget Bites

If you're trying to stretch your budget—or want a low-key dinner option—here are some ideas. I normally don't recommend international chains, but if you're on a tight budget in this expensive country, inexpensive and familiar comfort food can hit the spot.

**Pizza** is a bad value at lunch but competitive at dinner, when a 2,500-ISK one-person pizza starts to look cheap compared to a 5,000-ISK entree at sit-down restaurant. Pizza joints downtown include the hip **$$ Pizza Place with No Name** (at Hverfisgata 12, a bit pricier) and the venerable **$$ Hornið** (at Hafnarstræti 15, close to Parliament and Lækjartorg). For a cheap meal, locals call **$ Domino's,** with multiple outlets (including a central one at Skúlagata 27, near Hlemmur; easy ordering in English online or call 581-2345, locations and offers at www.dominos.is).

Just like back home, Reykjavík's suburban **IKEA** store has a handy and very cheap **$ cafeteria.** Local families pack in for inexpensive (if small) main dishes, including Swedish meatballs and Icelandic *plokkfiskur* (fish gratin or hash). Downstairs by the cash registers are Reykjavík's least-expensive hot dogs and soft-serve ice cream. IKEA is just off the main route from Reykjavík to the airport, the Blue Lagoon, and the Ásvallalaug swimming pool (daily 9:30-20:30, Kauptún 4 in the suburb of Garðabær, bus #21 to the IKEA stop—catch it at Mjódd or in Hafnarfjörður).

As in other expensive European cities, **international food** can be a good value here. **$ Noodle Station,** a small local chain, serves just one dish: big portions of a vaguely Vietnamese noodle soup, with your choice of beef, chicken, or vegetables. There's a location close to the Hlemmur bus junction (Laugavegur 86—see map on page 80), and another in a strip mall on the main road through Hafnarfjörður. For a larger selection of Asian dishes, consider **$ Krua Thai,** a couple of blocks downhill from the big Hallgrímskirkja church (daily 11:30-21:30, Skólavörðustígur 21a—see map on page 89), tel. 551-0833).

Of course, the absolute cheapest option is to assemble a picnic at a **supermarket.** Discount supermarket **Bónus** has two downtown branches, at Hallveigarstígur 1 and Laugavegur 59 (both open Mon-Thu 11:00-18:30, Fri 10:00-19:30, shorter hours Sat-Sun). **Hagkaup** runs several 24-hour supermarkets (closed on holidays) including one a 10-minute drive from downtown at Skeifan 15. There are also supermarkets in the Kringlan and Smáralind indoor shopping malls, outside the center.

sized salads. Eat outdoors on a nice day, or in the warm, greenhouse-like interior. Befitting the location, they grow some of their own vegetables and herbs (daily 10:00-22:00, early May and Sept until 18:00, closed Oct-April; take bus #2, #5, #15, or #17 to the Laugardalshöll stop and walk 10 minutes downhill to the parking lot and garden entrance; tel. 553-8872).

**$ Múlakaffi** serves old-style Icelandic cuisine with all the polish of a 1970s school lunchroom. You can stuff yourself for about 2,000 ISK, even at dinnertime. Choose a main dish at the counter—it might be fish cakes, cod cheeks, or pasta with meat sauce—then help yourself to as much soup, salad, bread, butter, and coffee as you like (dishes are listed at www.mulakaffi.is). This place has been here—in a commercial zone amidst office blocks and strip malls—for decades. You'll see tradespeople here on a midday break and older men who meet to chat and read the papers together (Mon-Fri 7:30-20:00, Sat 10:00-14:00, closed Sun, Hallarmúli 1, bus #2, #5, #15, or #17 to Nordica stop, tel. 553-7737).

## Farther Out, in Hafnarfjörður

This bedroom community, about 15 minutes' drive south of Reykjavík, isn't worth going out of your way to get a meal. However, if you're sleeping in Hafnarfjörður—or passing through on your way back from side-trips to the Blue Lagoon, South Coast, or Golden Circle—it can be easier to grab a bite here than to look for parking downtown. See the "Hafnarfjörður" map, for locations.

**$$ Von** ("Hope") is the top choice for foodies. This small, ambitious restaurant serves modern fish and meat dishes and is proud of their seafood and ox cheek. Local office workers come for good weekday lunch specials (reservations recommended for dinner, Tue-Sat 11:30-14:00 & 17:30-21:00, Sun 11:30-14:00, also open Sun evenings June-Aug, closed Mon year-round, Strandgata 75, along the water at the south end of downtown, past the fake stave church, tel. 583-6000, www.vonmathus.is).

**$ Pallett,** an inviting hangout café in the same complex as Von, is run by an Icelandic-British couple. They serve great coffee, affordable soup and sandwiches, and—on weekends—a full traditional English breakfast at midday (Mon-Fri 8:00-23:00, Sat-Sun from 10:00, Strandgata 75, tel. 571-4144).

**$ Bike Cave** is a casual hamburger restaurant tucked in the town center, with a spacious interior (including a glassy winter garden) and intriguing burgers (daily 9:00-22:00, Strandgata 34, tel. 571-3144).

**$ Súfistinn Kaffihús** is a simple, two-story café with soups, sandwiches, and quiches on the old main street, close to the town library (Mon-Fri 8:00-23:30, Sat from 10:00, Sun from 11:00, Strandgata 9, tel. 563-3740).

**$$$ Fjörukráin** ("The Waterside Tavern") is a Viking-themed dinner-only restaurant, often busy with groups (you can't miss it—look for the Norwegian stave church-like roof). It's kitschy and the prices are high for what you get, but the interior is a work of art and a visit can be fun (daily 18:00-22:00, Strandgata 55, tel. 565-1213).

**REYKJAVÍK**

# Reykjavík Connections

## BY PLANE
### Keflavík Airport (International Flights)

Keflavík Airport (pronounced KEPP-la-VEEK, code: KEF, tel. 425-6000, www.kefairport.is) is Iceland's only real international airport and the center of Icelandair's hub-and-spoke operation that carries thousands of passengers a day between North America and Europe. The airport's status as a transfer point gives Icelanders a much broader range of flight options, all year long, than they would otherwise have in this small country. Budget carrier Wow Air and several other airlines also serve the airport. Extra flights are added each summer to carry European tourists to Iceland—during summer months, the airport can get very crowded.

Arrival and departure areas are both on the ground floor, on opposite sides of the main terminal building. You'll find a couple cafés and a convenience store, car rental offices, a tax-refund desk, and ATMs, but no TI. A 24-hour bank is located inside (after security) where you can change any leftover Icelandic crowns when you leave the country—they're hard to exchange outside Iceland. The airport has free Wi-Fi.

**Nearby Gas Stations:** When returning a rental car be aware that the airport itself has only a couple of teeny self-serve pumps hidden near the car-rental return. It's smarter to fill up in downtown Keflavík or at the bigger gas stations a five-minute drive away along the main road from Reykjavík.

The Orkan gas station along the main road, next to the Bónus supermarket, can't process US chip-and-signature credit cards at the pump but sells prepaid gas cards inside its 24-hour shop. The N1 station in downtown Keflavík takes signature cards, but has shorter hours.

**Breakfast Near the Airport:** Many flights from the US arrive early in the morning. Hótel Keflavík, near the harbor in the town

**Keflavík Airport Area**

- ❶ Hotel Aurora Star
- ❷ Hótel Keflavík
- ❸ Alex Guesthouse

of Keflavík, offers a buffet open to nonguests (no reservations needed, 2,800 ISK, daily 5:00-10:00, Vatnsnesvegi 12, tel. 420-7000). The Viking World museum on the Reykjanes Peninsula also does a breakfast buffet that includes admission (see page 122).

## Getting Between Reykjavík and Keflavík Airport

The airport is about a 45-minute drive from downtown Reykjavík (30 minutes from Hafnarfjörður). For details on renting a car, see page 177. Without a rental car, your options are private airport buses, shared door-to-door van service, taxis, or an infrequent public bus.

Don't worry about making an early flight: The whole system is designed for people to get from Reykjavík with plenty of time to make a 7:00 or 8:00 departure. Buses, shuttles, and taxis are ready to go by 3:00 or 4:00 in the morning.

**By Airport Bus:** Two companies—Reykjavík Excursions and Gray Line—run buses between Reykjavík and the airport. Buses run whenever there are flights, even at odd hours. From the airport, buses typically depart when full, which can mean a wait.

From Reykjavík, buses depart according to a schedule that varies depending on the flight density.

**Reykjavík Excursions** runs the **Flybus** (tel. 580-5400, www. flybus.is) between the airport and the company's terminal in Reykjavík (called BSÍ, at Vatnsmýrarvegur 10, about a 10- to 15-minute walk from downtown).

**Gray Line** runs **Airport Express** buses (tel. 540-1313, www. airportexpress.is) to and from their terminal at Holtavegur 10, next to a Bónus supermarket in a distant part of Reykjavík.

Taking these buses makes good financial sense for solo travelers and for families, as children ride free or at a sizable discount. But the buses can be slow, disorganized, and stressful. The companies try to fill every seat. At busy times, the aisle will be crowded with hand bags, the luggage compartment will be jammed full, and boarding may be a mob scene. Bring patience.

Both companies have desks in the airport arrivals hall where you can buy tickets; you can also book and pay in advance online. A round-trip ticket (about 4,000 ISK) saves over two one-ways (about 2,500 ISK).

Gray Line's regular price is a tad cheaper, but Reykjavík Excursions tickets are discounted if you buy them from the flight attendant on board Icelandair. (Icelandair and Reykjavík Excursions have a longstanding business alliance, so you won't hear or read a word about Gray Line on Icelandair flights.)

In Reykjavík, the buses stop primarily at each company's main transfer point, but Gray Line also picks up and drops off downtown for no extra charge. En route between Reykjavík and the airport, both companies' buses stop on request at the bus shelter across from the Viking Village Hótel in downtown Hafnarfjörður (at Strandgata 55). If you need to be picked up there, pay in advance and reconfirm with the company, as buses bypass this stop if there are no requests.

*Door-to-Door Service:* For an extra 500 ISK each way, each company will tack on the transportation between their transfer point and major hotels and hostels in central Reykjavík. This usually involves a separate minibus trip between the transfer point and the hotel, and takes about 30 extra minutes. It's cheaper than a taxi, and easier than taking the city bus. The transfer procedures can be confusing (you'll need to carry your luggage from one bus to the other). If you're staying in an Airbnb, put in a nearby hotel as your pick-up and drop-off point, then walk from the hotel to your lodgings. If you're staying way out in the suburbs, the transfer service may not serve any point near you.

**By Shared Minibus Service:** Door-to-door minibus service is midrange both in price and speed. One company offering this is **Back To Iceland Travel,** which charges 3,200 ISK per adult and

1,600 ISK per child for a one-way trip—barely more than the airport bus. You may have to wait at the airport for other passengers to arrive, and the minibus will pick up and drop off others on the way between Reykjavík and the airport, so it's not as quick as a taxi. But you'll get more personal attention than on the airport bus and door-to-door service. Book in advance on their website; they'll be waiting for you with your name on a sign when you leave the baggage-claim area (mobile tel. 846-3837, www.btitravel.is).

**By Taxi:** Groups of at least four adults (who can split the cost) save time and pay only a little more to take a taxi to or from the airport. Anyone up for paying extra to avoid the craziness of the airport buses should also consider a taxi. Reykjavík's two main taxi companies both offer fixed-price service to and from the airport for about 15,000-16,000 ISK (1-4 passengers) or 19,000-21,500 ISK (5-8 passengers). If you reserve in advance, they'll wait for you at the airport with a sign. When reserving, tell them your destination and ask their advice; if your starting or ending point is in the southern part of the capital area (for example, in Hafnarfjörður), using the meter may be cheaper than these fixed rates. Contact **Hreyfill** (tel. 588-5522, www.hreyfill.is) and **BSR** (tel. 561-0000, www.taxireykjavik.is). Other smaller taxi and transfer companies may offer slightly lower rates.

**By Public Bus:** Strætó, the public bus company, runs buses (#55) between downtown Reykjavík and Keflavík Airport every 1-2 hours, taking about 70 minutes. At some times of the day and on weekends, they run only between the airport and the Fjörður stop in Hafnarfjörður, where you change to bus #1. The public bus is meant more for commuters than for international travelers and goes infrequently, but it's the cheapest way into town and has space for luggage. As it's considered a long-distance route, you can pay the bus driver with a credit card (1,760 ISK or four bus tickets; connecting city buses are free if you ask the drive for a transfer slip). For schedules, see www.straeto.is (enter the airport as "KEF" in the journey planner).

The Strætó bus stop is out in the open air along row A of the car rental lot. To find it, walk out from the arrivals side of the terminal under the roofed walkway, then hang a left and look for the tiny "S" sign (it's not signposted from inside the arrivals hall).

## Reykjavík City Airport

Reykjavík's domestic airport (code: RKV) is just south of downtown. Planes landing from the north fly directly over Parliament at a height of only a few hundred feet. While the runways are long enough to land an Icelandair 757, the airport is only used for smaller planes flying domestic routes and to the Faroe Islands and east Greenland. Check-in at the pint-sized terminals feels informal; arriving even an hour early feels like overkill, and there's no security checkpoint for domestic flights.

It's important to know that the airport has two terminals on *opposite* sides of the runway. If you go to the wrong terminal, you'll have to take a taxi to get to the other (you can't walk). Air Iceland Connect uses the larger main terminal on the *west* side of the runways (take bus #15 to the Reykjavíkurflugvöllur stop). If you're flying on Eagle Air—for example, to the Westman Islands—you'll go from a separate, smaller terminal on the *east* side of the runways (take bus #5 to the Nauthólsvegur stop; the terminal is behind the Icelandair Hótel Reykjavík Natura and the control tower). Parking is free at both terminals.

To make an early-morning domestic flight, before buses start running, call a taxi (reserve the night before; see the taxi recommendations earlier, under Keflavík Airport). Figure about 2,000 ISK for a taxi between downtown and either terminal (or between terminals). When you get in the taxi, remember to specify which airline/terminal you're heading to.

## BY BUS

Reykjavík has several bus stations. Buses run by **Reykjavík Excursions,** including all of their excursion buses and the scheduled FlyBus to the airport, use the old **BSÍ** bus terminal at Vatnsmýrarvegur 10, about a 15-minute walk from downtown (or take bus #1, #3, #5, #6, #14, or #15 to BSÍ). Two smaller companies, Sterna Travel and TREX, also use BSÍ for their scheduled and excursion buses.

Buses run by **Gray Line** use their terminal at **Holtavegur 10,** in the Reykjavík suburbs near the container-ship harbor. Gray Line runs minibuses to hotels around town to pick travelers up and shuttle them to the terminal. You can get within a five-minute walk of the terminal by public bus (#12 or #16 to the Sund or Holtagarðar stops), but it's easier to use their shuttles.

Long-distance buses run by **Strætó,** Iceland's public bus service, depart from the Mjódd bus terminal in the eastern Reykjavík suburbs. It's next to a small indoor shopping mall, also called Mjódd (MEE-ohd). Many city bus routes stop at Mjódd, including #3, #4, #11, #12, #17, #24, and #28 (no extra charge for transfer ticket).

Strætó's downtown city bus junction at **Hlemmur** doesn't serve long-distance routes, but is a good place to catch a bus to the long-distance terminal at Mjódd.

## BY CRUISE SHIP

There's no scheduled boat service from Reykjavík, but cruise ships frequently stop here in summer. The cruise ship terminal is at Skarfagarðar, a five-minute drive east of downtown; by bus, take #16 to the Klettagarðar/Skarfagarðar stop. Smaller cruise ships occasionally use a berth in the Old Harbor, just steps from downtown. The weekly ferry from Iceland to Denmark leaves from Seyðisfjörður, in eastern Iceland.

# NEAR REYKJAVÍK

# NEAR REYKJAVÍK

Most visitors to Iceland settle into a home base, typically Reykjavík, and see most of the countryside on day trips. The most popular destinations—all in western or southern Iceland—are all doable as day trips from Reykjavík, whether you rent a car or join an excursion.

Two of the best side-trips for getting a glimpse of Iceland's dramatic landscape are the Golden Circle (linking historical and geological wonders, in the country's lava-rock interior—covered in this book) and the volcano-and-glacier-lined South Coast (where you can hike up to the face of a glacier, stroll along black sand beaches, and walk behind a thundering waterfall).

There's also the famous Blue Lagoon spa—a serene, milky-blue oasis in a volcanic landscape (also covered in this book)—and

the West Iceland region around Borgarnes, with an eclectic variety of sights. In the Westman Islands, just off Iceland's South Coast, you can see the effects of a recent volcanic eruption and perhaps meet a real, live puffin.

Below, I've given you a few tips for planning side-trips on your own with a car, as well as your options for joining guided excursions.

**Summer Bonus:** In summer you'll enjoy very long hours of daylight; from early June to mid-July it never really gets dark. You can pack a day full by sightseeing close to your home base in the morning, then setting out on a side-trip in the late afternoon. In

**Near Reykjavík**

SNÆFELLSNES PENINSULA

Grábrók

WEST ICELAND

Viðgelmir Lava Tube

Reykholt

Borgarnes

50 Kilometers

50 Miles

Geysir

Þingvellir

Gullfoss

GOLDEN CIRCLE

Reykjavík

REYKJANES PENINSULA

Keflavík

Blue Lagoon

Hvolsvöllur (Lava Center)

Seljalands-foss

Þórsmörk

Skógar-foss

SOUTH COAST

Sólheima-jökull

Heimaey

WESTMAN ISLANDS

Dyrhólaey

Vík

*North Atlantic Ocean*

Reynisfjara

NEAR REYKJAVÍK

the peak of summer, for example, it's possible to leave Reykjavík for the Golden Circle as late as 16:00, see most of the sights along that route, and be back in town before the sun goes down.

**Winter Wake-up:** In winter, daylight is brief (as short as 4 hours). If roads are clear, it's smart to leave Reykjavík in the dark and time your arrival at the first attraction for sunrise. Be alert to weather conditions, as roads may close due to snow, high winds, or ice.

**Car vs. Excursion:** Although a car rental may seem pricey (roughly $350 for a one-week rental in summer, plus insurance, fuel, tolls, and parking), consider this: Per person, the bus transfer to and from the airport is $40; you'll pay $100 for a basic Golden Circle excursion and $150 for the South Coast. If you're in Iceland for three nights, and take two day-trip excursions, you'll spend close to $300 (double that for a couple). Suddenly a rental car doesn't seem that expensive.

## WITH A CAR

For travelers day-tripping on their own by car, I've outlined detailed self-guided driving tours with suggested hour-by-hour schedules and opinionated descriptions to help you assess your options and plan your drive.

My directions assume you're staying in Reykjavík. But if you prefer sleeping outside the city, you can drive to these day-trip

## Decoding Icelandic Place Names

Most Icelandic place names are simply a pileup of geographical features. For example, the word for the famous tongue-twister volcano Eyjafjallajökull can be broken down into three smaller words meaning "Island-Mountain Glacier." You can learn a lot about a place simply by decoding its name (and often just its suffix). For example, if you see *fjörður,* expect a dramatic seaside setting; *vík* is on the water, but less thrilling; *fjall* is mountainous; and *hver* means things could get steamy. Here are some of the building blocks:

| | | | |
|---|---|---|---|
| *á* | river, stream | *fell* | hill, mountain |
| *akur* | field | *fjall* | mountain |
| *ár* | river | *fjara* | beach, shore |
| *austur* | east | *fjörður* | fjord |
| *bær* | town | *fljót* | large river |
| *bjarg* | cliff | *flói* | gulf, bay |
| *borg* | outcrop, fortification | *flúðir* | rapids |
| *braut* | avenue | *foss* | waterfall |
| *brú* | bridge | *gata* | street |
| *bú* | estate, farm | *gerði* | fence, hedge |
| *dalur* | valley | *gígur* | crater |
| *eldfjall* | volcano (fire mountain) | *gljúfur* | canyon, gorge |
| *ey* | island | *grænn* | green |
| *eyja* | island | *heiði* | treeless highland, heath, sometimes "pass" |
| *eyri* | point, spit | *hellir* | cave |

destinations from a home base anywhere in the southwestern part of the country—for example, from the Reykjavík suburb of Hafnarfjörður, or from Keflavík, near the international airport.

Before heading out, be sure to read the tips on driving in Iceland in the Practicalities chapter.

## WITH AN EXCURSION

A variety of companies offer excursions around Iceland. These are great if you want to sit back, enjoy the scenery, and learn from a knowledgeable guide (or, in a few cases, a well-produced recorded commentary). With careful planning, you can cobble together half-and full-day excursions that will get you to many of Iceland's top sights.

| hlíð | mountainside, slope | sandur | sandy area |
|------|---------------------|--------|------------|
| holt | hill | skagi | peninsula |
| höfn | harbor | skarð | mountain pass |
| hraun | lava | skógur | forest |
| hús | house | staður | place, farm, town |
| hver | hot spring | stígur | trail |
| hvítur | white | stræti | street |
| jökull | glacier | strönd | coast, sandy beach |
| krókur | hook, river bend | suður | south |
| laugar | hot spring, pool | svartur | black |
| lækur | creek | tún | hay field |
| lón | lagoon | vatn | lake (also "water") |
| mýri | swamp, marsh | vegur | road |
| nes | promontory, headland | vestur | west |
| norður | north | vík | bay, inlet |
| reykur | steam | völlur | field, plain (plural vellir) |

These place name elements recur throughout the country, and in a few cases entire names are recycled (for instance, there's a Reykholt near Borgarnes in western Iceland, and another near Geysir along the Golden Circle). When that happens, the place name might get an add-on modifier for clarity. The town of Vík ("Bay"), on the South Coast, is called Vík í Mýrdal (the "Bay in Marshy Valley") to distinguish it from other less-visited Víks around the country. And if you're heading for Borgarfjörður Eystri (literally the "more eastern Borgarfjörður"), don't follow your GPS to plain old Borgarfjörður...nearly 400 miles to the west.

The most popular excursion destinations are the Golden Circle, the Blue Lagoon, the South Coast, the Snæfellsnes peninsula (north of Reykjavík), and the Reykjanes Peninsula (south of Reykjavík). In winter, you'll find evening trips in search of the northern lights. Some tours run all year, but winter offerings are generally sparser.

Most excursions start in Reykjavík, but there are also options from Akureyri, Mývatn, and other small towns around the Ring Road.

You may see tours advertised for the glacier lagoons and Skaftafell National Park in Southeast Iceland; while these are amazing sights, they're too far from the capital for a reasonable day trip (at least 10 hours round-trip from Reykjavík)—you'll spend far more time in the bus than at your destination. Save these for another trip...when you come back and drive around the Ring Road. Or, if you're serious about glaciers, add an overnight or two in the southeast and do it right.

## BIG VS. SMALL COMPANY

The two biggest players are **Reykjavík Excursions** (www.re.is, owned by Icelandair and promoted on their flights) and **Gray Line** (www.grayline.is). Their offerings are slick and consistent, but the 50-seat buses are typically jam-packed (though Gray Line offers some minibus departures). An advantage, though, is predictability and price; what these tours lack in intimacy they make up for in efficiency and lower ticket costs.

Several smaller outfits are more personal, generally use smaller vehicles—and charge a little to a lot more. Well-established and respected companies include family-run **Nicetravel** (www.nicetravel.is); environmentally focused **Geo Iceland** (www.geoiceland.com); small-bus, small-group **Iceland Horizon** (www.icelandhorizon.is); and pricey, boutique **Season Tours** (www.seasontours.is).

**Choosing an Excursion:** For starters, look at each company's brochure and website. As the offerings are constantly in flux, check reviews on TripAdvisor.com (in the "Things to Do" section) for recent firsthand accounts. Guide to Iceland (www.guidetoiceland.is), a consortium of several travel outlets, can be a good one-stop source for tours; they also have a booking desk at the Reykjavík TI.

**Add-on Options:** Beyond the standard sightseeing loops, excursion companies mix and match a staggering variety of add-on activities: hiking, caving, horseback riding, snorkeling, glacier walking, and snowmobiling. The possibilities are endless. You can do the Blue Lagoon on the way to the airport; add the Fontana baths in Laugarvatn, snorkeling, or an ATV ride to a Golden Circle trip; or go on a tour of *Game of Thrones* shooting locations.

**Prices:** Excursions run from about $80 to $250 (more for boutique experiences). For example, an express, six-hour Golden Circle tour costs about $100; a 10-hour South Coast tour costs around $150; and a bus trip to the Blue Lagoon, including the hefty admission, runs at least $120.

**When to Book:** For the standard tours—such as the Golden Circle or South Coast—you generally don't need to book a seat more than a day or two in advance, so you may want to wait until you arrive in Iceland—and can check the weather report. One exception is the Blue Lagoon, which can fill up faster than other excursions. Your hotel may be happy to book these tours for you (be aware that they get a commission).

More specialized tours (ice caving, glacier hikes) can book up quite a bit earlier; for these, keep an eye on online booking calendars, which typically count down the number of slots available for each tour. If it looks like they're selling fast, book yours before it's too late.

## WITH AN UNGUIDED EXCURSION

A number of private companies run regularly scheduled buses throughout Iceland's countryside—offering transportation to otherwise difficult-to-reach, remote areas, but without any guiding. Developed primarily to get hikers to trailheads, some of these buses can also work for independent travelers who want to put together day trips on their own. For more information, see the "Transportation" section of the Practicalities chapter.

# BLUE LAGOON & REYKJANES PENINSULA

The Blue Lagoon—arguably Iceland's most famous attraction—is tucked into a jagged volcanic landscape in the middle of nowhere, about a 45-minute drive south of downtown Reykjavík and not far from the international airport. People flock here from around the globe to soak, splash, and bob in the lagoon's thermal and, yes, milky-blue waters. While many visitors consider the Blue Lagoon a must, others disagree—it's pricey, time-consuming, and not everyone's cup of tea.

The Blue Lagoon and Keflavík Airport both sit on the Reykjanes (RAKE-ya-NESS) Peninsula, which extends into the sea south of Reykjavík. A few low-impact sights are scattered around the volcanic terrain beyond the Blue Lagoon—including Kleifarvatn lake; the thermal fields at Seltún; Grindavík, a humdrum town with some good lunch options; and Keflavík, the peninsula's main town. While the scenery is more impressive in other parts of the country, a quick drive around Reykjanes provides those on a tight time frame with an efficient glimpse of the Icelandic landscape.

## PLANNING YOUR TIME

Be aware that the Blue Lagoon requires reservations—you can't just show up and hope to slip in. To have your choice of slots, book several days ahead.

**Blue Lagoon Strategic Strike:** Given the Blue Lagoon's proximity to the international airport, a smart, time-saving strategy is to schedule your visit to coincide with your flight: If arriving on a morning flight, hit the Blue Lagoon on your way into Reykjavík. Or if you're flying out in the afternoon, soak in the Blue Lagoon on your way to the airport. If you have a layover of several hours, it

## Blue Lagoon: To Visit or Not to Visit?

Travelers are split on the Blue Lagoon. For some, a visit to this iconic thermal pool is the highlight of their time in Iceland. For others, it's outrageously expensive and overrated. Here are the pros and cons:

On one hand, the Blue Lagoon is a unique and memorable travel experience, thanks to its stunning volcanic setting, silky-blue water, and luxury-spa class. While you could visit any municipal swimming pool in Iceland to splash in hot water, the Blue Lagoon is as refined as those are functional—it is, in a sense, the ultimate expression of Icelandic thermal bathing. And it's simply fun: sipping a drink, smearing fancy mud on your face, and feeling pebbles under your feet as 100°F water ebbs your stress away. As a bonus, it's easy to reach on the way to or from the airport.

On the other hand, the Blue Lagoon is expensive (absurdly so to Icelanders), overly crowded with an almost exclusively touristic clientele, grossly commercial, and inconveniently located for those staying in Reykjavík. The reservation requirement is cumbersome, and the minerals in the water can wreak havoc on your hair. If you believe that one big pool of hot water is pretty much the same as any other, you'll be much happier to pay one-tenth of the price to enjoy one of Reykjavík's many municipal swimming pools—which also offer a far more authentic cultural experience. (For more on the municipal pool experience, read the description on page 160.)

**BLUE LAGOON & REYKJANES**

may not be worth the trouble to go all the way into Reykjavík—but a visit to the Blue Lagoon (or sights in the town of Keflavík) makes a far better alternative to hanging out at the airport.

**Combining the Blue Lagoon with the Reykjanes Peninsula:** If you're staying longer in Reykjavík and want to make a day of it, book your Blue Lagoon reservation for 13:00 and follow this plan.

| | |
|---|---|
| 10:00 | Leave Reykjavík for Kleifarvatn lake (45 minutes) |
| 11:00 | Visit Kleifarvatn and Seltún geothermal field |
| 11:30 | Drive to Grindavík (30 minutes) and have lunch |
| 12:45 | Drive to the Blue Lagoon (10 minutes) |
| 13:00 | Soak in the Blue Lagoon—aaah |
| 16:00 | Return to Reykjavík—or, before heading home, take in one of the museums in the town of Keflavík |

# Blue Lagoon

While Iceland has a wide variety of thermal baths, the Blue Lagoon's setting amongst rocky lava makes it unique. Bathing at the Blue Lagoon is, for many travelers, the ultimate Icelandic experience, and worth ▲▲▲.

If you're excited to visit the Blue Lagoon (Bláa Lónið), you're not alone: The sight's popularity and don't-miss-it reputation have driven prices way up. The lagoon has expanded, but at a pace that can't keep up with tourist demand (over 3,000 people visit each day). Reservations are required, and some slots sell out days in advance. (The bottleneck isn't the lagoon itself, but the number of lockers.) While the reservation requirement is a hassle, it keeps the lagoon from getting too congested—even on the busiest days, you can find pockets of hot water where you can escape the tour groups. Once inside, you can stay as long as you want.

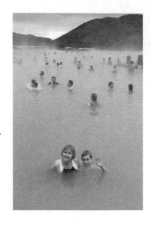

The Blue Lagoon is a delight. Nestled in a lunar-like landscape, this steamy oasis is a sprawling hot-water playground for grown-ups. Chunky rocks disappear beneath the opaque water, where they're coated with white silica slime. The naturally heated water is thoroughly relaxing. You'll smear mineral deposits on your

face, while giggling at your fellow silica-masked bathers. The hardest "work" you'll have to do is keeping your Icelandic microbrew or *skyr* smoothie above the water, as you behold the surrounding rocks hissing like teakettles. Before leaving the lagoon, some travelers are already planning their next layover in Iceland...giving them juuust enough time for a future soak.

## GETTING THERE

**With a Car:** If you're renting a car—and traveling with others who can split the cost—you'll save by driving to the lagoon over going by bus. It's about 45 minutes from downtown Reykjavík, and only 15 minutes from Keflavík Airport, off highway 43, on the way to the town of Grindavík. Some signs use only the Icelandic name: *Bláa Lónið*. The lagoon's huge parking lot is free.

**By Excursion Bus:** Both **Reykjavík Excursions** and **Gray Line** sell packages that include standard admission and round-trip travel between Reykjavík and the lagoon for about 11,700 ISK. You're allowed to use your return ticket to continue to Keflavík Airport instead of going back to Reykjavík (luggage storage is available at the Blue Lagoon—see page 115). Buses run hourly between Reykjavík and the Blue Lagoon but less frequently between the lagoon and airport—check schedules carefully and plan ahead (Reykjavík Excursions tel. 580-5400, www.re.is; Gray Line tel. 540-1313, www.grayline.is). Note that these companies have access to the same time slots for the Blue Lagoon as individuals—if the lagoon is sold out in one place, it'll be sold out everywhere.

## ORIENTATION TO THE BLUE LAGOON

**Cost:** Prices vary with demand. Most visitors opt for the **standard** package (typically 7,500 ISK, but can be as low as 5,400 ISK in off-peak hours). If you choose this package, you'll need to bring your own towel or rent one for 700 ISK. For an extra 2,000 ISK, the **comfort** package bundles towel rental, a dollop of green algae mud for your face (otherwise 450 ISK), and a free drink from the bar in the lagoon (otherwise 500-1,200 ISK). For another 2,000 ISK, the **premium** package adds bathrobe and slipper rental.

**Hours:** Daily 8:00-22:00, June-Aug until 23:00 or 24:00, Oct-Dec until 20:00, last entry one hour before closing. You need to leave the water at closing time, but have another 30 minutes after that to dress.

**Information:** Tel. 420-8800, www.bluelagoon.com.

BLUE LAGOON & REYKJANES

# The Origin of the Blue Lagoon

The Blue Lagoon dates only from the early 1970s, when the local power authority drilled for hot water to heat homes on the Reykjanes Peninsula. They hit a good high-temperature source, but as often happens, the water wasn't suitable for piping directly into home radiators—it was salty (due to sea-water intrusions) and had a high mineral and clay content. Instead, they set up a heat-exchange system where the geothermal water was used to heat fresh, cold water that could then be piped to homes. After running through the system, the partly cooled geothermal water was simply dumped into the lava field near the plant.

Within a few years, locals realized this was a great place for a free dip and started to bathe in the water. Silica clay gives the water its milky texture, and sunlight gives it a blue appearance. (The name "Blue Lagoon"—borrowed from the notorious 1980 Brooke Shields movie—was originally used in jest.) Authorities caught on, fenced off the lagoon, built a changing shed, and started to charge admission, which at first was no more than at a local swimming pool. Word spread, and within a few years the lagoon had become a major tourist attraction. The power authority privatized  the lagoon, controversially selling it to a group of local politicians. They raised capital and did an admirable job developing and marketing the lagoon, adding cosmetics lines, a gift shop, a hotel, and a fancy restaurant.

Today, almost all the Blue Lagoon's guests are tourists; only a small percentage are Icelanders, who find the facility too expensive and distant and don't like what it does to their hair. Meanwhile, three similar premium pools in Iceland have sprung up: **Fontana** (at Laugarvatn, on the Golden Circle route); **Mývatn Nature Baths** (partway around the Ring Road, in North Iceland); and **Krauma** (at Deildartunguhver, in West Iceland—see page 160). These somewhat cheaper, less upscale alternatives are farther afield and lack the lava setting (though Mývatn comes close); most travelers stick with the original.

**Reservations:** Book as far in advance as you can to get the widest selection of times. You have to commit to an entry time when you book, but once you're in the lagoon, you can stay until closing time. Evening entries are cheaper and less likely to be sold out. Tickets are only partially refundable, and changing a reservation costs 1,400 ISK. If you're running ahead of schedule for your reservation, you can try to enter earlier—if it's not too crowded, they may let you in (no promises).

**Arrival and Luggage Storage:** The lagoon's parking lot is connected to the main building by a 100-yard-long path cut through the lava field. A small building near the parking lot has a WC, pay luggage storage, and a waiting room for those taking buses from the lagoon.

**Eyewear and Jewelry:** Avoid wearing valuable eyeglasses in the water; if you must, secure them with a strap (if they fall off, you won't be able to find them in the opaque water). Be careful not to rub delicate lenses while they're in the Blue Lagoon water, as the clay can scratch them—instead, wait to rinse them in freshwater when you get out. (On a bright day, a pair of cheap sunglasses makes the lagoon more pleasant.) Because the water is opaque, there's no need for goggles. Leave jewelry in your locker to avoid tarnishing.

**Hair Concerns:** As with ocean water, the minerals in the Blue Lagoon leave your hair dry and brittle. The effect goes away within a day or two. Don't stress about this too much—the lagoon is more fun if you relax and let your hair get wet. Still, especially for those with long hair, it's smart to slather on the free conditioner (from dispensers in the shower stalls) before and after you bathe, or keep long hair tied up and out of the water. A bathing cap offers the best protection. In addition to conditioner, the lagoon provides free body wash and the use of hair dryers.

**Kids:** Children under age two are not allowed in the Blue Lagoon, and the facility is not really designed for kids (no slides, kiddie pools, or play areas). The water is opaque, so if a child goes under, you won't be able to see him or her. The same goes for toys, glasses, goggles...and anything else that might slip out of little hands.

**Eating:** The main building has an overpriced **$ self-service cafeteria** (with prepackaged sandwiches), plus the expensive, sit-down **$$$$ Lava Restaurant** (reservations recommended, same contact info as lagoon). You can get much more value by eating in Grindavík, a 10-minute drive away (described later in this chapter).

**Sleeping:** The lagoon runs the nearby **$$$$ Silica Hotel,** but it's very expensive. If you want to stay close, you'll find lower prices in towns like Keflavík and Grindavík (see "Hotels near the Airport" in the Reykjavík chapter).

**Expect Changes:** The Blue Lagoon is undergoing an ambitious expansion project. While the lagoon itself and the changing areas will remain essentially the same, they're adding a new wing with in-water spa treatments and a 60-room luxury hotel.

**Looking without Bathing:** If you're in the area and just want a peek at the dreamy setting, you can park, enter the main building, and visit the gift shop, cafeteria, and restaurant without a ticket. There's a good view of the bathing area from the cafeteria. A path from the parking lot leads through the non-bathing section of the lagoon. Also, as you drive toward the complex, there's a point where the water from the power plant comes up through the lava and right up to the road; you could get out for a photo, if you can pull off without blocking traffic.

## VISITING THE BLUE LAGOON

The procedures for a visit to the Blue Lagoon are basically the same as at other Icelandic pools (see "Pool Rules" sidebar on page 160). Watch the helpful video on the website (www.bluelagoon.com), which walks you through the process.

As you enter, you'll get an electronic wristband that serves as your locker key (and lets you charge drinks, face mud, and other extras—pay when you leave). Once in the **changing area,** follow green lights to available lockers. Attendants are also there to direct you. Once you've changed and showered (in a private cabin, if you prefer), head out to the lagoon.

The **lagoon** is *big.* The water ranges from waist to chest deep. The temperature varies more than in a regular swimming pool, with hot and cool spots—the average is around 100°F. While the water is not chlorinated, new water continually circulates into the lagoon—refilling the entire pool about every 40 hours. Bathers congregate by the warm spots where the hot water enters. Splish and splash around, exploring the nooks and crannies of the interconnected pools. There are many hidden areas to explore, including a little roofed grotto, and a few areas with benches that resemble hot pots at the municipal baths. Find the scalding, thundering waterfalls, and dare yourself to linger beneath them. There's also a sauna and a steam room.

The **bar** is in the far-right corner of the lagoon. Be sure to stay hydrated; look for water fountains under the bridges.

At the **mud station** (to the left), there are three options:

Every bather is entitled to a free ladleful of the **white** silica mud that collects in the lagoon. Smear this exfoliant on your face, let it set for about 10 minutes, then wash it off. Bathers who bought a "comfort" or "premium" ticket also get a blob of **greenish** algae, which supposedly reduces wrinkles and rejuvenates the skin (same procedure: wear for 10 minutes, then rinse). You may also see roving attendants handing out a **black** "lava scrub" face wash. (Keep all of these out of your eyes.) While it adds to the experience, all that mud is really just a sales pitch for the extremely expensive spa products for sale inside.

After you've showered and dressed, pay for any extras you indulged in. At the **exit** turnstile, touch your wristband to the panel, then insert it in the slot. Now comes the hard part: Try to keep your relaxed body awake for the drive back to your hotel or the airport.

# Reykjanes Peninsula Driving Tour

The Reykjanes Peninsula has enough sights to fill a day trip, and it's easy to combine with a visit to the Blue Lagoon. It's not the most scenic or historic part of Iceland—don't visit this area at the expense of more dramatic scenery only a bit farther away, such as the Golden Circle or South Coast. But Reykjanes is handy for those who don't have time to venture far beyond the airport area.

My self-guided driving plan assumes you'll tour the peninsula first and visit the Blue Lagoon later, but it works just fine in reverse, too. The major excursion bus companies all offer guided tours of the peninsula for about 12,500 ISK.

## FROM REYKJAVÍK TO THE BLUE LAGOON

This loop route is fairly straightforward. First, you'll drive about 45 minutes to the rugged Kleifarvatn lakeshore, with some interesting natural features (especially the Seltún geothermal field). Then you'll loop along the peninsula's south coast to Grindavík (about 30 minutes), a harbor town with some appealing lunch options. From there, it's a 10-minute drive to the Blue Lagoon. When you're done bathing, you can head straight back to Reykjavík (45 minutes), or consider a quick detour to some of the museums in Keflavík. (To see my suggested timing for this route, see page 112.)

• *Leaving the city, drive south on highway 41 through **Hafnarfjörður**— a suburb of Reykjavík that feels like its own small town—following the route toward the airport.*

*As you crest the hill at the end of Hafnarfjörður, look ahead to see the red-and-white towers of the aluminum plant at **Straumsvík**. This was Iceland's first metal smelter, opened in 1969. Before you reach the smelter, follow the signs for* Krýsuvík *and turn left on highway 42. Continue as it makes several turns through an industrial area.*

# Reykjanes Peninsula

- - - - Recommended Driving Route

*GARÐSKAGAVITI LIGHTHOUSE*

Faxaflói

Reykjavík
City

Garðabær  41

Hafnarfjörður

STRAUMSVÍK
ALUMINUM PLANT

Garður

Sandgerði  45

429  See detail map in
Reykjavík chapter

Keflavík

Keflavík
Airport

REYKJA-
NESBÆR

Njarðvík

Vogar

421  41

42

42  417

Pass

Reykjanes   Peninsula

▲ Keilir

Seltún
Geothermal
Field

BEACH

Kleifarvatn

Hafnir  44

Ásbrú
(FORMER
US BASE)

43

Hafnaberg
Cliffs

"Bridge Between
■Continents"  426

Blue Lagoon
(Bláa Lónið)

Þorbjörn

Gunnuhver
Hot Springs

425

Grindavík

Grænavatn

42  427

427

To Þorlakshöfn,
Eyrarbakki
& Selfoss

REYKJANESVITI
LIGHTHOUSE

Krýsuvíkurbjarg
Cliffs

To Eldey Rock

North Atlantic Ocean

2 Kilometers

2 Miles

*BLUE LAGOON & REYKJANES*

*The forbidding-looking mountains ahead of you enclose your destination, the lake called Kleifarvatn. A low pass winds through the mountains to the lake; for these few miles, the road isn't paved—drive slowly as you dodge potholes.*

## Kleifarvatn Lake

Kleifarvatn (CLAY-vahr-VAHT) lake offers a nice sample of Iceland's distinctive volcanic scenery. In good weather, you can walk along the black sand beach and even dip your toes in the water. There's something peculiar about Kleifarvatn: It has no outlet (it's fed by underground springs, and the water level varies). The area around the lake is totally undeveloped, and is a good (if lonely) place to look for the northern lights on clear,

dark nights. There's a small parking lot near the end of the first long stretch of sandy beach, as well as parking lots at the overlooks from the headlands a little farther on. Don't drive off-road here.

• *A little past the end of the lake, take the turnoff to the right and park to explore the...*

## ▲Seltún Geothermal Field

This steaming, bubbling, boiling (and very smelly) landscape hints at the geothermal power just underfoot. A boardwalk and marked

paths take you on a 15-minute circuit through the field. Stay on the path, as the water and steam here are boiling hot. Partway through the loop, you can climb steeply up to a hilltop viewpoint overlooking the entire area, with Kleifarvatn lake just beyond—but the up-close boardwalk stroll through the steam zone is plenty satisfying. The environment here is not just natural, but also the product of botched attempts to exploit the geothermal field for energy—first in the 1750s, and most recently in the 1940s. In 1999, one of the boreholes from the last attempt got plugged up and exploded violently, creating a 30-foot crater now filled with water (at the first overlook). There are picnic benches here, and a WC (in summer).

• *Just after leaving Seltún, watch on the left for the Grænavatn parking lot. Grænavatn ("Green Lake") is a small lake that was formed inside a volcanic crater. It's worth a quick stop for a look at its green water (the color comes from algae at the bottom) and surrounding jagged hilltops.*

*Continue south on highway 42 until it tees at highway 427, where you'll turn right. About 10 minutes from Seltún, you'll see a dirt road branch off to the left, signposted* Krýsuvíkurbjarg. *This road (too rough for two-wheel-drive cars) leads out to a high coastal cliff with a large seabird colony. Hikers not in a hurry could park along the shoulder of the dirt road and walk out (about 2.5 miles each way).*

*Highway 427 continues through attractive, moss-covered lava fields and then traverses a dark, inhospitable upland before arriving in the town of Grindavík.*

## Grindavík Town

Grindavík (pop. 2,000) is important for its harbor, which was improved in the 20th century and is one of the few usable ones on Iceland's southern coast. Follow *Höfnin* signposts to reach the harbor, where you'll see fishing boats moored and large fish-processing factories. If you like, spend a few more minutes driving around

BLUE LAGOON & REYKJANES

## History of the Reykjanes Peninsula

The Reykjanes Peninsula is geologically new and active, and the extensive lava fields here have at most a thin layer of vegetation. (Looking at it from an approaching plane, or on Google Maps, you'll see lots of brown.) During Iceland's early centuries, when farming was the mainstay of the economy, few people lived here. But the peninsula was a good base for rich offshore fishing grounds. As fishing became more important, the temporary settlements on the peninsula became permanent. Villages sprang up, particularly at Keflavík and Njarðvík on the north side, and at Grindavík in the south. Many of the people who settled here were poor and landless, and today's Icelanders, perhaps wrongly, still think of the peninsula as a proletarian region with little "old money" wealth—no sheep, no fine churches.

During World War II, military planners realized that the broad, flat wastelands near the town of Keflavík were an ideal place for an air base. Planes crossing the Atlantic could refuel here efficiently, and there was space for very long runways (long enough to land a space shuttle). After the war, the US military established a base next to the airport. Until 2006, when the base was closed, up to a few thousand Americans lived there, in a mostly self-contained community. The military base and the airport became the peninsula's largest employers, and the towns of Keflavík and Njarðvík grew.

this spread-out town; keep an eye out for the old church, the new church, the police station, the primary school, and the municipal swimming pool.

**Sights in Grindavík:** The town museum, **Kvikan** ("Saltfish Museum"), backs up to the harbor. It has exhibitions on the town's history (including life-size dioramas of the fishing industry), the history of salted cod (once the backbone of the local economy), Icelandic geology and geothermal energy, and novelist Guðbergur Bergsson (b. 1932), who was born here but has spent much of his life in Spain. The building also serves as the local TI, dispensing maps and brochures, and there's a contemporary art exhibition space upstairs. While nicely presented and fairly interesting, the museum is worth visiting only if you have time to kill before your Blue Lagoon appointment (1,500 ISK; daily in summer, Oct-April Sat-Sun only, Hafnargata 12a, tel. 420-1190, www.grindavik.is/kvikan).

**Eating in Grindavík:** The unassuming **$ Bryggjan** café at the harbor specializes in lobster soup, served with bread and butter and coffee or tea; they also have sandwiches and cakes. It's cozy, and decorated with fishing gear and memorabilia from both Grindavík and the Faroe Islands (the owner is half Faroese; daily 7:00-23:00, Miðgarður 2, tel. 426-7100). **$ Hjá Höllu** ("Halla's Place") is a popular local lunch joint with a small, inventive, ever-changing menu that includes vegetarian options—ask them to translate. It's on the town's main road, in the tiny mall next door to the Nettó supermarket, which also houses a liquor store, pharmacy, and hair salon—enter from inside the mall (Mon-Fri 8:00-17:00, Sat from 11:00, closed Sun, Víkurbraut 62, tel. 896-5316, www.hjahollu.is). For something more formal, try the **$$ Salthúsið** sit-down restaurant, a block behind Nettó, with a spacious, woody interior and a deck that's inviting on a nice day (daily 12:00-22:00, off-season until 21:00, Stamphólsvegur 2, tel. 526-9700, www.salthusid.is).

## Onward to the Blue Lagoon

The Blue Lagoon is a 10-minute drive north of Grindavík: Hopefully you've timed things so that you arrive promptly for your reservation.

• *Road signs direct you to* **Bláa Lónið** *along highway 426, which winds through the lava around the west side of the mountain called Þorbjörn.*

*It's also fine to take highway 43, going north past the* **Svartsengi geothermal plant**, *which feeds the lagoon. The plant is not open to the public, but you can make an unmarked turn off highway 43 and drive up as far as the visitor parking lot, getting a view of the red-painted water pipes that deliver hot water to area communities, and the turbine halls that generate electricity. (To actually visit a geothermal power plant, plan a trip to Hellisheiðarvirkjun, between Reykjavík and Selfoss; see page 62.)*

*Even if you're not getting wet at the Blue Lagoon, you can park for free at the complex and have a look around.*

## FROM THE BLUE LAGOON TO KEFLAVÍK AND BACK TO REYKJAVÍK

From the Blue Lagoon, most travelers get on the road to Reykjavík. If you're tempted to drive around the desolate **southwestern tip** of the Reykjanes Peninsula, note that the route is less interesting than it looks on the map. Both the Reykjanesviti lighthouse, and the nearby path up to the headland, are closed to visitors; the Gunnuhver geothermal area is impressive but Seltún is better; and the bridge over a tectonic fissure, which claims to let you "walk between continents," is gimmicky. I'd skip this circuit, but if you do travel it, follow the *Reykjanesviti* signs down paved road 425 to Gunnuhver (don't take the Gunnuhver turnoff before that, which leads down a mucky dirt road).

• *To **return to Reykjavík** from the Blue Lagoon, head out to highway 43 and head north. After about 10 minutes, highway 43 tees into highway 41, the main road between Keflavík and Reykjavík. Turn right to head straight back to Reykjavík (about 45 minutes from the Blue Lagoon).*

*To stop in **Keflavík and Njarðvík** (described below), follow highway 43 as described above, but instead of turning right on highway 41, turn left. You'll soon see the towns of Keflavík and Njarðvík on your right (about a 15-minute drive from the Blue Lagoon).*

## Keflavík and Njarðvík (Reykjanesbær)

The peninsula's main settlement (pop. 15,000) isn't a must-see, but has some attractions that can easily fill a few hours. Once separate towns, Keflavík and Njarðvík have grown together; in the 1990s they merged governments under the new name Reykjanesbær.

In 2006, the town expanded even more when the US military left its base near the airport and turned the area over to civilian use. That neighborhood is now called **Ásbrú**; if you're curious, you can follow signs into it and drive around (turning off highway 41 at a roundabout). The streets still have English names and you can drive past the old military PX, the base's theater, and the yellow-painted housing blocks.

Keflavík and Njarðvík have several museums that can be a good end to this driving tour. To reach them, turn off highway 41 and head into town, following signs for the museums. For a map of this area, see the end of the Reykjavík chapter.

**Icelandic Museum of Rock 'n' Roll:** This chronicles the coming-of-age of Icelandic pop music, from the 1930s to the present. The museum fills a large space in the local music school and concert-hall complex. Exhibits cover the biggies (Björk, Sigur Rós, and Of Monsters and Men), as well as many Icelandic musicians who aren't known internationally (Páll Óskar Hjálmtýsson and Björgvin Halldórsson). The free videoguide with headphones lets you watch and listen to the performers. There's also a small theater that screens documentary films, and a drum set you can try out. The museum sells coffee and candy bars, but doesn't have a real café (1,500 ISK, daily 11:00-18:00, Hjallavegur 2, Reykjanesbær, tel. 420-1030, www.rokksafn.is).

**Viking World:** This museum houses the *Icelander,* a replica of the medieval Scandinavian ship unearthed at Gokstad, Norway in the 1880s (the original is in Oslo). While the boat itself is worth seeing, the rest of the attraction—with a few artifacts, some conceptual exhibits, and a Viking dress-up area—lacks substance. The museum opens early and offers a breakfast buffet (museum—1,500 ISK, museum and breakfast—1,800 ISK, daily 7:00-18:00, breakfast until 11:00, Víkingabraut 1, tel. 422-2000, www.vikingworld.is). More interesting is the **"Settlement Age Zoo"** (Landnámsdýragarður) just across the parking lot—a cute (and free) petting farm, with animals living in miniature sod-roofed huts (early May-mid-Aug daily 10:00-17:00).

**Duus Museum:** At the northwestern end of Keflavík, this local history and art museum has a collection of more than 100 model boats made by a retired local sea captain (1,500 ISK, daily 12:00-17:00, Duusgata 2, tel. 420-3245, http://sofn.reykjanesbaer.is/duusmuseum).

• *When you're ready to head back, it's a straight, 45-minute shot directly to Reykjavík along highway 41.*

# GOLDEN CIRCLE

The Golden Circle is Iceland's classic day trip. If you have just one day to see the Icelandic countryside from Reykjavík, this route offers the most satisfying variety of sightseeing and scenery per miles driven. And you'll be in good company: Travelers dating back to the Danish king Christian IX, who visited Iceland in 1874, have followed the same route outlined in this chapter.

The Golden Circle loop includes this essential trio of sights: Þingvellir, a dramatic gorge marking the pulling apart of the Eurasian and North American tectonic plates (and also the site of the country's annual assembly in the Middle Ages); Geysir, a bubbling, steaming hillside that's home to Strokkur, Iceland's most active geyser; and Gullfoss, one of Iceland's most impressive waterfalls. You can round out the trip by adding any of several minor sights, taking a dip in a thermal bath, or going snorkeling or scuba diving at Þingvellir. This chapter explains your options and links them with driving directions.

Note that the Golden Circle loop is well-trod and extremely touristy. Long lines of tour buses and rental cars follow each other around the route each day, and you'll see the same faces more than once. Despite the crowds, the attractions hold their appeal.

**On Your Own or with an Excursion:** Driving the Golden Circle in your own car offers maximum flexibility, but some may find it more relaxing to join an organized bus trip. The tour companies listed on page 108 offer full-day Golden Circle tours (10,000-15,000 ISK depending on group size). Reykjavík Excursions and Gray Line also offer half-day trips—but these cost only slightly less, rush you through the sights, and are worth it only if you're short on time.

# Golden Circle Driving Tour

The entire circuit involves about four hours of driving, not including stops. The basic self-guided route is simple: From Reykjavík, you can take your pick for the first leg of the drive (straightforward vs. scenic), either 40 minutes or one hour to Þingvellir. After touring Þingvellir, it's about an hour to the thermal fields at Geysir, then 10 minutes farther to the gushing Gullfoss

waterfall. From there, you'll backtrack to Geysir and circle back around to Reykjavík in about 1.75 hours, passing a few lesser sights (the most interesting of which is the Kerið crater). My suggested route goes clockwise—starting with Þingvellir—but it can also be done in the other direction.

## PLANNING YOUR DRIVE

Here's a suggested plan (with stops) for those wanting to get an early-ish start and be home in time for dinner:

| | |
|---|---|
| 9:00 | Leave Reykjavík and head for Þingvellir national park, taking the scenic Nesjavallaleið route (1 hour) |
| 10:00 | Visit Þingvellir |
| 11:30 | Drive from Þingvellir to the village of Laugarvatn (30 minutes) and have lunch |
| 13:00 | Head to Geysir geothermal field (20 minutes), and watch Strokkur erupt a couple of times |
| 14:00 | Drive to Gullfoss (10 minutes) and visit the waterfall |
| 15:00 | Head in the direction of Selfoss (1 hour), stopping briefly at Skálholt Church and Kerið crater (or any other sight along the way that interests you—all described later) |
| 16:30 | Return to Reykjavík (about 45 minutes from Selfoss) |

## Golden Circle Tips

This drive is peppered with additional sights and activities; you can easily alter my suggested plan to suit your interests. In addition to the sights described in this chapter, this route also passes by the Halldór Laxness house (commemorating an esteemed Icelandic author) and the Hellisheiði Power Plant (both covered in the Reykjavík chapter). Visiting every possible sight could take two or three days. Before setting out, review the possibilities, prioritize, and come up with a plan that hits what you want to see in the time you have. Here are some things to consider:

**Avoiding Crowds:** The geothermal field at Geysir—the smallest sight—is the most crowded spot on the route. An early start helps keep you ahead of the tour buses; in summer, when days are long, you could instead do this trip in the afternoon/evening, when crowds are lighter (see "Evening Options," later).

**Activities:** Several activities along the Golden Circle require extra time—and in some cases, prebooking. To allow time for any of these, skip some of the minor sights along the drive. The Silfra fissure, at Þingvellir, provides top-notch **scuba or snorkeling** opportunities (book well in advance—see details on page 138). Several horse farms are just outside Reykjavík, making it easy to incorporate **horseback riding** into your Golden Circle spin (again, this should be pre-arranged—see page 108). There are also several **thermal baths** along the way (see sidebar later in this chapter).

**Evening Options:** In the summer, some intrepid travelers—determined to wring the absolute maximum travel experience out

See detail maps of Þingvellir, Geysir & Gullfoss

F-338  35  To North Iceland via Kjölur Route (4-Wheel Drive Only!)

**Gullfoss**

**Geysir**

Kálfstindar

Laugarvatn

37

35

FONTANA BATHS

Apavatn

Reykholt

359  30

Lyngdalsheiði

37

Skálholt

CATHEDRAL

SECRET LAGOON

Flúðir

BURG POOL

SLAKKI PETTING ZOO

31

36  35

**Kerið Crater**

Hvítá River

30

32

BOBBY FISCHER'S GRAVE

Note: Driving route road width exaggerated for clarity

**Eateries**
1. Þingvellir Café
2. Fontana Thermal Baths Cafeteria
3. Efstidalur II Restaurant
4. Skjól Café
5. Gullfoss Café
6. Friðheimar Tomato Farm
7. Ölverk Brewery/Pizza
8. Fjöruborðið Restaurant
9. Hafið Bláa Restaurant

Akureyri  Egilsstaðir
ICELAND
Reykjavík
Vík
50 KM
50 Miles

**GOLDEN CIRCLE**

1

To Vík and Landeyjahöfn (Ferry to Westman Islands)

26

Hella

33

• • • • Golden Circle Main Route
‑ ‑ ‑ ‑ ‑ Optional Scenic Route

of every moment—set out on this loop in the late afternoon...making the most of the abundant daylight. And since the major Golden Circle sights (Þingvellir, Geysir, Gullfoss) don't technically "close," you can visit them essentially anytime—plus, they're less crowded in the evening (some of the lesser sights and thermal baths do have closing times). Another fine evening activity is to have a memorable dinner in the countryside at one of my recommended restaurants—stretching your day and allowing a late return to Reykjavík.

**With More Time:** If you have an extra day or two, consider splitting the Golden Circle into shorter, more manageable day trips: For example, on one (highbrow) day you could do Þingvellir along with the Halldór Laxness house and the Fontana baths, and on the next (nature-focused) day you could do Geysir, Gullfoss, and the hike to the Reykjadalur thermal river.

**Weather and Road Conditions:** The route crosses three mountain passes (Mosfellsheiði or Nesjavallaleið, then Lyngdalsheiði, and finally Hellisheiði). These passes can be icy and slippery, especially from October to April. Check the road conditions map at Road.is before you start off. In treacherous conditions, take a bus tour and leave the driving to pros. If you do drive the Golden Circle in winter, it's smart to set off from Reykjavík an hour before sunrise so you get maximum value out of the daylight hours.

If highway 365 (Lyngdalsheiði, between Þingvellir and Laugarvatn) is closed or in bad shape, you can avoid it by taking a long way around on lowland roads (highways 36 and 35). This adds about a half-hour to the trip, which makes it difficult to cram the entire Golden Circle into a short winter day. You may need to lower your expectations, and do only part of the circuit (either Þingvellir or Geysir/Gullfoss).

**Name Note:** Be aware that there are two Reykholts in Iceland: one here on the Golden Circle, and the other about 100 miles away, in West Iceland.

# Golden Circle Loop

Below, I've linked the main stops with driving directions. Let's get started.

## FROM REYKJAVÍK TO ÞINGVELLIR

There are two ways to get from Reykjavík to Þingvellir: through Mosfellsheiði (highway 36) or along the road called Nesjavallaleið (highway 435). Nesjavallaleið takes a little longer (one hour) and is narrow and curvy in parts (with many blind summits), but is much more scenic. Because of its high elevation, Nesjavallaleið is open only from May to September. If it's closed, it will appear in red on the road conditions map at Road.is. The Mosfellsheiði route is kept open all year. If conditions are appropriate and you're confident driving in Iceland, I'd definitely take Nesjavallaleið.

## Option 1: A Straight Shot via Mosfellsheiði

You'll start this 40-minute route heading north out of Reykjavík on highway 1 toward Borgarnes and Akureyri, then turn right on highway 36 just past the town of Mosfellsbær, following the *Þingvellir* signs. This leads up through Mosfellsdalur ("Moss Mountain Valley") and over a low, broad pass (900 feet above sea level) to Þingvellir.

The Mosfellsdalur valley is still rural, with several horse farms. As you drive through, look left up the hillside (or turn up the side road called Mosfells-vegur) to see the unusual church called **Mosfellskirkja,** designed

# Thermal Bathing Along the Golden Circle

If you're trying to pack the maximum Icelandic experience into your Golden Circle day, consider adding a visit to a thermal bath. This loop drive passes near four extremely different options (each one described in this chapter). Skim these options before you depart, to strategize where you might squeeze in a dip...and remember to bring your swimsuit and towel (or rent one—available at all listed here except Reykjadalur).

**Fontana Thermal Bath,** in Laugarvatn, is the upscale choice. While not as ritzy as the Blue Lagoon, it's a "premium" option that feels a notch up from standard municipal swimming pools.

**The Secret Lagoon,** in Flúðir (a 10-minute detour from the main Golden Circle route, near Reykholt), is a big, rustic outdoor pool packed with young travelers unwinding after a busy day of sightseeing. This is the only bathing experience on this route where it's smart to prebook.

**Borg swimming pool** is a municipal facility right along the main road between Reykholt and Selfoss—nothing fancy, but cheap, handy, and (more than the others listed here) authentically Icelandic.

**Reykjadalur**—the "Smoky Valley" above the town of Hveragerði—is the adventurous choice: It's a remote, steaming, natural thermal river that requires a one-hour hike each way.

Of course, if you're heading home to Reykjavík at the end of your Golden Circle day, you can have your pick of the capital area's many **public swimming pools** (options are described on page 63); two good suburban pools, Lágafellslaug and Árbæjarlaug, are on the outskirts of town and convenient to the Golden Circle route.

Before visiting any of these, be sure to get up to speed by reading the "Pool Rules" sidebar on page 160.

by architect Ragnar Emilsson in the 1960s. It's full of triangular shapes—including the bell tower and roof—as a reference to the Trinity.

Note that this route passes by the former home of Iceland's most famous author, **Halldór Laxness** (open to tourists; for details see page 61). Otherwise, it's a (fairly dull) straight shot to Þingvellir. When you begin to see the Þingvallavatn lake—Iceland's largest—on your right, you know you're getting close.

## Option 2: Scenic and Rugged via Nesjavallaleið

This one-hour route—more with photo stops—is much more interesting than Mosfellsheiði. It climbs high up (to about 1,500 feet) over a craggy mountain range, descends steeply past the

Nesjavellir geothermal plant, and then narrows as it hugs the shore of Þingvallavatn lake. Most of Nesjavallaleið (NESS-ya-VAHT-la-laythe) was built as a service road for a giant hot water pipe that feeds Reykjavík's heating system.

Start out by leaving Reykjavík south on highway 1 toward Selfoss. As the town thins out into countryside, turn left following a small sign for highway 435 and *Nesjavellir*. The road crosses the giant **hot-water pipe,** then curves around to follow straight along it. You'll drive parallel to the pipe—and some high-tension wires—for quite some time. In August and September, the bracken along the sides of this road is a good place to look for blueberries and crowberries. The road rises and eventually hits a ridge, part of a volcanic system called Hengill; from here the road climbs in a series of bends. Before the crest, you can stop at a pullout in the small, mountain-ringed Dyradalur valley, with signboards and picnic benches; an important path for travelers once led through the gully you see at the end of the valley (called Dyrnar—"The Doors").

As you come over the ridge, you'll see the **Nesjavellir geothermal power station** far below you. This plant, built in the early 1990s, sends 250 gallons of boiling water through the pipe to Reykjavík every second, and also generates electricity. For a better look, take your pick of two overlooks: one at the end of a little dead-end side lane, and the other reached by short paths from a parking lot by the side of the road. (Another power plant—Hellisheiði, at the conclusion of this Golden Circle spin—has a real visitors center; see page 62.)

The highway descends steeply into the valley, ending at a T-junction with highway 360, where you'll turn left toward *Þingvellir*. (Note that if you're doing the Golden Circle in reverse, highway 435 is signposted here only as *Hengilssvæði*.)

Now the road winds tightly along the shore of **Þingvallavatn** lake, with fine views, no guardrails, and several narrow, blind summits. You'll pass some nice summer homes. Building here is forbidden, but houses constructed before the ban were grandfathered in. Eventually, the road leaves the lake and ends at a junction with highway 36, where you'll turn right; from this junction, it's another four miles to Þingvellir.

## ▲▲▲Þingvellir

The gorge at Þingvellir (THING-VETT-leer), dear to all Icelanders, is both dramatic and historic. It's dramatic because you can readily see the slow separation of

the North American and Eurasian tectonic plates— the earth's crust is literally being torn apart. And it's historic because, during the Settlement Age, it was here at "Assembly Plains" (as its name means) that chieftains from the different parts of Iceland gathered annually to deal with government business (at a meeting called the AlÞingi). Today the area has been preserved as a national park. Visitors can walk along the rifts created by the separating plates, stand at the place where the original Icelanders made big decisions, hike to a picturesque waterfall, see a scant few historic buildings, and even go for a snorkel or scuba dive into a flooded gorge (book ahead).

### Orientation to Þingvellir

**Cost and Hours:** Park—free and always open, tel. 482-2660; visitors center—free and open daily 9:00-20:00, Sept-May until 18:00, tel. 482-3613, www.thingvellir.is.

**Arrival at Þingvellir:** Regardless of which route you took from Reykjavík, you'll wind up on the same road as you approach Þingvellir. You can park on either the upper (west) or the lower (east) side of the Öxará river. The two sides are no more than a half-mile apart if you use the footbridges over the river, but a five-mile drive by car. Parking is 500 ISK for the entire day (machines take credit cards; if you have trouble paying, go into the visitors center for help).

The first turnoff you'll reach is the large **P1 parking lot** on the upper side, with a pay WC; on maps, this spot is sometimes called Hakið. If it's not too crowded, it's easiest to park here, stop in at the visitors center, get oriented at the overlook, then hike down to the sights.

If you can't find a spot at P1, continue a few miles to the intersection with the park offices/café; turn right—onto road 361—to reach several **smaller parking lots** on the lower side (P2, P4, P5, and a lot for Silfra divers). This area is less congested and more convenient for picnicking. (Lot P3, which you'll see along the main

GOLDEN CIRCLE

# Þingvellir

To Café & Park Office, Highway 361, Geysir & Gullfoss

Öxarárfoss Waterfall

Path to P3

To Café & Park Office, Highway 361

362

P P3

200 Meters

200 Yards

TO AMERICA

Öxará R.

P P2 WC

TO EUROPE

GOLDEN CIRCLE

Drekkingar-hylur

A l m a n n a g j á  (E v e r y m a n ' s  G o r g e)

FLAG

LAW ROCK

Flosagjá

To Café & Park Office

P4 P

Peningagjá

CAMP RUINS

National Cemetery

361

Parish Cemetery

ÞINGVELLIR CHURCH

ÞINGVALLABÆR RESIDENCE

P Parking for Divers

VISITORS CENTER

WC

P P1

Öxará R.

WC P5

VIEWING PLATFORM

To Highway 36 & Reykjavík

Silfra (Diving)

DIVING ROUTE

To Geysir & Gullfoss

Þingvallavatn (Lake)

To Visitors Center & Reykjavík

36

## Self-Guided Tour

1 View Over Þingvellir
2 Almannagjá ("Everyman's Gorge")
3 Law Rock
4 Öxarárfoss Waterfall
5 Church & Cemetery

road between P1 and the others, is designed for hikers who want to take the Langistígur path, which descends into the fissure near the big Öxarárfoss waterfall.)

If you're with a group, consider drawing straws and having the loser drop everyone off at P1 (allowing them the convenience of a one-way stroll); the driver can park at one of the lower lots and hike up to meet the group.

**Length of This Visit:** For a quick visit, you can enjoy the overview, hike the gorge, and see the Law Rock in less than an hour. Add a half-hour to hike up to the waterfall (about a mile one-way from P1), and a half-hour to cross the river to the church (the least interesting and most skippable).

**Eating:** In good weather, Þingvellir is a nice place for a picnic. There are benches, wooded areas, and free portable toilets near P2 and P5. If you want to picnic here, B.Y.O.—the visitors center (at P1) has a very basic **$ snack stand** with premade sandwiches. Otherwise, the only eatery nearby is the **$ café** at the national park office a couple of miles away, at the junction of highways 36, 361, and 550. It's small and sometimes crowded, but acceptable in a pinch (daily 9:00-22:00, Sept-May until 18:00).

## Self-Guided Tour

This plan assumes that you're parking at the upper P1 lot (even if you park elsewhere, hike up here to begin your visit since it offers a nice overview). Start at the **visitors center,** where you'll find a modest and free exhibit with helpful maps for getting your bearings.

• *Exiting the visitors center, walk over to the overlook with the railing.*

**❶ View Over Þingvellir:** Look down at the lake and the land that's subsided to its north. You can see how the Öxará ("Ax River")

empties into the lake. Þingvellir's church (and some ruins of the old chieftains' encampments) lies just across the river below you. The five-gabled farm building dates from 1930.

Directly below you is Þingvellir's **great fissure;** look at how the North American and Eurasian tectonic plates are moving apart. Imagine pulling a big, chewy cookie apart very slowly; you'd start to see cracks in the dough, and eventually crumbs would start to slide into the gap. Here, you can see long, narrow fissures in the earth, running roughly north-south. The lake itself sits in the largest fissure of all. The lake bed (and the land to the north and south) basically has slid into the gap between the

GOLDEN CIRCLE

plates. The deepest parts of the lake bed are actually below sea level.
• *Follow the boardwalk as it switchbacks down between the cliffs, descending through the little side channel that leads into...*

❷ **Almannagjá** ("Everyman's Gorge"): As you walk, you're tracing the boundaries of continents. To your left is America. To

your right is Europe. You may see brochures claiming that at Þingvellir you can "touch America with one hand and Europe with the other," or jump between the continents. The idea inspires fun photographs, but it's not quite true: The whole area is shaped by the interaction between the two tectonic plates, and no single fissure forms the boundary between them.

On the left, the vertical cliff face is original rock as it was laid down by volcanic eruptions and compressed over the eons. On the right, you can see how the rock—once even with the cliff on your left—has fallen away into the gap due to the subsidence that also created the lake. On the right (fallen) side of the gorge, you can scramble out to various walkways and viewpoints.

• *As you approach the valley floor, follow the boardwalks to the right to stand in the area just below the flagpole. This marks the likely location of...*

❸ **The Law Rock** (Lögberg): Within about 60 years of the first settlements, Iceland was home to somewhere between 10,000 and 20,000 people—almost all of them farmers, scattered across the island on isolated homesteads. In about A.D. 930, local chieftains *(goðar)* began to gather at an annual meeting called the Alþingi ("all-thing"), which took place more or less where you're standing. For this reason, Þingvellir can be thought of as Iceland's first capital. Today, this site remains important for Icelanders—it's their Ancient Agora, their Roman Forum, their Independence Hall.

Gaze over the marshy delta below you, and time-travel back a thousand years. It's the middle of June, and you're surrounded by fellow chieftains, some having traveled on horseback more than two weeks, over challenging terrain, just to be here. Each chieftain has brought along an entourage of *þingmenn* (assemblymen). The field below you is dotted with temporary turf huts.

The meeting is about to begin, and you're immersed in a hairy mosh pit of hundreds—maybe thousands—of unwashed Norsemen (and Norsewomen). The collective body odor is overwhelming. But for two weeks, you've all agreed to set aside your grudges and work together to find consensus on critical issues of the day. This is your one chance all year to learn the latest news and gossip. And while everyone's here, there are sure to be some big parties, business wheeling and dealing, marriages arranged...and, quite likely, some duels. Merchants, tradesmen, and panhandlers are milling about, trying to drum up a little business. The whole event has a carnival-like bustle.

The crowd quiets with the appearance of the *allsherjargoði* (grand chieftain)—a direct descendant of Ingólfur Árnason (who was, according to the sagas, the first Icelandic settler of Reykjavík). As the high priest of the Norse pantheon, the *allsherjargoði* calls the assembly to order, and sanctifies the proceedings before the gods. Then the "law speaker" *(lögsögumaður)* takes his position at the Law Rock and recites the guidelines for the assembly, outlines the broad strokes of Icelandic law, and recaps the highlights of last year's session. The acoustics created by the cliff behind him help bounce his voice across the throngs; other speakers, strategically located at the back of the crowd, carefully listen to, then repeat, whatever the law speaker says.

As the Alþingi continues, the law speaker also presides over the Law Council *(Lögrétta)*, on the opposite riverbank. A more select group of chieftains reviews and debates existing legislation, and weighs in on legal disputes, and the law speaker is responsible for memorizing whatever is decided. (Mercifully, he serves only a three-year term.) Eventually, Christianity brings literacy and the Latin alphabet, and the law speaker's role gives way to that of a sort of "high attorney"—*lögmaður*.

The Alþingi gatherings took place throughout the Commonwealth Era. But things changed after 1262, when the chieftains entered into union with Norway—pledging fealty to the Norwegian king under an agreement called the Old Covenant. The Alþingi still convened annually at Þingvellir, but morphed into an appeals court; it continued this way until 1798.

Þingvellir became a national park in 1930, to celebrate the millennial anniversary of the first Alþingi. And in 1944, the mod-

## Iceland's Conversion to Christianity

In A.D. 1000 (or 999, depending on how you reckon the calendar), the Alþingi had its most important session. Iceland's longtime ally Norway—whose king had recently converted to Christianity—was exerting tremendous pressure on Iceland to follow suit. When Norwegian missionaries failed to convert the entire island, the impatient king took several Icelandic traders hostage. Losing its primary trade partner would have been devastating to Iceland, and at the next summer's Alþingi, all hell broke loose between the pro- and anti-conversion factions. Civil war was in the air.

Eventually, both sides agreed to let the law speaker, a pagan named Þorgeir Ljósvetningagoði, make the decision for all of Iceland. According to the sagas, Þorgeir covered himself with a fur pelt and slept on it (literally) for one night and one day. Upon emerging, he addressed the assembly with his decision: Iceland was now Christian, but Icelanders could still worship their pagan gods privately, and continue a few key pagan practices (including the consumption of horse meat, the infanticide of unwanted children, and animal sacrifices to the old gods). And so, in one fell swoop, Þorgeir brought Iceland into the Christian fold, and averted a conflict with Norway that could well have wiped out the island's still-fragile civilization. This stands as one of the most peaceful mass religious conversion in history.

ern, independent Republic of Iceland was proclaimed right here. The stands below the flag are for official ceremonies; one of the information boards at the railing displays photographs of some of these ceremonies.

By the way, those original settlers couldn't possibly have known that the place they selected for their gathering also happened to straddle America and Europe. They chose this site mainly because it had recently been seized from a convicted murderer and designated for public use. Þingvellir is also fairly central (relatively accessible in summer from every corner of Iceland) and had ample water, grazing lands, and firewood to supply the sprawling gatherings. Its location along the cusp of continents is just one of those serendipities of history.

• *Follow the wide, gravel path straight ahead, and cross the river on a small bridge over a waterfall (the bottom end of Öxarárfoss, which we'll visit next). To your left is* **Drekkingarhylur** *("Drowning Pool"), where women suspected of witchcraft were drowned between the late–16th and mid-18th centuries.*

*If you're short on time, you could turn back here. Ideally, continue along the path. After about 300 yards, just before reaching parking lot P2, branch off on the small path to your left. Follow it for a few minutes as it crests the rise to your left. Then, a hundred yards to your left, is the large waterfall called...*

**❹ Öxarárfoss:** This is where the river—which rises up on the plateau—plunges over the cliff face into the valley. Old sagas say that the early settlers changed the course of the river to improve the water supply at Þingvellir, but no one is exactly sure whether this is true and how that might have been done.

• *You've already seen the most interesting parts of Þingvellir—you can head back the way you came (past the P2 lot). With more time, cross the footbridges on your left (below the Law Rock) to reach the...*

**❺ Church and Cemetery:** The current **church** was built in 1859, but there were churches here for centuries before. The origi-

nal church was supposedly built using timbers sent here from Norway's St. Olaf (King Olav II, 995-1030). If the church is open, step inside to see the humble, painted interior (generally closed Sept-May). Local parishioners lie in the small cemetery in front of the church. The multigabled house just beyond it, called **Þingvallabær,** was built in 1930 as a residence for the local priest, who was also the park warden. It's now used for ceremonial functions.

Behind the church, the round, elevated area up the stairs is a **cemetery** lot. This was planned as a resting place for national heroes, but the idea never took off, and only two people (well-known writers) were ever buried there.

Along the riverbank near the church, the **mounds** contain the remains of the temporary dwellings that were set up here each year for the annual assembly. From here, looking back the way you came, enjoy great views of the sheer cliff that defines the fissure.

• *Between the church and the river, a waterside path allows further exploration. Following this path takes you to the P5 lot, where a steep shortcut (on a rocky path through the woods) leads back up to the P1 lot where you started. (Also nearby is Silfra, a favorite destination of divers—described next.) For an easier route, you can backtrack along the river, then take the bridge on your left to reach the Law Rock, then hike back up through Everyman's Gorge.*

## Silfra Snorkel or Dive Trip

One of the many fissures at Þingvellir, Silfra is renowned among snorkelers and scuba divers for the clarity of the water. Thanks to the purity of the glacial water that fills it, you can see underwater for more than a hundred yards.

To snorkel or dive in Silfra, you'll need to join a tour (such as those offered by Dive.is, the largest operator). Snorkelers must be relatively fit and comfortable in the water, while divers need to be certified and experienced. There have been a few fatal accidents at Silfra in recent years (even involving snorkelers)—don't overestimate your abilities.

The water is a constant 35-39°F, so you'll be outfitted with some serious gear: a neoprene dry suit, hood, gloves, fins, mask, and snorkel. (The better companies have basic changing cabins in the parking lot; otherwise, there's limited privacy.) The suit keeps your body warm enough, but expect your face to go numb and your hands to get cold. After changing into your gear, you'll walk a few minutes to the entry stairs and descend into the fissure with your guide. A gentle drift current slowly takes you along the fissure and into a lagoon, where you'll need to kick against the current to U-turn to the metal exit stairs. You'll be in the water for about 30-40 minutes (prices for Dive.is: 20,000 ISK for guided snorkeling, extra 5,000 ISK for pickup in Reykjavík, 35,000 ISK for package that includes pickup, Silfra, and bus tour of Golden Circle, more for divers; tel. 578-6200, www.dive.is).

**Getting There:** Silfra is at the lakeshore near the east bank of the river. The entry point to Silfra is between parking lots P4 and P5. Follow the directions on page 131 (turning off onto road 361 to reach this area) and look for the designated lot.

## FROM ÞINGVELLIR TO GEYSIR AND GULLFOSS

This section of the drive circles around the far end of the lake, where you can clearly see the intercontinental rift—as if God dropped his hoe and dredged out a tidy furrow between America and Europe.

• *Leaving Þingvellir, return to highway 36 and continue east for about 10 minutes around the lake's north shore, crossing smaller fissures. Soon you'll pass the intersection with road 361 (a right turn here takes you back to Þingvellir's lower parking lots) and, immediately after that, the* **national park office,** *with a café.*

*Continuing along the east side of the lake, you'll reach a point where highway 36 turns off to the right. Stay straight toward Laugarvatn on highway 365. This road crosses an upland heath called **Lyngdalsheiði** at about 750 feet above sea level (if the road is closed, see "Weather and Road Conditions" under the "Golden Circle Tips" on page 125 for an alternate route).*

*On your left, enjoy some otherworldly, craggy mountain scenery— the **Kálfstindar ridge**. A half-hour after leaving Þingvellir, you'll reach a roundabout. Follow signs onto route 37 toward Geysir (not Selfoss) to descend into the sleepy, unassuming village of Laugarvatn.*

## Laugarvatn

Set by a small lake of the same name, Laugarvatn was long the home of Iceland's college for sports teachers (the program has now been moved to Reykjavík), and has many summer cottages owned by the country's labor unions for use by their members. There are hot springs in and around the lake, and Fontana, a nicely designed premium bath, makes good use of them.

**Fontana Thermal Baths:** Sitting right along the Laugarvatn lakeshore, Fontana is one of Iceland's few "premium" baths (and

worth ▲)—a step up in comfort (and price) from municipal swimming pools, and a bit more tourist-oriented. Beyond the visitors center—with ticket desk, changing rooms, and a good cafeteria—is the outdoor bathing area, overlooking the lake. The complex has three modern, tiled pools, artfully landscaped with natural boulders, as well as a steam room (where you can hear the natural hot spring bubble beneath your feet), and a dry sauna. To cool off or get a change of pace, bathers are encouraged to take a dip in the thermal waters of the lake (4,200 ISK, mid-June-mid-Aug daily 10:00-23:00, mid-Aug-mid-June daily 11:00-22:00, tel. 486-1400, www.fontana.is).

For some, Fontana may be a good alternative to the Blue Lagoon—it's cheaper, smaller (easier to navigate), less pretentious, much less crowded, and doesn't require reservations. But it's also less striking—more functional than spa-like—and lacks the Blue Lagoon's romantic, volcanic setting. Thermal bath fans may want to do both. You can fit the Golden Circle and a leisurely soak at Fontana into a single day if you sightsee quickly and skip the minor stops.

**"Thermal Bread Experience":** Fontana follows the Icelandic tradition of baking sweet, dense rye bread right in the thermal sands at its doorstep. Twice daily, you can pay to join the baker as they dig up a pot of bread, then taste it straight out of the ground (1,500 ISK, daily at 11:30 and 14:30). But note that you can eat the very same bread as part of their regular lunch buffet.

**Nearby Thermal Beach:** The lake in front of Fontana—heated by natural hot springs—is free to bathe in (at your own risk). Facing the lake, head right to find a small, black sand beach next to the fenced-off geothermal area (keep well clear of this area of boiling-hot water). The water near the springs is warm, but it gets colder as you go deeper. At a minimum, consider rolling up your pants and dipping your feet. On the wooden walkway between the geothermal plant and the lakeshore, notice—but don't touch—little boiling pools in the mud.

**Eating in or near Laugarvatn:** This village is a good place for lunch along the Golden Circle route. One of the best options is

the **$$ Fontana Thermal Baths cafeteria,** in the bath's entrance lobby, and open to the public (no bath entry required). You can get unlimited soup and bread for 1,500 ISK, or spring for their full 3,500-ISK lunch buffet (more expensive at dinner, daily 12:00-14:30 & 18:00-21:00). There are a few other places to eat in town and a small grocery store.

Or consider driving 10 more minutes to **$$ Efstidalur II** ("Uppermost Valley"), a large, family-run restaurant located on a dairy farm just off highway 37 between Laugarvatn and Geysir. The upstairs section specializes in burgers and has pricier main courses. Downstairs is the ice cream counter, with windows overlooking the cows in the barn. It's a popular, bustling place—family-friendly and often crowded with groups (daily 11:30-21:00, mid-Sept-mid-May until 20:00, well-signposted up a gravel driveway, tel. 486-1186, www.efstidalur.is).

• *From Laugarvatn, highway 37 leads 20 minutes onwards to the geothermal field at Geysir (passing the Efstidalur II eatery described earlier). Along the way, the road changes numbers to highway 35.*

## ▲▲Geysir Geothermal Field

When people around the world talk about geysers, they don't realize they're referencing a place in Iceland: Geysir (GAY-sear), which literally means "the gusher." While the original Geysir geyser is no longer very active, the geothermal field around it still steams, boils, and bubbles nonstop, periodically punctuated by a dramatic eruption of scalding water from the one predictably active geyser, Strokkur. Watch Strokkur erupt a couple times, look at the rest of the field, use the WC, and then continue on.

**Cost and Hours:** Free and always open.

**Safety Warning:** Make sure to keep children very close; hold their hands whenever possible. Impress upon them that they should not touch any of the water, which is boiling hot, and that they must stay behind the ropes. At Strokkur, standing upwind will keep you out of any spray.

**Arrival at Geysir:** Approaching Geysir, you'll see the geothermal field on your left, and a visitors complex with parking lots on your right. Park as close to the geothermal field as you can (the lots at the far end of the visitors center are closer to the best geyser action), then walk across the road and explore.

**Services and Eating:** Across the road from the geothermal area is a complex with a clothing and souvenir store, free WCs, a golf course, two hotels, and a handful of restaurants at different price ranges. While these are OK, I'd opt for one of the Laugarvatn eating options (described earlier), or wait for **$ Skjól** ("Shelter"), a café connected to a hostel and campground along highway 35 between Geysir and Gullfoss (just before the junction with highway 30). Talkative owner Jón Örvar is known for making good, affordable, splittable pizzas; he also serves other simple meals like burgers and fish-and-chips. This place attracts many hikers and outdoorsy folk (June-Aug daily 9:00-14:00 & 18:00-23:00, shorter hours off-season, mobile 899-4541, www.skjolcamping.com).

**Visiting Geysir:** The geothermal field itself lacks the boardwalks and other maintenance you would normally expect at a sight this popular. That's due in part to a dispute between the government (which owns part of the site) and private landowners, who have been bickering publicly for years about whether to charge for parking and admission. Outdoor signboards explain the geology.

The area's centerpiece is a geyser called **Strokkur** ("Butter Churn"), which erupts about every 10 minutes (but don't set your

GOLDEN CIRCLE

**GOLDEN CIRCLE**

watch by it). The eruptions themselves, which shoot about 50 feet in the air, are relatively short—in every sense—and won't wow anyone who has seen Old Faithful at Yellowstone. What's nice about Strokkur, though, is the short wait between gushes, and how close you can get. Each eruption is a little different. It's surreal to stand around in a field with people who have come from the far reaches of the globe, just to share this experience...of staring at a hole in the ground. Everyone huddles in a big circle around Strokkur, cameras aimed and focused, waiting for the unpredictable spurt. When it finally happens, it's over in a couple of seconds, as abruptly as it started. After each show, the crowd thins out a bit, and new arrivals shuffle in to take their place, shoulder-to-shoulder, cameras cocked, waiting...waiting...waiting.

Just a few yards up the hill above Strokkur, check out a few other **fumaroles and hot pools,** including Konungshver and the colorful Blesi. The miniature Litli-Geysir, along the path from the main parking lot, bubbles and boils but doesn't erupt.

Steaming uneasily off to the side is the **original "great" Geysir.** This was the only one known to medieval Europeans, and is the origin of the word *geyser.* It was dormant for most of the 20th century, but after a nearby earthquake in 2000 it started erupting occasionally. It blows higher and longer than Strokkur, but rarely and unpredictably, so don't expect to see anything. (Geysir is on the far side of the field if you're coming from the main parking lot; there's another, smaller parking lot close to it.)

GOLDEN CIRCLE

For a commanding view over the Geysir area, continue past Konungshver, climb over the stile, and make your way 10 minutes up to the top of one of the rocky outcroppings that overlook the geothermal field and surrounding terrain. The snowy mass of Vatnajökull looms to the west.

• *From Geysir, continue to the Gullfoss waterfall, a straight shot 10 minutes onward along highway 35.*

## ▲▲Gullfoss Waterfall

The thundering waterfall called Gullfoss (GUTL-foss, "Golden Falls") sits on the wide, glacial Hvítá river, which drains Iceland's interior. The waterfall has two stages: a rocky upper cascade with a drop of about 35 feet, and a lower fall where the water drops about 70 feet straight down into a narrow gorge. Somewhat unusually for a waterfall, the gorge runs transverse to the fall line, effectively carrying the water off to the side. Dress warmly: Cold winds blow down the valley, and the spray from the falls can soak you. Winter visitors should watch for slippery areas. If you have ice cleats, this is a good place to put them on.

**Cost and Hours:** Free and always open, tel. 486-6500, www. gullfoss.is.

**Arrival at Gullfoss:** Two different viewing areas—connected by a wooden staircase—let you admire the falls; each has its own

free parking lot and viewpoints. Both are equally worth seeing, but if you're short on time, focus on the lower one—which lets you get up close and feel the spray. To quickly hit the lower viewpoint, as you approach the area, just after the blue *P* sign,

watch for the unmarked right turn to the lower parking lot. With more time, continue to the official, well-signed upper parking lot, with pay WC, café, and gift shop (with free WCs for customers).

**Eating:** The large **$ café** by the upper parking lot serves soup (their bottomless bowl of lamb soup is popular), salad, and sandwiches (daily 9:00-21:30, Sept-May 10:00-18:00).

**Visiting the Waterfall:** From the upper parking lot, boardwalks lead along the edge of the plateau, high above the falls, to a couple of good **upper viewpoint** spots. On a clear day, you can see glaciers in the distance. The view upriver gives a sense of Iceland's vast, lonely interior Highlands.

From here, stairs lead down to the **lower viewpoint.** This area gets you close to the falls. It's closed in winter, when ice can make it dangerous (don't try it). A narrow trail leads through the spray from the falls to a level area between the upper and lower stages of the waterfall. If you walk out here with children, keep them close.

It would be easy to dam or divert the river above the falls for electricity generation. In the early 1900s, British investors tried to buy the waterfall, but their plans fell through. The government acquired the land and the falls have been left in their natural state. Near the base of the staircase, look for the relief sculpture of **Sigríður Tómasdóttir,** a local farmer who helped thwart plans for the dam.

GOLDEN CIRCLE

## FROM GULLFOSS BACK TO REYKJAVÍK

This stretch features a few mildly interesting stops to consider on the way (all described next)—but if you're in a hurry, these are skippable. It's about one hour from Gullfoss to Selfoss, then another 45 minutes back to Reykjavík (without stops).

For a late lunch, consider **$$ Friðheimar** ("Peaceful Homes"), a very popular, borderline-pretentious tomato farm 30 minutes from Gullfoss, offering lunch daily (12:00-16:00) right in the greenhouse, surrounded by rows of tomato plants, with pots of fresh basil on each table. The brief menu is all tomato: tomato soup with bread, fresh pasta with tomato sauce, and tomato ice cream or cheesecake with green tomato sauce (popular with tour groups—reservations strongly recommended, along highway 35 in the village of Reykholt—just north of junction with highway 31, tel. 486-8894, www.fridheimar.is).

• *From Gullfoss, turn back along highway 35 and pass by Geysir again. Shortly after Geysir, make a left turn to stay on highway 35 toward Reykholt and Selfoss. Your next big stop along the route is the Kerið crater (see page 148), about 45 minutes from Gullfoss. Along the way, consider the detours described next.*

## Sights Just Off the Golden Circle

The next three sights—a thermal pool, a church, and a petting zoo—are short detours from highway 35 and the main Golden Circle route.

### Secret Lagoon (Gamla Laugin)

Claiming to be the "oldest swimming pool in Iceland" (from 1891), the Secret Lagoon is a big, rustic, three-foot-deep, 100°F pool in front of a dilapidated old house (with a modern entrance/ changing facility). The pool is surrounded by an evocative thermal landscape; a boardwalk leads around the pool, past steaming and simmering crevasses. Greenhouses stand nearby. Compared to the over-the-top-romantic Blue Lagoon, or even Reykjavík's mu-

nicipal swimming pools (which are one-third the price), this is a very straightforward experience: Its proximity to the Golden Circle and clever marketing make it more popular than it probably should be. On the other hand, the bathers here seem very happy—sipping drinks, bobbing on colorful pool noodles, happy to enjoy this après-Golden Circle hangout. Far from "secret" (it's included on several day tours from Reykjavík), the pool can get quite crowded with a younger clientele. It's smart to reserve ahead online—when it's full, it's full.

**Cost and Hours:** 2,800 ISK, daily 10:00-22:00, Oct-April 11:00-20:00, last entry one hour before closing, tel. 555-3351, www.secretlagoon.is.

**Getting There:** The Secret Lagoon is a 10-minute drive off the main Golden Circle route. From highway 35, just before the village of Reykholt, turn left at highway 359, signed *Flúðir*. Follow this about five miles into the small village of Flúðir, watching on your left for the turnoff to *Hvammur* and *Gamla Laugin*. The Secret Lagoon is tucked amid the big greenhouses, on your right.

### Skálholt Church

This church was the old seat of the bishopric of southern Iceland. The current church was built in the 1960s and is flanked by a retreat center run by Iceland's Evangelical Lutheran state church. Unless you're heavily into Icelandic history, this is a low-key site—worth a few minutes only if you want to mix something non-geological into your day.

**Cost and Hours:** Church entry-free, 300 ISK donation requested if visiting crypt—OK to put foreign bills in the box; daily

9:00-18:00, pay WC in complex next to church, tel. 486-8870, www.skalholt.is.

**Getting There:** About 30 minutes south of Gullfoss on highway 35, detour left onto highway 31 for a couple of minutes, following *Skálholt* signs through farm fields. The church is just over the hill, overlooking a lake-and-mountain panorama.

**Visiting the Church:** As you drive up, you can see from the rich farmland around the church how it was able to support a medieval religious community. Almost nothing is left of the original buildings, many of which were destroyed by earthquakes in the late 18th century. It's peaceful here, and tour buses bypass the place. The locally designed stained-glass windows in the church are very colorful.

If you visit, be sure to go downstairs to the **crypt,** with a small exhibit of historical and archaeological artifacts. There's also a period sketch of the 18th-century church, which survived the earthquakes but was torn down soon after. From the crypt, you can exit directly outdoors through the only original part of the building, a short tunnel (a feature also found in some other medieval Icelandic buildings). An old-style, turf-roofed wooden chapel on the grounds is usually open (but empty).

## Slakki Zoo

Slakki is a combination petting zoo and indoor minigolf complex, housed partly in cute buildings meant to look like a typical old-style Icelandic farm. It's best for little kids between ages two and seven. There's a decent café, tiny playground, and good photo ops, and kids can get to know a big, noisy, green parrot. Families with small children could make this their main target for a Golden Circle day trip...and still manage to glimpse some of the better-known sights on the way.

**Cost and Hours:** Adults-1,000 ISK, kids-500 ISK, daily 11:00-18:00 in summer, May and Sept Sat-Sun only, closed Oct-April, off Skálholtsvegur in the hamlet of Laugarás, tel. 486-8783.

**Getting There:** The zoo is less than a mile past Skálholt Church along highway 31.

• *To continue to the Kerið crater on highway 35, after passing Skálholt, drive about 15 minutes, then watch for the little Kerið sign, which comes up very quickly (you might see an Icelandic flag and people hiking along a ridge on your left as you approach).*

**GOLDEN CIRCLE**

## ▲Kerið Crater ("The Tub")

The most worthwhile stop on the way back to Reykjavík is a volcanic cone, from an eruption about 6,500 years ago, that has collapsed and filled with water—creating a tiny crater lake. It's right next to (but not visible from) the road. It's vividly colorful: red walls draped with green vegetation, overlooking deep aquamarine-blue water. You can see it in a single glance, take a half-hour to walk around the rim, or descend 150 feet down a set of stairs to the surface of the lake.

As Kerið (KEH-rithe) is on private land, it's unusual among Iceland's outdoor sights in charging admission (which caused a great stir when it was announced). But it's cheap, and the owners have improved the parking lot and pathways; most visitors find it worth the cost.

**Cost and Hours:** 400 ISK when staffed, not staffed at night or in darkness, mobile tel. 823-1336, www.kerid.is.

**Nearby:** About five minutes north of the crater is the **Borg public swimming pool,** in the Borg sports complex at the junction of highways 35 and 354, between Skálholt and Kerið—look for the water slide just past the main turnoff into the hamlet of Borg (1,000 ISK; June-late-Aug Mon-Fri 10:00-22:00, Sat-Sun until 19:00; otherwise Mon-Thu 14:00-22:00, Sat-Sun 11:00-18:00, closed Fri; tel. 480-5530, www.gogg.is).

• *As you head south from Kerið toward Selfoss on highway 35, you'll drive past a dramatic slope on your right. Look at the mountainside to see the huge boulders that have slid down the slope over the ages—and see if you can spot the one lonely summer house taking its chances among them. About 15 minutes after Kerið, you'll reach...*

## Selfoss

Selfoss (pop. 7,000) is the largest town in southern Iceland, and set next to rapids on the Ölfusá river. (The water that flows over Gullfoss winds up here.) The Golden Circle route bypasses the town center, which is fine as there's not much to see, but you can easily drive across the bridge if you need to stop for supplies. Chess fans enjoy visiting the grave of troubled grandmaster Bobby Fischer in the Laugardælakirkja churchyard a mile northeast of Selfoss.

**Eating near Selfoss:** If you're in the mood for langoustine-by-the-sea, it's about a 15-minute detour to two *humar*-focused restaurants: **Fjöruborðið,** in the seaside village of Stokkseyri, and **Hafið Bláa.** For locations, see map on page 126.

• *It's a 45-minute drive from Selfoss back to Reykjavík. At the main roundabout in Selfoss, turn right onto highway 1. Soon after leaving Selfoss, on the left you'll see* **52 white crosses** *at the base of a conical hill (Kögunarhóll). These commemorate motorists and pedestrians killed on this busy, poorly lit road—statistically one of Iceland's most dangerous—between 1972 and 2006. Consider this a sobering reminder to drive with extra caution.*

*In a few minutes, you'll approach the small town of* **Hveragerði**. *While the town itself (pop. 2,000) is dreary, it sits at the mouth of a valley with evocative hillsides and offers an opportunity to hike to a thermal river (Reykjadalur); the town also has a great brewery/pizzeria (both described later). To stop at these, turn off highway 1 and follow the main drag all the way through Hveragerði. You'll come out at the upper end of town and keep going, following* Reykjadalur *signs about 2.5 miles, until the road dead-ends at the Reykjadalur parking lot, with a little café and basic WCs.*

## ▲Reykjadalur Thermal River

This natural thermal area—literally "Steamy Valley"—is aptly named. For outdoorsy hiker/bathers, Reykjadalur (RAKE-yah-dah-lrr) is worth ▲▲. The hike to the river is just over two miles one way along a well-maintained path, with a 600-foot elevation gain (allow at least three hours total for this experience).

Stepping out of your car at the end-of-the-road parking lot, you're surrounded by steaming hillsides. From here, cross the bridge, then hike approximately one hour up the valley. Eventually you'll reach some basic changing cabins next to a hot stream. The water is shallow—you'll need to lie down to be submerged—but wonderfully warm. Reykjadalur is far from undiscovered, so you'll likely have plenty of company. Relax and enjoy the experience...but remember it's an hour's hike back down to your car. The little café in the parking lot, Dalakaffi, is a nice place for cake and coffee (Sun-Fri 13:00-18:00, Sat from 11:00, www.dalakaffi.is).

**Warning:** Stay on marked paths at all times. This entire area is very geologically active, and anyone wandering off the path could end up stepping into a hidden, underground pool of boiling water.

**Eating in Hveragerði:** The main reason to visit nearby Hveragerði is to eat at **$$ Ölverk** ("Beerworks"), a wonderful little microbrewery/pizzeria tucked in a dreary strip mall a couple of blocks into town. In addition to a chalkboard menu of their own beers, and some others by local brewers, they dish up tasty pizzas from a brick oven. Casual and family-friendly, it works well for an easygoing, memorable dinner on your way back to Reykjavík (daily 11:30-23:00, take the main road through Hveragerði and watch for the pizzeria on your right at Breiðumörk 2b, tel. 483-3030, www. olverk.is).

• *Leaving Hveragerði, the road climbs steeply in a series of wide bends to a high upland plateau (1,200 feet) called...*

## Hellisheiði

This plateau separates southern Iceland from the Reykjavík area. The weather can be dodgy up here, so check the road conditions in advance. About halfway across the plateau, you'll see pipes and steam from **Hellisheiðarvirkjun,** a geothermal plant owned by the Reykjavík energy utility; if it's not too early or late in the day, you could stop at the visitors center (see page 62). From here, it's less than 30 minutes—across a lunar landscape—to Reykjavík. On your way into town, consider stopping in the suburb of **Hafnarfjörður** for dinner (see recommendations in the Reykjavík chapter).

# ICELANDIC EXPERIENCES

Gazing into a volcanic crater lake, leaping across a tectonic fissure in the earth's crust, or following a track across a lava field are among the experiences you can have in Iceland. Not to mention descending into the underground magma chamber of an extinct volcano, or boiling an egg in the ashes of a new one. Explore waterfalls, glaciers, geysers, rivers, fjords, and cliffs. The surrounding ocean teems with giant whales and adorable puffins. Or you could luxuriate in an outdoor bath filled with earth-warmed water.

Iceland is a small land that packs in a lot of experiences—and there are things you can do here that you can't do anywhere else (not easily, at least). This chapter is a rundown of some of the quintessential Icelandic experiences, designed to inspire your trip planning and point you to more thorough coverage elsewhere in this book.

Even with a car—and especially without—many of these experiences require going through a tour operator. I've listed some established outfits. But the scene changes frequently, so check online to see if newer variations on these experiences now exist (for instance, the "Things to Do" reviews on TripAdvisor can offer a helpful roundup).

A good one-stop resource is Guide to Iceland, a for-profit consolidator of travel providers that works in partnership with the Reykjavík TI. Guide to Iceland has a desk in Reykjavík's City Hall that can explain the offerings of many different companies—allowing you to comparison-shop easily in person—or you can search their website (www.guidetoiceland.is), which also hosts many evocative blogs. They charge no additional commission and will match a better price if you find one. They work with some, but not all, tour providers in Iceland, so it's smart to also do your own research.

Note that while Reykjavík is usually a good home base, many

# The Many Ways Iceland Can Kill You

Several times a year, Iceland is captivated by a full-scale land and helicopter search for travelers sucked out to sea by a wave, separated from their snowmobile tour group, or lost in the wilderness. More so than in any other country in Europe, in Iceland nature can threaten your very existence.

To encourage safe travel, Iceland operates the SafeTravel.is website with detailed advice and up-to-the-minute alerts. Their "112 Iceland" app is free; they also staff a desk at the Reykjavík TI (inside City Hall). There's also a national emergency number with help in English—112.

Travel smart and keep the following risks in mind. For more on driving, see page 177.

**Wind:** The signature feature of Icelandic weather is wind. For Icelanders, good weather means no wind or a light breeze; bad weather means it's blowing hard. Even in summer, you'll likely encounter winds that are uncomfortable or dangerous to walk or drive in. Check the forecast at the Icelandic weather service's web page (http://en.vedur.is). If it's windy and icy at the same time, use extra care.

**Falls:** In winter, Reykjavík's sidewalks generally aren't cleared or salted, and are very slippery and icy. Falls are common. Paths in the countryside ice over, too. Cautious travelers visiting from December through February can pack a pair of ice cleats to strap over their shoes.

**Exposure and Getting Lost:** When traveling in less inhabited parts of the country, be prepared for the unexpected. Your car could break down or run out of gas, or you could take a wrong turn. Travel with extra clothing (even summer days can turn cold and windy, especially at higher elevations) and keep your mobile phone charged (reception is good all around the Ring Road). Carry a paper map as a backup. Before heading into wilderness areas, upload your itinerary to SafeTravel.is.

**Sneaker Waves:** Iceland's South Coast has some very dangerous beaches with strong waves that regularly pull unsuspecting tourists out to sea. The most notorious are two blacksand beaches around Dyrhólaey. One of these, called Kirkjufjara, was chained off for good after a drowning in 2017. The other, at Reynisfjara, is still open, and although picturesque and popular with tourists, it's imperative to obey all signs, stay *much* farther from the water

excursions head to destinations quite far away—which means long hours in a bus and higher prices. Staying closer to your objective and booking a tour that originates nearby may be a better option. For example, if you're interested in glacier activities, consider spending a night or two on the South Coast or in Southeast Iceland.

As you join the hordes of international visitors who treat Ice-

Pinole Branch
Contra Costa County Library
2935 Pinole Valley Road
Pinole, Ca. 94564
510-758-2741

**Customer ID: 21901026867949**

**Items that you checked out**

Title: Rick Steves' snapshot.    Reykjavi k
ID: 31901063442760
**Due: Friday, November 05, 2021**
Messages:
Item checked out.


Total items: 1
Account balance: $0.00
10/15/2021 4:40 PM
Checked out: 2
Overdue: 0
Hold requests: 0
Ready for pickup: 0

_____

Renew online or by phone
ccclib.org
1-800-984-4636
Have a great day!

11/17/21

than you think is safe, and never turn your back to the ocean.

**Trail Hazards:** There are very few ropes, guardrails, or warning signs in Iceland—but if you see any, take them seriously. Step carefully, and watch out for loose stones, crevices, and sharp lava rocks.

**Scalding Thermal Water:** The water in Iceland's geothermally active areas can be boiling hot, and the danger is often unmarked. Every year or two a tourist falls in and gets severely burned, typically in a less-visited geothermal area without ropes or walkways. If you value your fingers, don't use them to test the water.

**Avalanches:** Icelanders have taken this danger more seriously since 1995, when two avalanches in the Westfjords killed 34 people. Wintertime travelers may encounter avalanche warnings in any settled area close to a steep mountain slope.

**Volcanoes:** On average, a volcano erupts in Iceland every five years. Some eruptions can be viewed from a safe distance, but others melt glaciers, let loose streams of boiling lava, give off poisonous gases, or spew ash and boulders that will damage you or your car. Volcanic eruptions and their consequences can and regularly do interfere with travel plans. A good place to start following along with eruptions (and earthquakes) is the Icelandic weather service's website.

**Earthquakes:** Minor earthquakes are frequent in Iceland, but catastrophic earthquakes are rare. In the past century, quakes of about six on the Richter scale have hit different parts of the country every decade or two.

**Angry Birds:** While not life-threatening, angry birds can be a nuisance. In late spring and early summer, Arctic terns *(kríur)* will dive-bomb your head if you get too close to their breeding grounds. Obey any closure signs near major nesting areas.

land as a newly discovered playground, do so considerately. Respect the land. The nature on display may seem raw and powerful, but it's also extremely fragile. Nobody yet knows precisely what long-term impact the recent influx of tourism will have on this special place. To be part of a sustainable long-term prosperity, treat Iceland as a precious treasure...because that's what it is.

# Glaciers

More than one-tenth of Iceland's surface is covered with glaciers *(jökull)*—mainly along the southern coastline and in the desolate

interior. The glaciers are most accessible at so-called tongues, where a slow-motion river of ice flows down a valley. There are several accessible glacier tongues along Iceland's southern coast, from near Skógar in the west to near Höfn in the east. If traveling on your own, you can **hike close to the tongue of a glacier** in two places: at the Skaftafell wilderness area, where you can walk to a branch of Iceland's largest glacier, Vatnajökull; or at Sólheimajökull, along the southern coast closer to Reykjavík.

There are also two **glacier lagoons**—where a glacier tongue terminates in a beautiful pool of water, and icebergs calve off and float around—a few minutes' drive apart in Southeast Iceland: Jökulsárlón and Fjallsárlón. At either, you can pull over for a good look at the lagoon, or pay to board a boat for an up-close trip between bobbing icebergs. Near Jökulsárlón is another enchanting glacial sight, the so-called **Diamond Beach,** where chunks of shimmering ice from the nearby lagoon wash up on a black sand beach. This is a magical look at the final stage of glacial ice's very long, very slow journey to the open ocean.

For safety's sake, the activities described above are the only glacier-related ones you should attempt on your own. Properly outfitted and with a guide, you have more options.

Several companies offer **glacier walks.** They'll equip you with cold-weather gear, serious crampons, and ice axes, then tie your group together and carefully amble across the ice. The most popular places for this are Sólheimajökull and Skaftafell in Southeast Iceland. The two big tour companies—Reykjavík Excursions and Gray Line—offer this, as do as a variety of smaller, more specialized operators, including Icelandic Mountain Guides (www. mountainguides.is), Arctic Adventures (www.adventures.is), Troll Expeditions (www.trollaferdir.is), Glacier Guides (www. glacierguides.is), Glacier Journey (www.glacierjourney.is), and Extreme Iceland (www.extremeiceland.is).

For a high-speed trip, consider **glacier snowmobiling.** Mountaineers of Iceland, one of the most established outfits, offers a variety of trips across Langjökull (near the Golden Circle), ranging from $250 to $500 (www.mountaineers.is—also offers ATV and

Super Jeep tours; or try Glacier Journey). You can even go on a **dogsled trip** across the glacier (consider Extreme Iceland).

Finally, if you're intrigued by all that ice, you can spelunk through an **ice cave** burrowed into a glacier ($200-300, 3-4-hour experience). There are three ice caves you can visit in Iceland. Into the Glacier takes visitors to an artificial cave in Langjökull in West Iceland; it's the only ice cave open year-round (www.intotheglacier. is). The glacier atop the Katla volcano in southern Iceland has a natural cave that's open from June to December—but it's melting quickly, so could close soon (tours depart from Vík; try Katlatrack, www.katlatrack.is). In the winter (Nov-March), Vatnajökull has a natural cave that you can explore with a tour that departs from the Jökulsárlón glacier lagoon (companies include Arctic Adventures, Extreme Iceland, and Glacier Journey; you'll pay more for pick-up in Reykjavík).

If you won't be venturing beyond Reykjavík, the **Museum of Icelandic Natural Wonders** has a simulated ice cave and glacier, and exhibits that focus on Iceland's glacial geology.

# Volcanoes

Travelers come to Iceland hoping for a glimpse of a volcano. When the volcano called Eyjafjallajökull spewed ash into the atmosphere in 2010—bringing European air travel to a halt—it grabbed the imagination of many. While you probably won't see any spewing ash or flowing lava while you're here, there are a variety of volcanic sights where you can learn more about the island's unique geology.

## VOLCANIC LANDSCAPES

Much of Iceland is plainly shaped by volcanic activity—you won't have to look hard to find lava landscapes. Here are a few of the most dramatic and accessible.

**Westman Islands:** This archipelago, just off the South Coast, is the most interesting volcano-related sight in Iceland, and a pilgrimage for those with serious interest. The Westman Islands saw some of Iceland's most spectacular volcanic activity in recent times. First, from 1963 to 1967, the islet of Surtsey literally rose from the Atlantic Ocean; while it can't be visited, on a clear day you can see the islet from the main island, Heimaey. Then, in 1973, the town of Vestmannaeyjar was rudely awoken in the middle of the night by a surprise eruption on the adjacent hillside. The locals were evacuated, and the eastern part of the town was gradually swallowed by flowing lava. Today, streets dead-end at steep walls of volcanic rock, and a few lucky houses are surrounded on three sides by jagged cliffs. The still-warm crater hovers above it all. And the

# Iceland's Volcanoes

Iceland is among the most volcanically active places in the world, with roughly one eruption every five years. Aside from liquid lava, Iceland's volcanoes eject gas, ash, cinders, and solid rock (like pumice). The biggest rocks are sometimes called "volcanic bombs." Volcanic eruptions can last from a couple of days to several years.

Grímsvötn, a hard-to-reach volcano under the Vatnajökull glacier (in Southeast Iceland), is currently Iceland's most active; it last erupted in May 2011. Bárðarbunga, another volcano under the same glacier, began rumbling awake as recently as late 2017. The more famous Eyjafjallajökull, on the South Coast, made news in 2010—costing airlines more than $1 billion in disruptions. Other well-known Icelandic volcanoes include Hekla (once nicknamed the "Gateway to Hell"), Krafla, Askja, and Katla, which has the most potential for a damaging eruption (as it could send waves of water washing over coastal hamlets).

Of the roughly 130 volcanoes in Iceland, the most common type is the stratovolcano—the classic cone-shaped peak with explosive eruptions that form a crater in the very top (such as Hekla and Katla). There are also a few dormant shield volcanoes—with low-profile, wide-spreading lava flows (one called Skjaldbreiður is near the Golden Circle). Eruptions from fissure vents (long cracks in the earth's crust) are also common in Iceland, such as the Holuhraun eruption of 2014 or the destructive Laki eruptions in the 1780s.

Iceland's entire surface is made of volcanic rock, most of it basalt—the rock that forms when lava cools. Iceland's towering cliffs and jagged islands and skerries are all made of basalt. When basalt cools in particular ways, it forms the hexagonal rock columns that you see at Reynisfjara (on the South Coast), near Dettifoss (in the north), and other places.

At the lake called Mývatn, in North Iceland, you can see pseudocraters (also called rootless cones), which form after lava flows over a pond or marsh. The water beneath the lava boils and a giant bubble breaks through the lava, leaving a crater-like depression.

New lava is shiny and oily-looking, while old lava loses its gleam. Old lava fields—recognizable by their unique, bumpy appearance—are often covered by a fuzzy layer of Icelandic moss.

ICELANDIC EXPERIENCES

Volcano Museum in town is literally built around a house buried by lava—letting you peek into a family home forever trapped in rock.

**Reykjanes Peninsula:** Your introduction to Iceland is one of the best looks you'll get at a volcanic landscape, as the area around Keflavík Airport is covered by jagged lava fields. The nearby Blue Lagoon is situated in this same rocky world (see the Blue Lagoon & Reykjanes Peninsula chapter). Closer to Reykjavík, the suburb

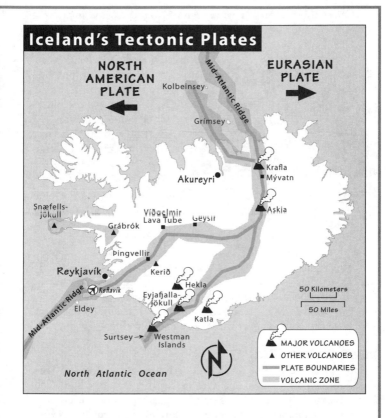

Iceland's Tectonic Plates

NORTH AMERICAN PLATE

EURASIAN PLATE

Mid-Atlantic Ridge

Kolbeinsey

Grímsey

Krafla
Mývatn

Akureyri

Askia

Snæfells-jökull

Víðgelmir Lava Tube

Geysir

Grábrók

Þingvellir

Reykjavík

Keflavík

Eldey

Surtsey →

Kerið

Hekla

Eyjafjalla-jökull

Katla

Westman Islands

Mid-Atlantic Ridge

North Atlantic Ocean

50 Kilometers

50 Miles

MAJOR VOLCANOES
OTHER VOLCANOES
PLATE BOUNDARIES
VOLCANIC ZONE

So why does Iceland have so many volcanoes? The answer lies beneath the surface. Iceland is located on the long, mostly underwater Mid-Atlantic Ridge—the meeting point of the Eurasian and North American tectonic plates. As the two tectonic plates move apart, magma from the earth's mantle rises to the surface (we start calling it "lava" when it erupts). Iceland is located on a mantle plume, where magma is especially close to the surface, which explains why land formed here and not elsewhere along the tectonic ridge.

of Hafnarfjörður is nicknamed the "Town in the Lava" because it sits on a lava flow.

**Mývatn:** This North Iceland lake is ringed by a variety of otherworldly features, from the "pseudocraters" at Skútustaðir (where giant bubbles of steam burst through molten rock) to the jagged formations along the lake's eastern shore, at Dimmuborgir, and at the huge, climbable Hverfjall crater.

**Climbable Craters:** Several craters around Iceland invite you to climb up onto their rims for spectacular views. One of the fin-

est examples, **Grábrók,** is alongside the Ring Road in West Iceland, just be- fore the pass to the north. **Kerið,** along the Golden Circle route, requires al- most no climbing and has a lovely lake inside. Near Mývatn, in the north, you can hike to the top of **Hverfjall** or drive just over the mountains and up the Katla Valley to reach **Víti** ("Hell"), a rugged crater encircling a deep-blue lake.

**South Coast:** All along the South Coast, you'll see plenty of volcanoes—but you may not realize it, since they're currently dor- mant and covered with thick glaciers. The most famous is Eyjafjal- lajökull, which blew its top in 2010. Several other large glaciers, such as Mýrdalsjökull and Vatnajökull, have volcanoes underneath. For a hike with the best possible views of glacier-topped volcanoes, head to **Þórsmörk,** where a huff up to the Valahnúkur viewpoint affords you panoramas over three different volcanoes.

## VOLCANO MUSEUMS

Iceland's best explanation of volcanic activity is at the **Volcano Mu- seum** in the Westman Islands. On the South Coast, the high-tech **Lava Centre** in Hvolsvöllur is both entertaining and educational. A short drive up the road is the much more modest **Iceland Erupts** exhibit, which focuses on the 2010 Eyjafjallajökull eruption and its ashy impact. Reykjavík's **Volcano House** shows films about the two most famous eruptions, and its **Museum of Icelandic Natural Wonders** (at the Pearl) is developing some volcano exhibits.

## VOLCANIC CAVE TOURS

Iceland offers three opportunities to enter dormant volcanic caves. While quite expensive for what you get (especially the first option), they're worthwhile for those interested in an up-close look.

**Þríhnjúkagígur** (a.k.a. **"Inside the Volcano"**; just southeast of Reykjavík, in the Bláfjöll mountains) offers the chance to descend into the magma chamber of a volcano that erupted about 4,000 years ago. The magma drained out and left a cavity so big that it could contain the Statue of Liberty. The first explorer entered in 1972. Now an elevator is rigged up in the opening every sum- mer, allowing tourists to descend 400 feet into the bottle-shaped chamber, with a floor measuring 160 by 220 feet (the size of three basketball courts). The trip package includes hotel pickup in Reykjavík, the 30-minute bus ride out, a fairly easy 45-minute hike each way from the road to the volcano, the elevator down (5 minutes each way), 30 minutes on the floor of the chamber, and an included lunch. The rock is entirely cool—there's no volcanic activity here anymore. At around $400, it's not cheap, but it's definitely memorable. Book in advance online (42,000 ISK, tours run mid-May–mid-Oct only, tel. 519-5609, www.insidethevolcano.com).

**Raufarhólshellir** (a.k.a. "The Lava Tunnel") is an approximately mile-long, underground lava tube created when a flowing river of molten rock was enclosed, then drained out, leaving behind colorful formations. It's about a 45-minute drive from downtown Reykjavík, roughly on the way to the South Coast. In 2017, the cave was closed to the public and converted into a private attraction—infuriating local spelunkers. Expect uneven footing and chilly temperatures; they'll loan you coveralls and a helmet (6,400 ISK for basic one-hour tour, 9,900 ISK includes Reykjavík bus transfer; 19,900 ISK "extreme" tour lasts 3-4 hours, is more physically demanding, goes deeper into the tunnel, and includes Reykjavík transfer; prebooking required, www.thelavatunnel.is).

In West Iceland is the similar **Víðgelmir** (a.k.a. "The Cave"). This cave is newer (about 1,000 years old rather than 5,000) and more extensive, but also more remote (about a 2-hour drive north of Reykjavík, or an hour east of Borgarnes). With a guide, you can walk about a half-mile into a lava tube.

# Thermal Waters

Iceland's volcanic activity goes hand-in-hand with naturally heated water—which Icelanders have cleverly harnessed in a number of ways, from thermal baths to sources of electricity and heat.

## THERMAL BATHS AND POOLS

Iceland has a wide range of options for enjoying its relaxing (and, yes, slightly stinky) thermal waters. Some bathing experiences cater primarily to tourists, chief among them the heavily advertised "premium baths." The most famous of these is the **Blue Lagoon** near Keflavík Airport (see the Blue Lagoon & Reykjanes Peninsula

# Pool Rules: Visiting an Icelandic Thermal Swimming Pool

Icelanders love going to their local swimming pools, which are heated with natural thermal water. These aren't elaborate water parks, but more like municipal swimming pools back home: functional facilities for taking a dip with family and friends. (Not so long ago, it was common for Icelanders to live in apartments with no shower or bathtub—instead, they had an annual pass for the pool and went daily.)

Of course, the big draw of Icelandic pools is the naturally steamy water, which is pumped right out of the ground. Even the lap pools stay at a warm temperature (around 85°F), while "hot pots" (smaller hot pools) are in the 100°F range. Bigger pools have more facilities, which can be indoors, outdoors, or both. Very windy or cold weather makes indoor bathing attractive. But if it's not too bad out, there's something cozy about submerging yourself in hot water while the wind ruffles your hair and snowflakes settle on your nose.

Iceland's public bathing culture has its own set of customs, which locals take very seriously. You'll quickly get the hang of the system. Here's a step-by-step primer:

**1. Bring a swimsuit and towel** (rentals are available but expensive). Also bring any other gear you need: bathing cap, goggles, flip-flops (although most Icelanders don't bother with them), or toys for children (you can bring a bag into the pool area and stow it discreetly). There's no need to bring soap or shampoo—there are liquid soap dispensers in the showers.

**2. Pay.** Most towns have a shareable 10-visit discount card, which can save money with as few as five adult entries. At some pools, you'll be issued a locker key or an electronic wristband that will open a locker; at others, you'll find keys in the locks.

**3. Change.** Changing rooms are sex-segregated. Young children may go with a parent of either sex. Before entering the locker area, take off your shoes. (Many Icelanders leave them on public shoe racks, but I carry mine along and put them in my locker.)

chapter), but a similar (if smaller) version is **Mývatn Nature Baths** in North Iceland—a must for those doing the Ring Road. A less impressive premium bath is **Fontana,** in Laugarvatn and handy to the Golden Circle route. A new facility called **Krauma** has opened at Deildartunguhver in West Iceland. Other tourist-oriented bath-

Find an available locker, disrobe and lock your clothes inside, and carry your swimsuit and towel with you to the shower area.

**4. Shower.** Store your towel in one of the cubbyholes provided (you'll leave it there until after you've showered on your way out of the pool) and keep your swimsuit handy. Soap down and shower thoroughly. Yes, you're expected to shower naked: Icelanders are relaxed about nudity, and showering is considered a (required) sanitary issue. (Only the Blue Lagoon, where almost all the visitors are tourists, has some frosted-glass stalls for bashful foreigners.) Note: Iceland's water is extremely soft. You don't need very much soap to get clean, and it can take a long time to wash it off.

**5. Swim and soak.** After showering, slip on your swimsuit and head for the pool area. Typically, people start out in the warm pools (usually a lap pool for swimmers, a shallower pool for recreation, and a wading pool for kids; these are typically around 29°C/85°F). Then they finish off with a soak in the hot tubs (38-40°C/100-104°F) or a visit to the sauna. Each tub is posted with the temperature; anything above 40°C is extremely hot. Stay as long as you want; if you feel dizzy or uncomfortable, take a break outside or in a cooler pool, and take advantage of the water fountain.

**6. Finish up.** When you're done, return to the shower room, take off your swimsuit, shower again, and retrieve your towel. Towel off *before* returning to the locker area (they like to keep it as dry as possible). Many pools have a centrifuge to wick the water out of your suit. Back at your locker, get dressed, but don't put your shoes on until you exit the locker room. Return any keys or armbands to the counter.

**7. Refuel.** Most pools have tables and chairs in the entry hall where you can eat a packed lunch or snack. Most also have vending machines, snack counters, or even full-fledged cafés.

**Note:** At the pool, Icelanders usually just talk to the people they came with and generally leave strangers alone. Everyone is polite and helpful, but don't expect to get into a long conversation. At some times of day, groups of local "regulars" (often senior citizens) may seem to take over one of the hot pots, but you're welcome to squeeze in, too.

ing experiences include the **Secret Lagoon,** a simple but cleverly marketed bath a short drive from the Golden Circle route at Flúðir.

While those baths have big marketing budgets and attract lots of international visitors, they're rarely frequented by Icelanders—who know that you can bathe in equally luxuriant 100°F water for a fraction of the price, albeit in simpler surroundings, at one of the country's many **thermal swimming pools** *(sundlaug)*. Every community of even a few hundred people seems to have scraped together the funds for their own well-maintained pool complex, often with a (warm) lap pool and at least one or two smaller hot pools (called "hot pots"). Many have a wide

variety of different pools, saunas and steam rooms, and colorful waterslides for kids. In addition to being affordable, these provide a pleasantly authentic Icelandic experience, allowing you to rub elbows with locals who come home from work or school, grab a towel, and head to the pool. I've listed several of these in the Reykjavík area, and throughout the country—including in Borg, right along the Golden Circle; in a remote corner of West Iceland, at Húsafell; in tiny Hofsós, just off the Ring Road, with an infinity pool overlooking a fjord; and in Iceland's second city, Akureyri.

Up-to-date opening hours for each pool are on the website of each town, but you usually have to hunt for them a bit amidst the other municipal services. These websites also won't show temporary closures (for special events, maintenance, etc.), so it's wise to confirm opening hours by telephone before making a trek to a distant pool.

Various websites list Iceland's thermal pools (try www.swimminginiceland.is or www.hotpoticeland.com). The free booklets *Áning—Accommodation in Iceland* and *Thermal Bliss* include extensive lists of pools (available at the Reykjavík TI or downloadable at www.icelandreview.com/publications). The *Reykjavík Grapevine* has a great article called "Every Swimming Pool in the Greater Reykjavík Area, Rated" (easily found at www.

grapevine.is). Or you can simply keep a lookout for the international-al "pool" symbol—a swimmer's head poking out above waves—anywhere you go. Even though the clientele is mostly Icelandic, visitors are welcome (just follow the rules—see sidebar).

Finally, Iceland has a few opportunities to (carefully) bathe in **natural thermal springs.** Above the town of Hveragerði, near the end of the Golden Circle route, you can hike an hour to soak in the thermal river of **Reykjadalur** (see page 149). In the Highlands, **Landmannalaugar** ("The People's Pools") has a famous natural thermal area, which takes quite some effort to reach (only with an off-road vehicle, and only in summer); this is best done on a guided excursion (about 20,000 ISK, offered by many companies mid-June–mid-Sept, includes pick-up and drop-off in Reykjavík). It's important to note that tourists routinely wind up in the burn unit of Reykjavík's hospital after being scalded at natural thermal areas. Watch your step, keep on marked trails, bathe only where you see others doing so safely, and remember that a thermal landscape comes with lots of hidden dangers.

## THERMAL SIGHTS

Wandering through a steaming, bubbling, colorful, otherworldly thermal landscape is a uniquely Icelandic treat. For such a small island, Iceland has a re-markable variety of these locations. Just watch your step—always stay on marked trails, as a thin crust can cover a boiling-hot reservoir—and be ready for some intense sulfur smells.

The most visited is **Geysir,** on the Golden Circle. But, while it's unique in offering the chance to watch a geyser spurt high into the air, it's crowded. For more interesting and varied thermal landscapes, consider the following options.

Perhaps the best thermal area is at **Námafjall,** just over the hills from Mývatn, in North Iceland. Much closer to Reykjavík, the **Seltún** geothermal area on the Reykjanes Peninsula is quite striking. "Honorable mentions" go to the sputtering shore of **Laugarvatn** lake, along the Golden Circle route; the bubbling spring at **Deildartunguhver,** in West Iceland; and the steaming valley of **Reykjadalur,** above the town of Hveragerði (just off the Golden Circle route). See "Thermal Bath Hikes," later.

To see how Iceland has harnessed the substantial power of its thermal waters, stop by a geothermal plant. **Hellisheiðarvirkjun** sits amidst a lunar landscape just outside Reykjavík, on the way to the Golden Circle and South Coast day trips, and boasts Iceland's most extensive visitors center about its geothermal energy industry. **Krafla,** with a modest information center, fills a dramatic valley in the north, near Mývatn.

# Whales, Birds, and Horses

## WHALE WATCHING

Many come to Iceland hoping to catch a glimpse of the elusive whales of the North Atlantic. The waters here are home to 23 different varieties of gentle giants.

On a typical whale-watching trip, you're most likely to see white-beaked dolphins, harbor porpoises, and mid-sized minke whales (the species also listed on local menus). If you have luck, you may spot a breaching humpback whale (most often seen from ports in North Iceland, such as Húsavík and Akureyri) or a black-and-white orca (Keiko, the killer whale of *Free Willy* fame, was captured in Iceland). On very rare occasions, some get a glimpse of one of the two biggest mammals on the planet: the blue whale or the fin whale.

Several companies offer whale-watching boat trips (generally 3-4 hours for about 11,000 ISK). These once were concentrated in North Iceland: in the tiny town of Húsavík, and Iceland's second city of Akureyri. The same trips (and many of the same companies) are now also well-established in Reykjavík, making it easier to whale watch without a long trek north. See the Reykjavík chapter for a rundown of your options.

Ideally, don't book your whale-watching trip too far in advance. Follow the weather report and choose a summer day that's as sunny and windless as possible; like you, whales and dolphins enjoy nice weather and are most likely to surface then. May through August are the best months, when whales are attracted to the small creatures feeding near the sun-warmed surface of the water. Windy weather or rough seas can turn the trip into four hours of seasickness, and you likely won't see more than a dolphin or two. From November to February, I'd skip the trip entirely. Dress warmly (though boat operators usually have extra outerwear to loan).

Be aware that whale-watching trips are a big commitment of time and money—best for those with a serious interest in the creatures. For a guaranteed, up-close look at (artificial) whales, stop by the expensive but enjoyable Whales of Iceland exhibit near Reykjavík's harbor.

ICELANDIC EXPERIENCES

## BIRDS AND BIRDING

Adorable, chubby little puffins—with their black-and-white markings and cartoonish beaks—are fun to watch. They usually arrive in Iceland in early summer, then take off again at summer's end—making the window for seeing them quite short. (For more on puffins, see the sidebar on the next page.)

The biggest puffin populations are in the Westman Islands (with about half of Iceland's estimated 10 million puffins—and one-fifth of the world's puffins); along the South Coast (particularly around the Dyrhólaey promontory, and farther east, at Ingólfshöfði cape); and along the Westfjords (at Látrabjarg, Hornbjarg, Hornstrandir, and Breiðafjörður). The islet called Lundey ("Puffin Island")—with a relatively small population of about 20,000 puffins—is ideally situated just a short boat trip from downtown Reykjavík, and a handy destination for a puffin cruise from the Old Harbor. Perhaps Iceland's best puffin experience is at the Westman Islands' Sæheimar Aquarium, where you can usually meet a real-life puffin named Tóti, who was rescued as a stranded puffling by local kids.

Birders find plenty of other seabird species to get excited about in Iceland. Along with puffins, the auk family includes the guillemot, the murre, and the razorbill (all of which have a black body and white belly, but lack that cute orange beak). Arctic terns are sleek flyers—gray on top, white on bottom, with a black crown and a reddish beak. They're notorious for aggressively dive-bombing tourists who wander too close to their nests, then pulling up at the last second. Arctic terns have the longest migration in the animal kingdom: They spend their summers in the Arctic...and then, come fall, fly to the "southern summer" in the Antarctic (over its life, an Arctic tern might fly as many as 1.5 million miles). Rounding out the flock are seagull-like fulmars and kittiwakes. Iceland has several freshwater bird species as well, including ducks, oystercatchers, and golden plovers.

For a one-stop look at (taxidermy-style) examples of all Icelandic bird species, head north to Sigurgeir's Bird Museum near Mývatn.

## ICELANDIC HORSES

Icelandic horses are small, strong, and docile, and descend from the ponies originally brought to Iceland in the Settlement Age. (Viking Age settlers carefully selected only the smallest yet strongest horses for the journey—able to fit on their ships, but capable of working hard once in Iceland.) Today, Icelandic horses are exported to enthusiasts worldwide, but since A.D. 982, no horses have been imported to the island—so every one you see is a purebred. Icelandic horses are renowned for their unique gaits: In addition to

# Puffins

Iceland's unofficial mascot is the Atlantic puffin *(Fratercula arctica)*—that adorably stout, tuxedo-clad seabird with a too-big orange beak and beady black eyes. Some 10 million puffins summer in Iceland—the largest population of any country on earth.

Puffins live most of their lives on the open Atlantic, coming to land only to breed. They fly north to Iceland between mid-May and early June, raise their brood, then take off again late in August. Puffins mate for life and typically lay just one egg each year, which the male and female take turns caring for. A baby puffin is called—wait for it—a puffling.

To feed their pufflings, puffins plunge as deep as 200 feet below the sea's surface to catch sand eels, herring, and other small fish. Their compact bodies, stubby wings, oil-sealed plumage, and webbed feet are ideal for navigating underwater. Famously, puffins can stuff several small fish into their beaks at once, thanks to their agile tongues and uniquely hinged beaks. This evolutionary trick lets puffins stock up before returning to the nest.

Stocky, tiny-winged puffins have a distinctive way of flying. To take off, they either beat their wings like crazy (at sea) or essentially hurl themselves off a cliff (on land). Once aloft, they beat their wings furiously—up to 400 times per minute—to stay airborne. Coming in for a smooth landing on a rocky cliff is a challenge (and highly entertaining to watch): They choose a spot, swoop in at top speed on prevailing currents, then flutter their wings madly to brake as they try to touch down. At the moment of truth, the puffin decides whether to attempt to stick the landing; more often than not, he bails out and does another big circle on the currents...and tries again...and again...and again.

Each August, the puffins head south at night, following the moon. On the Westman Islands, pufflings are often distracted by the town lights and crash-land on streets and rooftops. Local children collect them and bring them to the aquarium, which allows them an overnight rest before being released into the wild to try again.

In addition to seeing puffins along the summer coastline, you may occasionally see them on restaurant menus. With such abundant numbers, Iceland doesn't protect the puffin. Considered by some Icelanders to be a delicacy, puffin tastes like chicken...but cuter.

ICELANDIC EXPERIENCES

the typical walk, trot, and gallop, Icelandic horses employ the *tölt*, which is fast and extremely smooth, and the *skeið*, a high-speed "flying pace." This "five-gaited" status is their claim to fame.

Even if you're not an equestrian enthusiast, a horseback ride is a nice way to enjoy the outdoors for a couple of hours, much  as Icelanders have for centuries. Horseback riding is big business, and dozens of farms all over Iceland offer rides for travelers—including a cluster just outside Reykjavík. Browse and book on company websites: Íslenski Hesturinn (The Icelandic Horse, tel. 434-7979, http://islenskihesturinn.is), Viking Horses (mobile 660-9590, www.vikinghorses.is), Laxnes (tel. 566-6179, www.laxnes.is), and Íshestar (tel. 555-7000, www.ishestar.is).

It's usually a half-day affair, either morning or afternoon. If you're based in Reykjavík, they'll pick you up, drive you out to the farm, outfit you with a helmet and riding gear, give you about an hour and a half on horseback, and drop you off afterwards, all for about 12,000-15,000 ISK (some tours throw in lunch; Laxnes and Íshestar lower the price if you drive out yourself). Beyond the Reykjavík area, your scores of options include some in dramatic surroundings: in the broad valley of Skagafjörður, through the glacial rivulets of Þórsmörk, along the beaches of the South Coast, and so on. Wherever you ride, check the weather forecast before booking.

For just a glimpse of an Icelandic horse, watch for roadside paddocks all around the island. Or head to the Reykjavík Family Park and Zoo (see page 59), ideally at feeding time. On weekends, the zoo lets little kids trot around the horse paddock, accompanied by a keeper.

## Hiking

Iceland is a wonderland for hikers, whether you're taking an easy stroll from your car to a waterfall, or embarking on a grueling but dramatic multiday trek. Before heading out on a challenging hike, make sure you have proper equipment, water, maps, and advice from an experienced local.

Be aware of current weather conditions—and don't underestimate the impact of Iceland's howling winds and bone-chilling (even in summer) temperatures. Read "The Many Ways Iceland Can Kill You" sidebar (earlier in this chapter).

## EASY HIKES

Throughout this book, I've focused on easy hikes that offer a big reward for minimal effort—mainly starting from a parking lot and looping through an accessible slice of Icelandic scenery. Some of my favorite, easy car hikes include the loop through Þingvellir along the Golden Circle route; the hikes up to the South Coast glaciers at Sólheimajökull and Skaftafell; the hike up to the lighthouse at Dyrhólaey promontory, on the South Coast; and walking up to Eldfell volcano on the Westman Islands. Along the Ring Road, there's a variety of enjoyable options around Mývatn lake—including the pseudocraters at Skútustaðir, the forested peninsula at Höfði, and the lava pillars at Dimmuborgir. Other Mývatn hikes include the Námafjall thermal field and adjacent hill-climb just over the mountains from the lake, and the hike out to the volcanic cone at Leirhnjúkur. Also consider the crater hikes described in the "Volcanoes" section, earlier.

Each of the great **waterfalls** I've described in Iceland comes with a hike—some short, some long—and often an opportunity to climb up to a higher vantage point: Gullfoss on the Golden Circle, Seljalandsfoss (and its neighbor Gljúfrabúi) on the South Coast, Skógafoss on the South Coast, Hraunfossar and Barnafoss in West Iceland, and along the Ring Road—Goðafoss and Dettifoss in North Iceland, and Svartifoss in the southeast.

## THERMAL BATH HIKES

To combine a hike with a natural thermal bathing experience, you can walk about an hour up the valley called **Reykjadalur,** just above the town of Hveragerði (an hour from Reykjavík and on the route of both the Golden Circle and the South Coast day trips). Your reward is a thermal river where you can recline in warm, rushing water. Less of a hike, and less rewarding, is **Seljavallalaug,** a tepid pool tucked into the side of a mountain about a 15-minute hike from the South Coast road. At both, expect minimal, grubby changing areas and plenty of adventurous hikers.

## SERIOUS HIKES

For serious hikers, Iceland offers dozens of premier hiking destinations—many in the Highlands, and inaccessible with a standard car. The two below are perhaps the best-known; for either you'll need a high-clearance four-wheel drive vehicle, or you can ride in a specially equipped excursion bus.

Perhaps the best combination of quality hiking and accessibility is **Þórsmörk**, a volcanic landscape with glorious mountain, valley, and canyon walks; the moderately challenging hike up to Valahnúkur is spectacular. Þórsmörk is a short detour from the South Coast, but most people get there via excursion bus from Reykjavík (5 hours each way).

More remote is **Landmannalaugar**, in the Highlands about 120 miles east of Reykjavík (much of it on difficult-to-traverse, gravel-and-rock roads; about 4.5 hours one-way, open only in summer). In this vivid area—striped with volcanic hues—a petrified lava field from 1477 butts up against pointy peaks, with excellent trails and some natural thermal pools. Hikes abound: You could trek to the crater lake called Ljótipollur ("Ugly Puddle"); huff your way up the extremely colorful Brennisteinsalda, with high-altitude views and an optional detour to the Stórihver thermal area near the top; or opt for an easier walk to the big lake called Frostastaðavatn.

To reach Landmannalaugar, you'll need a 4x4 vehicle, or you can join an excursion (typically Aug-Sept, starting at 20,000 ISK, offered by various outfits). You can also take a bus operated by Iceland On Your Own (www.ioyo.is), Trex (www.trex.is), or Iceland By Bus (www.icelandbybus.is). While you can get a glimpse of the area in a very long day trip from Reykjavík, serious hikers overnight at the Landmannalaugar hut/campground.

Both Þórsmörk and Landmannalaugar are key stops along a variety of popular multiday hikes (with overnights in staffed huts) that traverse the glacial landscape of the south. One of the most popular routes, called **Laugavegur**, takes three to five days (34 miles over challenging terrain) and connects Þórsmörk and Landmannalaugar. Another favorite is the two-day, 14-mile **Fimmvörðuháls** hike, from Þórsmörk south, over the saddle between Eyjafjallajökull and Mýrdalsjökull, to Skógar on the South Coast—right over the site of the first stage of the 2010 Eyjafjallajökull eruption.

For something closer to the capital, you could ascend **Esja**—the big, long ridge that looms just north of Reykjavík. The most popular hike here is the four-mile round-trip to Steinn ("The Stone"), with an elevation gain of 650 feet (don't attempt this in cold weather).

For details on these, and good overall information about hiking, see the websites of FÍ (the Iceland Touring Association, www.fi.is) and NAT (Nordic Adventure Travel, www.nat.is). Companies offering guided hikes in Iceland include Icelandic Mountain Guides (www.mountainguides.is) and Trek Iceland (www.trek.is).

## Other Outdoor Experiences

To reach spectacular scenery without the climb, you can choose from a variety of wheeled tours. Tours by **mountain bike,** by **ATV,** or by **"Super Jeep"** (a monster 4x4 vehicle that can go just about anywhere) give you access to some of the more remote areas mentioned earlier.

Various companies also offer **rafting and kayaking tours,** either in the canyon just below Gullfoss (the thundering waterfall on the Golden Circle), or in North Iceland on two rivers that drain the Hofsjökull glacier, south of Sauðárkrókur in the Skagafjörður region. Companies include Arctic Rafting (www.arcticrafting.com) and Viking Rafting (www.vikingrafting.is).

For divers, **scuba diving or snorkeling at Silfra**—a fissure flooded with crystal-clear glacial water, at Þingvellir on the Golden Circle—is a highlight (see the Golden Circle chapter).

## Northern Lights

The northern lights are a magical, occasional, serendipitous sight on clear, crisp nights in Iceland from about the end of August to the middle of April. You can't really plan to see the northern lights—they don't always appear, and when they do, are often obscured by cloud cover. While often visible in Reykjavík, the north-

ICELANDIC EXPERIENCES

# Nature's Light Show

Like floating curtains of translucent cloth, the northern lights arc across Iceland's wintery sky in shades of green, pink, purple, and even red. The lights are caused by charged particles from the sun that collide with the earth's upper atmosphere and cause it to glow. If these particles were able to hit earth's surface, the radiation would be catastrophic, damaging our DNA and increasing the risk of cancer. Fortunately, the earth's magnetic field deflects most of these particles; but near the poles, where the field is weakest, some can seep through, creating the northern lights. They are strongest along a ring-shaped band that crosses Iceland, Greenland, northern Canada, Alaska, Russia, and northern Scandinavia, and diminish as you move farther north toward the magnetic pole. Their intensity varies with the sunspot cycle; the last maximum was in 2013, and the next will be in 2025.

Iceland is a good place to see the northern lights, but not the best; its advantage is that it's relatively easy to get to, and its main disadvantage is its frequent cloudy weather. Perhaps that's why there's no mention of the phenomenon in the Icelandic sagas. However, a few Icelandic folk traditions mention the lights: For example, pregnant women avoided looking at the northern lights for fear their babies would be born cross-eyed. While other ancient people also saw the northern lights as a sign of war or famine, today they are a tourist attraction—and a reminder that life on our fragile planet depends on the protection of a magnetic field.

ern lights stand out better farther from the center of town and in the countryside, where there's less light pollution. All things being equal, spending a night or two in a more remote area could increase your chances.

The dreamy northern lights images that you see are done using long exposures and sometimes Photoshop (tweaking the aurora colors to a Kermit-the-Frog green). What you'll actually see will probably be closer to the color of a Thai green curry—more coconut milk than Kermit.

With all the interesting things to do in Iceland, it would be a shame to spend your energy chasing after the northern lights every evening. I suggest planning your trip as if you won't see them, and considering it as a bonus if you do. Whether you'll see the lights or not is mostly out of your control, but consider the tips below to improve your odds.

**Come during aurora season.** Visit Iceland in aurora season (from a little before the fall equinox to a little after the spring equinox). Some say that September/October and February/March are the best months. At the least, they have longer days and nicer temperatures, so you can enjoy regular sightseeing more. If you're planning to rent a car, go in fall, when the road conditions are better.

**Maximize your chances.** It's easy to miss the northern lights simply by not bothering to look for them.

On any clear, dark night, go outside and scan the sky every half hour or so up until bedtime. You can follow the aurora and cloud-cover forecast on the Icelandic weather service's English-language website (http://en.vedur.is; click on "Weather," then "Aurora forecasts"). The American aurora forecasts at www.swpc.noaa.gov also cover Iceland.

**See the lights without a car.** If you're staying in Reykjavík and you don't have a car, consider taking a northern lights bus tour (around 7,000 ISK). Tours only run when conditions look good—call around dinnertime to find out. You'll leave town at 21:00 or 22:00 and you won't be in bed until almost four hours later. Read a few reviews before you go, and remember that even if the forecast is good, you may see nothing at all. (If so, the bus company will likely give you a voucher for another trip—not much help on a short visit.) For some, the trip is a nice chance to snuggle up with a travel partner on a bus and listen to an entertaining tour guide who serves hot cocoa. For others, it's a disappointing few hours of yawning and wishing they'd turned in early.

**See the lights with a car.** If you're staying in Reykjavík and have a car, you could put together your own northern lights tour by driving out into the suburbs or a little way into the countryside. Þingvellir and Kleifarvatn are plenty dark and within a 45-minute drive of town. If you stay within greater Reykjavík, drive out toward the tips of Seltjarnarnes or Álftanes (by Bessastaðir, the presidential residence), where city lights are a little dimmer.

ICELANDIC EXPERIENCES

# PRACTICALITIES

This section covers just the basics on traveling in Iceland (for much more information, see *Rick Steves Iceland)*. You'll find free advice on specific topics at www.ricksteves.com/tips.

## MONEY

Icelanders rarely use cash; they pay with plastic even for small purchases such as parking meters and hot dogs. In Iceland, I use my credit card nearly exclusively, for everything from hotel reservations and car rentals to everyday expenses such as meals and sightseeing.

If you need cash, Iceland uses the *króna* (meaning "crown"; plural *krónur*): 100 ISK = about $1. To very roughly convert prices in Icelandic *krónur* to dollars, simply lop off the last two zeros: 2,000 ISK = about $20, 6,000 ISK = about $60. (Check www.oanda.com for the latest exchange rates.)

The standard way for travelers to get *krónur* is to withdraw money from an ATM (labeled *Hraðbanki*) using a debit card, ideally with a Visa or MasterCard logo. Don't withdraw more Icelandic currency than you need. Most merchants prefer plastic, and you'll scramble to spend unused *krónur* at the end of your trip. To keep your cash, cards, and valuables safe, wear a money belt.

Before departing, call your bank or credit-card company: Confirm that your card(s) will work overseas, ask about international transaction fees, and alert them that you'll be making withdrawals in Europe. Also ask for the PIN number for your credit card—you may need it for Europe's "chip-and-PIN" payment machines (see below; allow time for your bank to mail your PIN to you).

**Dealing with "Chip and PIN":** Most credit and debit cards now have chips that authenticate and secure transactions. European cardholders insert their chip card into the payment slot, then enter a PIN. (Until recently, most US cards required a signature.) Any American card with a chip will work at Europe's hotels, restaurants, and shops—although sometimes the clerk may ask for a signature.

**Drivers Beware:** Note that your US credit and debit cards may not work at some Icelandic gas pumps, even with a chip. Know your credit card's PIN, and be prepared to move on to another gas station. Especially in rural areas, don't let your tank get too low. If you have trouble buying gas at the pump, try asking inside the gas station for a prepaid gas card, which you should be able to purchase with any US card.

**Dynamic Currency Conversion:** If merchants or hoteliers offer to convert your purchase price into dollars (called dynamic currency conversion, or DCC), refuse this "service." You'll pay more in fees for the expensive convenience of seeing your charge in dollars. If an ATM offers to "lock in" or "guarantee" your conversion rate, choose "proceed without conversion." Other prompts might state, "You can be charged in dollars: Press YES for dollars, NO for *krónur*." Always choose the local currency.

## STAYING CONNECTED

The simplest solution is to bring your own device—mobile phone, tablet, or laptop—and use it just as you would at home (following the tips below, such as connecting to free Wi-Fi whenever possible).

**To call Iceland from a US or Canadian number:** Whether you're phoning from a landline, your own mobile phone, or a Skype account, you're making an international call. Dial 011-354 and then the local number. (The 011 is our international access code, and 354 is Iceland's country code.) If dialing from a mobile phone, you can enter + in place of the international access code—press and hold the 0 key.

**To call Iceland from a European country:** Dial 00-354 followed by the local number. (The 00 is Europe's international access code.)

**To call within Iceland:** Just dial the seven-digit phone number.

**To call from Iceland to another country:** Dial 00 followed by the country code (for example, 1 for the US or Canada), then the area code and number. If you're calling European countries whose phone numbers begin with 0, you'll usually have to omit that 0 when you dial.

**Tips:** If you bring your own mobile phone, consider signing up for an international plan; most providers offer a global calling plan that cuts the per-minute cost of phone calls and texts, and a flat-fee data plan.

Use Wi-Fi whenever possible. Most hotels and many cafés

# Sleep Code

Hotels are classified based on the average price of a typical en suite double room with breakfast in high season.

| | | |
|---|---|---|
| **$$$$** | **Splurge:** | Most rooms over 35,000 ISK |
| **$$$** | **Pricier:** | 28,000-35,000 ISK |
| **$$** | **Moderate:** | 20,000-28,000 ISK |
| **$** | **Budget:** | 15,000-20,000 ISK |
| **¢** | **Hostel/Backpacker:** | Under 15,000 ISK |

Unless otherwise noted, credit cards are accepted and free Wi-Fi is available. Comparison-shop by checking prices at several hotels (on each hotel's own website, on a booking site, or by email). For the best deal, *always book directly with the hotel.*

offer free Wi-Fi, and you'll likely also find it at tourist information offices (TIs), major museums, and public-transit hubs. With Wi-Fi you make free or inexpensive domestic and international calls via a calling app such as Skype, FaceTime, or Google+ Hangouts. When you can't find Wi-Fi, you can use your cellular network to connect to the Internet, send texts, or make voice calls. When you're done, avoid further charges by manually switching off "data roaming" or "cellular data."

Without a mobile device, you can make calls from your hotel and get online using public computers (there's usually one in your hotel lobby or at local libraries). Most hotels charge a high fee for international calls—ask for rates before you dial. Or you can use a prepaid international phone card (one brand in Iceland is called AtlasFrelsi).

For more on phoning, see www.ricksteves.com/phoning. For a one-hour talk on "Traveling with a Mobile Device," see www.ricksteves.com/travel-talks.

## SLEEPING

I've categorized my recommended accommodations based on price, indicated with a dollar-sign rating (see sidebar). I recommend reserving rooms in advance, particularly during peak season. Once your dates are set, check the specific price for your preferred stay at several hotels. You can do this either by comparing prices on sites such as Hotels.com or Booking.com, or by checking the hotels' own websites. To get the best deal, contact my family-run hotels directly by phone or email. When you go direct, the owner avoids any third-party commission, giving them wiggle room to offer you a discount, a nicer room, or free breakfast. If you prefer to book online or are considering a hotel chain, it's to your advantage to use the hotel's website.

For complicated requests, send an email with the following

information: number and type of rooms; number of nights; arrival date; departure date; and any special requests. Use the European style for writing dates: day/month/year. Hoteliers typically ask for your credit-card number as a deposit. In general, hotel prices can soften if you do any of the following: offer to pay cash, stay at least three nights, or travel off-season.

In Iceland, hotels are usually large (big enough for groups), impersonal, and corporate-owned. If you want a more mom-and-pop feeling, look for guesthouses and farmstays. An ample breakfast buffet is generally included.

A short-term rental—whether an apartment, house, or room in a local's home—is an increasingly popular alternative, especially in expensive Iceland. Aggregator websites such as Airbnb, FlipKey, Booking.com, and the HomeAway family of sites (HomeAway, VRBO, and VacationRentals) let you browse properties and correspond directly with Icelandic property owners or managers. Of these, Airbnb is definitely the biggest name in the Iceland short-term rental market.

## EATING

I've categorized my recommended eateries based on price, indicated with a dollar-sign rating (see sidebar).

Traditional Icelandic cuisine isn't too far removed from its Viking Age roots—relying heavily on anything hardy enough to survive the harsh landscape (lamb, potatoes), caught in or near the sea (fish, seabirds), or sturdy enough to withstand winter storage (dried and salted fish). Today's chefs have built on this heritage, introducing international flavors and new approaches to old-style dishes. In recent years, Reykjavík has emerged as a foodie destination—with both high-end, experimental "New Icelandic" cuisine and a renewed appreciation for the country's traditional, nose-to-tail "hardship" cuisines. The capital offers a wide variety of dining options, but even in the countryside, you're never far from a satisfying meal.

Food and drink prices in Iceland are strikingly high, but it is possible to eat well here without going broke. There's no tipping, taxes are built into prices, and restaurants cheerfully dispense free tap water, making eating out more reasonable than it might seem.

In Reykjavík, lunches are a particularly good value, as many eateries offer the same quality and similar selections for far less than at dinner. Make lunch your main meal, then have a lighter evening meal. Many places offer a lunch special—typically a plate of fish, vegetables, and a starch (rice or potatoes) for 2,000-3,000 ISK. An unlimited soup-and-bread buffet—typically available for less than 2,000 ISK—is another good budget lunch option, commonly offered at cafés, bakeries, touristy rest stops, and other basic eateries.

## Restaurant Price Code

I've assigned each eatery a price category, based on the average cost of a typical main course. Drinks, desserts, and splurge items (steak and seafood) can raise the price considerably.

**$$$$**    **Splurge:** Most main courses over 5,500 ISK

**$$$**    **Pricier:** 4,000-5,500 ISK

**$$**    **Moderate:** 2,500-4,000 ISK

**$**    **Budget:** Under 2,500 ISK

In Iceland, a takeout place or soup-and-bread buffet is **$**; a sit-down café is **$$**; a casual but more upscale restaurant is **$$$**; and a swanky splurge is **$$$$**.

Picnicking is a good way to stretch a limited budget. Seek out the budget supermarket chains Krónan and Bónus. But be wary of grocery shopping at the omnipresent convenience stores, which are well-stocked but far more expensive.

If you drink alcohol, prices are high, especially for wine and spirits. If you plan to seriously imbibe during your visit, make a point of stopping at the airport duty-free store on your way into the country.

## TRANSPORTATION

If you're staying in Reykjavík and plan only a few brief forays outside the city, you can get by without a car. But most visitors find that renting a car gives them maximum flexibility for getting out into the Icelandic countryside—the highlight of any visit to this country. You won't find convenient public transportation options for reaching some sights (including the Golden Circle); instead you'll likely need to rely on pricey excursions, or rent a car (often the more cost-effective choice).

**By Car:** Two people splitting the cost of a rental car and gas will likely save a lot over the cost of bus excursions, while enjoying the flexibility of stopping whenever and wherever they want. It's cheaper to arrange most car rentals from the US. For tips on your insurance options, see www.ricksteves.com/cdw, and for route planning, consult www.viamichelin.com. Bring your driver's license. Many tourists think of a trip to Iceland as more of an "expedition" than it really is, and shell out for a high-clearance SUV when they would do just fine with a teeny two-wheel-drive car. You won't need four-wheel drive for the itineraries in this book in summer, or even for a quick winter stopover if you stick to Reykjavík.

Local road etiquette is similar to that in the US. The website www.drive.is has a helpful (if overlong) video with tips for safely navigating the country's many unpaved roads and one-lane bridges.

The Icelandic Road Authority (Vegagerðin) website (www.road.is) shows up-to-date snow, ice, and wind conditions on all the major roads in the country. Visiting this site is a must before setting off on any car trip, even in summer. Ask your car-rental company about the rules of the road or check the US State Department website (www.travel.state.gov, select "International Travel," then "Country Information," then search for your destination and click "Travel and Transportation").

**By Bus:** You can select from a full menu of **guided bus tours** to get into the countryside. You'll pay a premium for a guide and a carefully designed experience, but these excursions take the guesswork out of your trip. The dominant operators are Reykjavík Excursions (www.re.is) and Gray Line (www.grayline.is), while several smaller companies offer a more intimate experience. Guide to Iceland (www.guidetoiceland.is), a consortium of several travel outlets, can be a good one-stop source for tours; they have a desk inside the Reykjavík City Hall's TI.

Iceland has a good network of scheduled **public buses** (painted yellow and blue and called *strætó*), run as a single system by city and local governments (www.straeto.is). Although the Strætó network is more geared to locals than visitors, it can be useful to those traveling from one town to another. However, these buses typically do *not* connect the big countryside sights (such as Þingvellir, Geysir, and Gullfoss on the Golden Circle). Reykjavík city buses are part of the Strætó network and use the same tickets and fare structure.

In summer months, several private companies offer direct, regularly scheduled, if still pricey **bus transport** to many popular outdoor destinations that are otherwise challenging to reach (even by car). Companies to consider include Reykjavík Excursions (under the name Iceland On Your Own, www.ioyo.is), Sterna Travel (www.icelandbybus.is), and Trex (www.trex.is).

## HELPFUL HINTS

**Emergency Help:** To summon the **police** or an **ambulance**, call 112. For passport problems, call the **US Embassy in Reykjavík** (tel. 595-2200, after-hours line for emergencies only—595-2248, http://is.usembassy.gov) or the **Canadian Embassy in Reykjavík** (tel. 575-6500, www.canadainternational.gc.ca/iceland-islande).

**Theft or Loss:** To replace a passport, you'll need to go in person to an embassy or consulate (see above). Cancel and replace your credit and debit cards by calling these 24-hour US numbers collect: Visa: tel. 303/967-1096, MasterCard: tel. 636/722-7111, American Express: tel. 336/393-1111. In Iceland, to make a collect call to the US, dial 00-800-2225-5288; press zero or stay on the line for an operator. File a police report either on the spot or within a day or two; you'll need it to submit an insurance claim for lost or stolen travel gear, and it can help with replacing your passport or credit and debit cards. For more information, see www.ricksteves.com/help.

**Time:** Iceland doesn't observe Daylight Savings Time (due to its far-north location). In summer, Iceland is one hour behind Great Britain and four/seven hours ahead of the East/West coasts of the US. In winter, Iceland is on par with Great Britain and five/eight hours ahead of the East/West coasts of the US.

**Climate:** Summer or winter, be prepared to bundle up (pack gloves, sturdy boots, and a waterproof jacket). While conditions overall are surprisingly moderate for the latitude, frosty temperatures and bone-chilling wind can happen at any time of year.

**Holidays and Festivals:** Iceland celebrates many holidays, which can close sights and attract crowds (book hotel rooms ahead). For information on holidays and festivals, check Iceland's tourism website: www.visiticeland.com. For a simple list showing major—though not all—events, see www.ricksteves.com/festivals.

**Numbers and Stumblers:** What Americans call the second floor of a building is the first floor in Europe. Europeans write dates as day/month/year, so Christmas 2020 is 25/12/20. For measurements, Iceland uses the metric system: A kilogram is 2.2 pounds; a liter is about a quart; and a kilometer is six-tenths of a mile.

## RESOURCES FROM RICK STEVES

This Snapshot guide is excerpted from my latest edition of *Rick Steves Iceland,* one of many titles in my ever-expanding series of guidebooks on European travel. I also produce a public television series, *Rick Steves' Europe,* and a public radio show, *Travel with Rick Steves.* My website, www.ricksteves.com, offers free travel information, a forum for travelers' comments, guidebook updates, my travel blog, an online travel store, and information on European rail passes and our tours of Europe. If you're bringing a mobile device on your trip, you can download my free Rick Steves Audio Europe app, featuring dozens of self-guided audio tours of the top sights in Europe and travel interviews about Europe. You can get Rick Steves Audio Europe via Apple's App Store, Google Play, or the Amazon Appstore. For more information, see www.ricksteves.com/audioeurope.

## ADDITIONAL RESOURCES

**Tourist Information:** www.visiticeland.com
**Passports and Red Tape:** www.travel.state.gov
**Packing List:** www.ricksteves.com/packing
**Travel Insurance:** www.ricksteves.com/insurance

**Cheap Flights:** www.kayak.com or www.google.com/flights
**Airplane Carry-on Restrictions:** www.tsa.gov
**Updates for This Book:** www.ricksteves.com/update

## HOW WAS YOUR TRIP?

To share your tips, concerns, and discoveries after using this book, please fill out the survey at www.ricksteves.com/feedback. Thanks in advance—it helps a lot.

# INDEX

INDEX

*Our website enhances this book and turns*

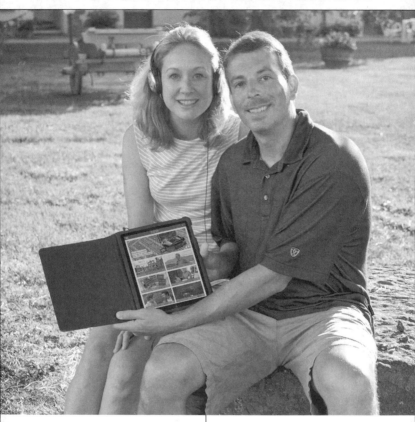

### Explore Europe

At ricksteves.com you can browse through thousands of articles, videos, photos and radio interviews, plus find a wealth of money-saving travel tips for planning your dream trip. And with our mobile-friendly website, you can easily access all this great travel information anywhere you go.

### TV Shows

Preview the places you'll visit by watching entire half-hour episodes of Rick Steves' Europe (choose from all 100 shows) on-demand, for free.

## *your travel dreams into affordable reality*

### Radio Interviews

Enjoy ready access to Rick's vast library of radio interviews covering travel

tips and cultural insights that relate specifically to your Europe travel plans.

### Travel Forums

Learn, ask, share! Our online community of savvy travelers is a great resource for first-time travelers to Europe, as well as seasoned pros. You'll find forums on each country, plus travel tips and restaurant/hotel reviews. You can even ask one of our well-traveled staff to chime in with an opinion.

### Travel News

Subscribe to our free Travel News e-newsletter, and get monthly updates from Rick on what's happening in Europe.

# Audio Europe™

## Rick's Free Travel App

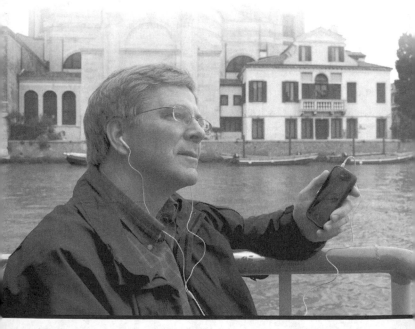

Get your FREE **Rick Steves Audio Europe**™ app to enjoy…

- Dozens of self-guided tours of Europe's top museums, sights and historic walks
- Hundreds of tracks filled with cultural insights and sightseeing tips from Rick's radio interviews
- All organized into handy geographic playlists
- For Apple and Android

With Rick whispering in your ear, Europe gets even better.

**Find out more at ricksteves.com**

*Gear up for your next adventure at ricksteves.com*

### LIght Luggage

Pack light and right with Rick Steves' affordable, custom-designed rolling carry-on bags, backpacks, day packs and shoulder bags.

### Accessories

From packing cubes to moneybelts and beyond, Rick has personally selected the travel goodies that will help your trip go smoother.

## *Experience maximum Europe*

### Save time and energy

This guidebook is your independent-travel toolkit. But for all it delivers, it's still up to you to devote the time and energy it takes to manage the preparation and logistics that are essential for a happy trip. If that's a hassle, there's a solution.

### Rick Steves Tours

A Rick Steves tour takes you to Europe's most interesting places with great

# great tours, too!

## *with minimum stress*

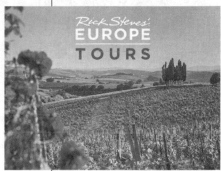

guides and small groups of 28 or less. We follow Rick's favorite itineraries, ride in comfy buses, stay in family-run hotels, and bring you intimately close to the Europe you've traveled so far to see. Most importantly, we take away the logistical headaches so you can focus on the fun.

travelers—nearly half of them repeat customers— along with us on four dozen different itineraries, from Ireland to Italy to Athens. Is a Rick Steves tour the right fit for your travel dreams? Find out at ricksteves.com, where you can also request Rick's latest tour catalog. Europe is best experienced with happy travel partners. We hope you can join us.

### Join the fun

This year we'll take thousands of free-spirited

See our itineraries at ricksteves.com

# A Guide for Every Trip

## BEST OF GUIDES

*Full color easy-to-scan format, focusing on Europe's most popular destinations and sights.*

Best of England
Best of Europe
Best of France
Best of Germany
Best of Ireland
Best of Italy
Best of Spain

## COMPREHENSIVE GUIDES

*City, country, and regional guides with detailed coverage for a multi-week trip exploring the most iconic sights and venturing off the beaten track.*

Amsterdam & the Netherlands
Barcelona
Belgium: Bruges, Brussels, Antwerp & Ghent
Berlin
Budapest
Croatia & Slovenia
Eastern Europe
England
Florence & Tuscany
France
Germany
Great Britain
Greece: Athens & the Peloponnese
Iceland
Ireland
Istanbul
Italy
London
Paris
Portugal
Prague & the Czech Republic
Provence & the French Riviera
Rome
Scandinavia
Scotland
Spain
Switzerland
Venice
Vienna, Salzburg & Tirol

THE BEST OF ROME

...me, Italy's capital, is studded with ...man remnants and floodlit-fountain ...ares. From the Vatican to the Colos-...m, with crazy traffic in between, Rome ...onderful, huge, and exhausting. The ...ds, the heat, and the weighty history

of the Eternal City where Caesars walked can make tourists wilt. Recharge by taking siestas, gelato breaks, and after-dark walks, strolling from one atmospheric square to another in the refreshing evening air.

...red *Pantheon*—which ...gest dome until the ...rly 2,000 years old ...day over 1,500).

...l of Athens in the *Vat-* ...edies the humanistic ...ence.

..., gladiators fought ... another; entertaining ...a Rome *ristorante*. ...rds at *St. Peter's* ...k seriously.

Rick Steves guidebooks are published by Avalon Travel, an imprint of Perseus Books, a Hachette Book Group company.

## POCKET GUIDES

*Compact, full color city guides with the essentials for shorter trips.*

| | |
|---|---|
| Amsterdam | Paris |
| Athens | Prague |
| Barcelona | Rome |
| Florence | Venice |
| Italy's Cinque Terre | Vienna |
| London | |
| Munich & Salzburg | |

## SNAPSHOT GUIDES

*Focused single-destination coverage.*

Basque Country: Spain & France
Copenhagen & the Best of Denmark
Dublin
Dubrovnik
Edinburgh
Hill Towns of Central Italy
Krakow, Warsaw & Gdansk
Lisbon
Loire Valley
Madrid & Toledo
Milan & the Italian Lakes District
Naples & the Amalfi Coast
Normandy
Northern Ireland
Norway
Reykjavík
Sevilla, Granada & Southern Spain
St. Petersburg, Helsinki & Tallinn
Stockholm

## CRUISE PORTS GUIDES

*Reference for cruise ports of call.*

Mediterranean Cruise Ports
Scandinavian & Northern European Cruise Ports

### Complete your library with...

## TRAVEL SKILLS & CULTURE

*Study up on travel skills and gain insight on history and culture.*

Europe 101
Europe Through the Back Door
European Christmas
European Easter
European Festivals
Postcards from Europe
Travel as a Political Act

## PHRASE BOOKS & DICTIONARIES

French
French, Italian & German
German
Italian
Portuguese
Spanish

## PLANNING MAPS

Britain, Ireland & London
Europe
France & Paris
Germany, Austria & Switzerland
Ireland
Italy
Spain & Portugal

Rick Steves books are available from your favorite bookseller.
Many guides are available as ebooks.